Praise for
Unfolding the Mystery of Your Life on the Five Wisdoms Path

With so many people now experiencing trauma, both psychological and physical, who better to rely on than the great Chögyam Trungpa Rinpoche, whose teachings remind us so clearly of our basic sanity? His wisdom lineage is alive and well in his students—but their challenge now is to bring direct experience of this wisdom to younger people. Irini Rockwell is doing just that: showing us how his incredibly creative teachings on the Five Wisdoms can be directly applied.

–Dzongsar Jamyang Khyentse

Irini Rockwell's book, *Unfolding the Mystery of Your Life on the Five Wisdoms Path,* is a valuable contribution to the field of personal development and spiritual growth. As a student of the great master Chögyam Trungpa Rinpoche, Irini received his teachings of Tantra directly, and has taught these practices and techniques for many years. The book offers readers a powerful tool for self-discovery, helping them identify their Buddha type and distinguish between neurotic tendencies and innate wisdom. This comprehensive guide, born from years of invaluable experience, has the potential to become a significant resource for those seeking healing, restoration, and a deeper connection with their innate Five Wisdoms, fulfilling its destiny as a source of great benefit to many.

–Dzigar Kongtrul Rinpoche

This rich and important book offers a remarkable map of the human mind and heart and explores patterns of relationality that influence our lives.

–Roshi Joan Halifax,
Abbot, Upaya Zen Center

Unfolding the Mystery of Your Life on the Five Wisdoms Path offers a modern roadmap through ancient teachings on discovering the power of your unique wisdom matrix. Rather than trying to become who you think you "should" be, Rockwell shows you how to relax into your natural brilliance to create more joy in your relationships, work life, and creative self-expression.

–Susan Piver, Author
The Four Noble Truths of Love and *The Buddhist Enneagram*

This book is an illuminating guide to personal and spiritual transformation and a beautiful journey into the heart of the Five Wisdoms. It is a treasure for anyone seeking to understand themselves more deeply. Irini Rockwell has a gift for making profound wisdom accessible and actionable.

–Tim Olmsted
Pema Chödrön Foundation founder and president,
Tergar Meditation Community senior instructor

Thorough, clear, and practical, Irini offers us guidance for unraveling our confusion, rediscovering our natural wisdom, and living a life interconnected with the vastness around us. Her commitment to Vajrayana Buddhism shines through on each page and her love of wisdom is a gift she freely and skillfully offers.

–Michael Carroll
Founder Wisdom Seat
Author *Awake at Work* and *The Mindful Leader*

The Five Wisdoms typology transcends all other personality systems—as it reveals the inseparability of our confusion and innate wisdom—and Irini Rockwell transcends all expositors. This book distills a lifetime of study and practice, and reveals the depth of Rockwell's extensive experience. No one is better qualified to guide you into this transformative arena, and to show you how these ancient teachings have immediate applicability in this modern world.

–Andrew Holecek
Author *Reverse Meditation* and *Dream Yoga*

Irini Rockwell is a torch-bearer of ancient wisdom in modern times. Through an unfolding of the Five Wisdoms and esoteric Tantric Buddhism, she offers lucid and practical guidance to bring an enlightened perspective to daily experience. Whether already on a spiritual path or intrigued about how such a journey might unfold, this book invites you to work with your obstacles and celebrate your wisdom.

–Jeffrey Fortuna, MA, LPC
Founder of Windhorse Integrative Mental Health

Irini invites her readers into a profound journey of self-discovery utilizing her deep knowledge of the five wisdoms of Tibetan Buddhism. Her book is both inspiring and immensely practical.

–Dr. Susan Skjei, Former Director,
Authentic Leadership Center at Naropa University

Irini Rockwell's new book represents a significant advancement in making Tibetan Buddhist wisdom accessible and applicable to modern life. Drawing from her decades of experience integrating Buddhist teachings with psychology, personal development, and embodiment practices, Rockwell offers a down-to-earth approach that resonates with a wide audience. Her work, which has impressed and inspired many over the years, including at the KenKon center in the Netherlands, seamlessly blends ancient wisdom with contemporary methods. This latest offering not only serves those interested in the Five Wisdoms or Tibetan Buddhism but also provides valuable insights for anyone on a journey of healing or self-discovery, making it a highly recommended resource for those seeking wisdom to navigate these challenging times.

–Sydney Leijenhorst
Founder, KenKon Integral Life and Training Centre

The Five Wisdoms of Tantric Buddhism that Irini Rockwell explores resonate beautifully with the Intelligences in the Integral City GPS. They also reveal the elements of water, earth, fire, and air and the seasons of winter, fall, spring, and summer. In this way, all Intelligences can be explored, understood, and practiced at great depth. Irini's sparkling humor, creativity, and full-bodied teachings inspire a way to live Gaia's Code of Care for Self, Others, Place and Planet.

–Marilyn Hamilton, PhD
Author *Integral City Book Series*

Irini Rockwell's book is a vibrant roadmap for self-discovery, blending Tibetan Buddhism and psychology with practical tantric exercises for everyday living. By working with the Five Wisdom Energies, we can enrich our lives and radiate sanity in our homes and workplaces. Irini is a dependable guide to tap into conscious and unconscious energies towards personal transformation and spiritual growth. We become more intimate with our true nature and have a deeper resonance with our experiences.

–Jean Gunner, Director of Buffalo Pediatric Associates
and Heart Wisdom at Work Founder

The work that Irini Rockwell offers is a deep dive and authentic reveal into our essential nature. Having read her books and participated in a Five Wisdoms workshop, I am discovering new found compassionate humor and spaciousness. The Five Wisdoms promote insight into human interactions in the present. What a gift! Often "self help" experiences are fleeting but with Irini's work my life holds more freedom to embrace, forgive, and love.

–Kate Kelly,
Senior Artist in Residence, Skidmore College

Irini's book has profoundly enriched my meditation practice and deepened my understanding of mind, body and spirit. Viewing feelings through the lens of energetic colors has given me a more nuanced comprehension of my own feelings and their impact on my relationships with others. This book serves as a valuable guide, encouraging us to observe the flow, variation, and transformation of energies that permeate every aspect of our interconnected universe.

–Peggy Galantowicz, M.A., LPC

This book presents a captivating journey into self-discovery and transformation. Irini Rockwell's loving and insightful guidance invites you to embrace your true essence, ignite your inner brilliance, and live a life of profound purpose and passion.

–Patricia Valinho
Five Wisdoms Training graduate

Unfolding the Mystery
of Your Life on
the Five Wisdoms Path

ISBN 979-8-9909935-0-1

Published by The Five Wisdoms Institute
www.fivewisdomsinstitute.com

Cover design by Nada Orlic at Erelis Design
www.erelisdesign.com

Page design by Robert Henry at Right Hand Publishing
www.righthandpublishing.com

Author photograph by Druppa

More from Irini Rockwell in the
Five Wisdoms series

The Five Wisdom Energies, a Buddhist Way of Understanding Personalities, Emotions and Relationships, Shambhala Publications, 2002

A Buddhist System for Uncovering Your Strengths and Letting Them Shine, Shambhala Publications, 2012

A Heart of Service: A Family's Epic Story, Timeless Press, 2017

The Five Wisdoms Institute:
www.fivewisdomsinstitute.com

Unfolding the Mystery
of Your Life on
the Five Wisdoms Path

Irini Rockwell

Chögyam Trungpa Rinpoche

This book is inspired by the teachings of Trungpa Rinpoche. It is with deep appreciation that I offer this tribute to him.

As he began to teach in the West, Trungpa Rinpoche was keenly aware that people were attracted to the trappings of ritualized Buddhism. Many were caught in spiritual materialism, using the teachings to aggrandize themselves. He moved to the United States in 1970 and quickly picked up on the culture: peoples' passions, hang-ups, and terms of the day. He also found that the counter-culture hippie generation was open to spiritual exploration. He saw their intelligence and goodness, but also their neurosis, anxiety, and fears. Most importantly, he saw that striving to reach higher or altered states as a way to transcend pain was basically missing the point. Thus, his main message was to cut through spiritual materialism (the title of his second book) and present authentic Buddhist teachings devoid of spiritual baggage. He was incomparable in his ability to present the essence of esoteric teachings in a non-traditional way. His work made these teachings more accessible resulting in a more immediate impact. In a letter he wrote in 1970, he says:

> My teaching concerns actual experience. I don't feel that I need to hide behind something, though some people are critical of me for coming out and showing myself as a human being...[he had just taken off his monk's robes]. But my role is a far deeper one than a mere cultural mission, a representative of the East to the West. I am not Tibetan but Human and my mission is to teach others as effectively as I can in this world in which I find myself.

To get away from conventional Buddhist language, he used the psychological language of lay people in the 1960s and 70s. He provoked inquisitiveness rather than giving pat answers and used language that allowed people to shed their ego rather than build it up. He encouraged people to focus on their experience in the present moment, the present situation (a word he loved), just as it is. He related to everyone as a full human being to engender the direct experience of the awakened mind. He was an emissary of nowness. He encouraged people to use their basic intelligence, trusting their own wisdom mind. In answer to a question he sometimes said, "Your guess is as good as mine." This was one way he kept things fresh.

Trungpa Rinpoche presented tantric teachings to the general public in such a way that only the initiated would realize their true origin. For instance, the large body of teachings on working with the arts are sourced in the advanced teachings of Mahāmudrā. As well, the Five Wisdoms are sourced in both Mahāmudrā and Ati, the most profound teachings Buddhism has to offer. For me, studying traditional tantric texts with Khenpo Tsültrim Gyamtso Rinpoche revealed his sources and further illuminated Trungpa's teachings.

Trungpa Rinpoche often used words to take us beyond what we think they mean, redefining them by his use of them. An ordinary word or phrase could be given extraordinary meaning. For example, adding "basic" to goodness makes it not just mundane goodness but the most primordial, profound, and absolute truth of all existence. He used "basic goodness" in some situations instead of the traditional Sanskrit word bodhicitta, translated as awakened heart.

He made the teachings immediate. In his books and talks, it often felt like he was talking directly to you and knew exactly what you were experiencing. On the other hand, at times many of us could not get any sense of it at all. It was completely incomprehensible! This points to the fact that tantric teachings are said to be self-secret; if we are not ready to hear them, we will not understand them. We can read the same words over and over again and each time we can find new meaning at a deeper level. Buddhism confirms what we know and takes us deeper.

Not only did Trungpa Rinpoche teach in an extraordinary way, he also created new forms of practice. He had befriended several Zen teachers and learned from their tradition. He brought in many of their forms and practices making his teachings totally unique.

Trungpa Rinpoche was larger than life. His legacy goes on. He is still very much with us. I feel tremendous gratitude that I continue to be his student. In this small way I am offering my contribution to the ongoing flourishing of his teaching.

Table of Contents

Introduction

I n the journey of life, we find ourself navigating through a maze of experiences, emotions, and choices, each leading us down a path that shapes our understanding of the world and what it means to be who we are. Along this intricate journey lies the opportunity to unlock the mysteries that lie within us, to delve deep into the essence of our being, and to uncover the profound wisdom that guides us on our path.

Unfolding the Mystery of Your Life on the Five Wisdoms Path invites you to embark on a transformative exploration of self-discovery and introspection, drawing upon the ancient teachings of the Five Wisdoms of Tantric Buddhism to illuminate the path to personal growth and spiritual awakening.

As we embark on this journey together, we will delve into the essence of the Five Wisdoms: the wisdoms of clarity, equanimity, intuition, action, and all-encompassing space. Each wisdom offers a unique perspective on the nature of reality, the complexities of the human experience, and the interconnectedness of all beings.

Through reflective practices, insightful teachings, and practical exercises, this book will guide you on a profound exploration of your inner landscape, helping you unravel the mysteries that lie at the core of your being. It will empower you to embrace your true essence and awaken to the boundless wisdom that resides within you.

For me, discovering the Five Wisdoms was an absolute game changer! It propelled me into decades of inquiry. I became deeply interested in the essence of who I am. Then I wanted to share my discoveries with others. You!

Unfolding the Mystery

On the Five Wisdoms Path, we gain a profound understanding of our energetic style, the potency of sitting with emotions without judgment, and the dynamics of relationships. Unfolding the mystery of ourself is the first step! There is no doubt that we become fascinated by how the wisdoms reveal ourself to ourself: how we shine and how we get stuck. We come to appreciate the unique gifts of our personality and what we have to offer. Then they become a language through which we understand all that we experience. As we align more and more with the wisdom aspect of the energies, our stuck places become our work points.

We could work with our personal problems—anxiety, not feeling good enough, emotional intensity, and the list goes on—in a psychological way. However, the wisdoms take us further because we discover that the nitty gritty of our mundane life acts as a bridge to spiritual awakening. They give us a psychospiritual understanding of human dynamics as well as transpersonal realization.

For example, Peter, a corporate CEO, is often angry. From the perspective of wisdom energies, his anger is also his clarity. His clarity is his shining aspect; his insistence on being right is his stuckness. It is not a matter of Peter trying to change, but rather to keep aligning with his intelligence, the best of himself. Awareness of when he gets angry is his work point. His success as a leader becomes more powerful when it comes from knowing himself.

A Life Worth Living

Have you found yourself asking these questions? Do you want ways to deal with your struggles so you have more ease in your life? Or do you want to delve into a transformative spiritual journey and fundamentally change your life? Or both? How do you make the link, the bridge, between the depth and the minute particulars of your day? Can you, in fact, bring an enlightened perspective to daily experience? How can the Five Wisdoms guide you to a life worth living?

Tantra is not about acquiring knowledge. It has three primary focuses: direct experience, energetic embodiment of wisdom, and cosmic interconnectedness. Practices ground our understanding in our being, engaging with the subtle energies of our body, our sense perceptions, and the elements that make up our body. We gain a quintessential understanding of tantric brilliance in the beautiful rub between the teachings, the practices, and daily experiences that bring about moment-to-moment realization. This is what keeps the teachings alive.

We come to realize the Five Wisdoms encompass the full spectrum of existence and illuminate every aspect of our lives. They give us a big map, a systemic view. We see how reality fits together. We awaken to the totality and interconnectedness of everything. It's as if we have been living in a black-and-white world and suddenly our world is in technicolor.

We will see that the Five Wisdoms teachings are at the core of Tantric Buddhism and so illuminate it. So, what luck that we are born at this particular time and place and have access to the untold life-transformative power of Tantra! I have found that awareness of the mix of energies in my personality and being able to "read" energy in people, situations, and environments has been exponentially helpful.

We all have the potential to work with ourself to discover the deeper answers of immediate relevance. That anyone can do this makes it very ordinary. It is also extraordinarily ordinary! As ancient as these teachings are, they have great relevance and value for us in the 21st century. Fundamentally, there is no need of separation between the depths of our wisdom and the mundane world. We can find wisdom in any situation, however tumultuous. I find bringing an understanding of the gold mine of Tantra into daily life both exciting and challenging. Tantra and the CEO. Yes! No problem. Sign me up!

The Five Wisdoms Energies can become the foundation for working with ourself, others, and situations. They provide an unparalleled opportunity to transform all that we see as negative or confusing into what is positive and wise and bring us into a life that is truly worth living. They expand our way of being in the world exponentially. Ultimately, we have a balance of the energies. We know how to align with the wisdom of each energy. We celebrate brilliance and have compassion toward neurosis with ourself and others. We put aside personal agendas and do what is most needed. We ride the energy of the moment.

As the events of the world take their shifts and turns and present us with daily challenges, the Five Wisdoms can be our guide, a rudder to keep us on course. We bravely put up our sails but we never know which way the winds will blow. We have no way of knowing what the outcomes will be. But one thing I know is that on the spiritual path, we always fall forward! If this is the right time and the right situation, then these teachings will ring true for you.

A Brief Summary

In Part I, *The Five Wisdoms and You*, the primary intention is to gain a deep intimacy with ourself guided by our understanding of the Five Wisdoms. In this part, we will discover where we shine and where we get stuck in our personality styles, and how we relate to others.

In Part II, *Where We Get in Trouble*, we see how we create and maintain our ego from a Buddhist psychological perspective, become aware of the trauma and stress in our world, and learn how we can be informed by understanding our nervous system.

In Part III, *Turning It Around With Somatic Intelligence*, we see how the path and practice of meditation are essential to awakenment, how elemental embodiment and sense perceptions put us in touch with our primal being, the psychophysical practice of transmuting intensified emotions into wisdom, and the tantric practices of working with subtle energy and its relationship to neuroscience.

In Part IV, *A Bigger World Awaits You*, we begin to see how our journey is both inevitable and essential. We come to understand the essence of the tantric path and explore such topics as a radical perspective on wisdom and its relationship with quantum physics, the dimensions of reality, the dynamic duo of feminine and masculine energies, and a Tantric understanding of passion.

In Part V, *Mandala: Our Ever-Shifting Kaleidoscope*, we look at the outer mandala of phenomena, the inner mandala of experience, and the inseparability of their outer and inner worlds. We go deeper into an understanding of the Five Wisdoms mandala and journey.

In Part VI, *Your Life Purpose*, we dig deep to find our life's purpose in terms of personal fulfillment, engaging with others, creating our world, and using the Five Wisdoms in all we do.

This introduction is a nutshell version of the full spectrum of possibility with the Five Wisdoms. Our journey could bring us into more understanding of our everyday lives as well as profound realizations. It might be a lot to chew on, but now that we have some broad strokes, we can choose how far we want to go.

My Journey

I am a deep diver, a visionary, a trailblazer, and a pragmatist. Though I have rooted myself in the profound teachings of Tantric Buddhism, my teachings expand beyond traditional presentations. As a creative person, I have been continually inspired to innovate. As a woman and a dancer, I have focused on making my teachings experienced and embodied. Responding to the prevalence of trauma in our world, I've brought in contemporary research on neurobiology. As a lifelong learner, I have delved into quantum physics and have delighted in the resonance between it and Tantric Buddhism. I pay attention to cutting-edge thinkers who contribute to our understanding of expanded states of consciousness and the fast-growing demographic of people who consider themselves spiritual but not religious. I feel Buddhism is lacking in not having teachings on personality and relationships, so I have made them a primary focus. Most importantly, I focus on making the teachings have everyday relevance.

In writing multiple books, I delved into the gold mine of these teachings. Not hiding behind jargon made me dig deeper into my own understanding to present the teachings with authenticity and in an accessible way. Understanding is a process, like digging for treasure. The treasure is already there, the digging is what takes effort. Once the treasure is found, it is like a box full of rough-cut diamonds. Cutting and polishing each diamond reveals its brilliance. I was both challenged and exhilarated by the process of unpacking each word to find the essence of its meaning, turn it into everyday language, and give it experiential relevance.

I invite you to journey with me to gain more understanding of your own relationship to the wisdom energies.

The QR code below links to the "Book" page on the Five Wisdoms Institute website. You will find downloadable graphics in bright colors, which will illuminate your understanding of the book. Enjoy!

www.fivewisdomsinstitute.com/books

PART I

The Five Wisdoms and You

CHAPTER 1

To Know Yourself

You know best about yourself, so you should work with yourself constantly. This is based on trusting your intelligence rather than trusting yourself, which could be very selfish. It is trusting your intelligence by knowing who you are and what you are. You know yourself so well, therefore any deception could be cut through... So you should come back to your own judgment, to your own sense of your expressions... You just witness what you are.

–Chögyam Trungpa Rinpoche

Our first step is to get to know our personal self. Only we have firsthand knowledge of us: the way we brush our teeth, take a shower, put on our clothes, eat, how we go about our day, talk to a friend or colleague. Perhaps we are aware of the constant buzz of our inner monologue about how we are doing—our top ten tunes—and what turns us on and what gets us stressed. There is a lot going on within us all of the time. In all of this, we are our own witness. Knowing ourself intimately gives us a sense of our personality. We don't have to know who we are to be who we are, but it helps. We can learn to embrace many aspects of ourself and appreciate the full spectrum of who we are.

We can go to therapists, personal growth trainings, and become involved in spiritual teachings, but the bottom line is we need to work with ourself. An inner subjective life is the gateway to self-understanding and regulation. Self-awareness is not selfish but the opposite. It is at the heart of empathy for others.

> A great deal of the chaos in the world occurs because people don't appreciate themselves.
>
> –Chögyam Trungpa Rinpoche

We might think that focusing on our personal self is ego-centered, but, perhaps surprisingly, when we make friends with our true self, we don't struggle with ourself. We just are. We might ask what understanding our personality has to do with understanding Tantric Buddhism. Or wonder if the basic point of a spiritual path is to relate to the ephemeral realm. Simply put, the Five Wisdom Energies manifest in three dimensions: outer, energetic, and spiritual or cosmic. The energetic dimension is of primary importance as it is the bridge between our perceived world, which is seemingly pretty solid, and the ethereal realm, which is mysterious and magical. So, understanding the energetic make-up of our personality is not only an entrance to Tantric Buddhism but also the means to our awakenment.

> We try to avoid our individuality, but that is a big problem. Individuality sometimes comes out of ego, like wanting to be an emperor, a king, or a millionaire. But individuality can also come from personal inspiration. It depends on the level of one's journey, on how far you have been able to shed your ego. We all have our own style and our own particular nature. We can't avoid it. The enlightened expression of yourself is in accord with your inherent nature.
>
> –Chögyam Trungpa Rinpoche

The Five Wisdoms categorize people into five basic qualities, though ultimately there are infinite combinations. They illuminate who we are: our personality, disposition, emotional landscape, habits, and tendencies. Being both inner-personal and inter-personal, they give us insight into our energetic makeup and the particular ways we perceive and interact with our world. We discover that we are all multi-dimensional. They are a vehicle for self-discovery and a ground for working with others. They are what we need in challenging times.

The Energetic Dimension

The Five Wisdoms are five types of intelligence, five ways of knowing. Conventionally we understand intelligence as a conceptual accumulation of knowledge, ideology, or philosophy. The subtle energetic dimension of the Five Wisdoms can only be understood through experience. We open the door to a subtle level of being. Energy, also known as chi in some traditions, is experienced firsthand through our five sense perceptions, intuition which is like a sixth sense, and our whole psychophysical being. We tune in, feel, intuit energy in the moment.

The energies within us are like an inner tributary system and act as channels or meridians in our body. Our thinking mind has very little awareness, let alone understanding of this embodied energy. Yet this energy is operating all of the time, processing and integrating. Through the Five Wisdoms system, we can experience the energies directly in our being in a very accessible and immediate way.

Vital, vibrant, and all-pervasive, energy is the foundation of our existence, both innate to us and also self-existing beyond a sense of personal self. Experiencing our world energetically is connecting to the basic vitality of our existence, the vibrant aspect of being and communicating with our world. The world we perceive, conceptualize, and think we understand is a sur-face reality, the tip of the iceberg. Underneath lies a magical realm, more elusive and yet more impactful.

Whether we are aware of it or not, energy is pervasive. Every philosophical, spiritual, and religious tradition, every art form, in every corner of the globe, in every century of human existence, teaches about this deeper reality. Energy transcends concepts and therefore duality. It is inherently in flux, imper-manent, ephemeral, and illusory. Truly, it is a realm full of play and enjoyment. Energy is like light; it radiates. Symbols for en-ergy are a hologram, prism, or rainbow where the colors/ener-gies are facets of the whole.

In daily life, we cultivate awareness, attending to the present moment by observing what is happening. With training, we be-come a psychophysical barometer, a finely-tuned sensing de-vice. We pick up on the energetic climate, the patterns of energy, of anyone or any situation. Our awareness of energetic reality gives us an upper hand in relating to people and situations. We learn to appreciate our natural traits and those of others. We see that everyone has a quality of personal emanation: they fill the space with a definite presence, a unique feel. Everyone engages in the world in a unique way with their capacities, aptitudes, and preferences. As my friend Dave once remarked, "No one gave me this information about who I was except for my mother: 'You know, you're like that.' It was good to receive this knowledge but not from her when I was 18."

Fundamentally energy is neutral; our attitude toward it—in ourself, others, and our world—is what determines whether we are open or closed, fluid or frozen, intelligent or confused. When open, we experience ourself as warm and clear. When closed, we feel confused and stuck. Perpetually we teeter on the razor's edge between our sanity and our confusion. They are two sides of the same coin. They coexist in a common matrix of energy so the basic, raw energy can go either way. There is a texture to our experience that has no allegiance to good or bad:

our world is claustrophobic, neurotic, confused or our world is brilliant, full of wisdom, spacious. Our wisdom is our brilliance, skill, genius, how we shine, the best of who we are. Our neurosis is the shadow, parts of ourself we like the least, how we are stuck, a mask, a persona. This is our work point.

Both troublesome and pleasant experiences arise from the energetic matrix. With practice, we begin to align with our sanity rather than getting lost in our confusion. The salient point is understanding the inseparability of confusion and sanity. It's an understanding of wisdom that fully embraces our confusion as our good energy.

We are not trying to change or eliminate our style itself but the frozen version of it. When we stay with our awareness, insight arises from the rub between our understanding and our experience. We remain open and don't jump to conclusions, elaborate, or analyze. We could pay attention to feedback from others as we are often the last to know who we are. When we are open and have positive attitude toward who we are, we are no longer a mystery to ourself and automatically know what to do and what not to do. Ultimately it's not so much about who we are but riding the self-existing energy, going with the flow.

The analogy of light and refractions of light is often used to elucidate energy. There is a sense of luminosity and radiation. So light is a conduit for wisdom. Just as the color of light radiates, so do energetic qualities. It's like a rainbow, something we can see but not grasp; it is both there and not there. Many things are simultaneously both there and not there. Apparent but empty.

Traditionally, a diamond or a crystal is used as a metaphor for the mind. A crystal is a colorless, sparkling brilliance that includes the full range of colors. It is clear yet if we place a red cloth behind it, it becomes red. Similarly, the mind is originally clear, but can take on the "color" or energy of a thought or an emotion.

Wisdom is characterized by three basic qualities: openness, clarity, and warmth. Openness, or non-dual awareness, is the fundamental way in which each of the energies becomes wisdom. Taking anything personally creates duality and thus inevitably elicits the neurotic aspect of the energies. An open perspective sees things as empty of fixation and full of clarity. When the inherent human qualities of openness, clarity, and warmth infuse each of the energies, they radiate as five types of wisdom, intelligence, or brilliant sanity. Rinpoche says, "Since there is already such space and openness and the total absence of fear, the play of the wisdoms is a natural process."

Five Wisdom Energies

Are you ready to see yourself through the lens of the Five Wisdom Energies? It's important to remember that we have a mix of all of them. These descriptions give their traditional name in Sanskrit, their essence, color, unique wisdom quality, confused or neurotic quality, intensified emotion, element, sense perception, and season. In reading the following Five Wisdom Energies, which ones seem familiar to you? Foreign to you? Attractive to you? Threatening to you?

Buddha: Spacious White Energy

The buddha wisdom is all-encompassing space, a quality of completely open potential which accommodates everything. It radiates a white energy, spacious and peaceful. It is the foundation, the basic space or environment for the other energies. In itself, it has an ungraspable quality. People with buddha energy are contemplative, receptive, easy going, simple, and content with just being. They have a sedate, solid quality. They prefer that nothing is happening: have no personal agenda, don't pick and choose, and don't become reactive.

In their confusion or neurosis, they are solidly immobile and dense: numb, paralyzed, blind, deaf, and dumb, dull, spaced-out, disinterested, lazy, humorless, stubborn, and in-sensitive. They want to be left alone, not bothered. They are afraid to stand out and want to vanish into space. They don't want to do anything so they are busy resisting all of the time. They take the path of least effort.

Buddha is associated with the element of space. It does not have a sense perception or season.

Vajra: Insightful Blue Energy

Vajra has a mirror-like wisdom, akin to a crystal-clear mir-ror, reflecting a brilliant blue color. People with vajra energy see things as they are, without bias. They are clear minded with an intellectual brilliance: sharp, precise, logical, analytical, and direct. They are always on the dot and take great delight in their own intellect, enjoying their insights. Maintaining an un-compromising perspective, they are full of integrity and truth-fulness. They can hold many possible perspectives and see disadvantages of various involvements or challenges that might occur. They love complexity and understanding sys-tems. They can correct or remedy any neurotic distortion in a precise and sharp way.

When neurotic, they are self-righteous, convinced of their own insight based on intellectual fixation or hardened princi-ples. They have rigid conceptual boundaries and are overly an-alytical, critical, opinionated, authoritarian, and demand perfection. They can be possessive of their own insight. They are serious, uptight, and duty bound with no humor. They can be severe towards themselves and are pervaded by a sense of guilt when not living up to their sense of perfection. Trapped in their mind, they can be austere and sacrifice their health and comfort. Interpersonally they are not strong on social graces, and can come across as cool or even unfriendly. Intensified emotionally, they can burst into hot anger, ready to blame and criticize. Or they withdraw into a passive aggressive cold anger with cold disdain. They destroy violators and go to war to create peace.

Vajra is associated with the element of water, either turbulent or frozen, as well as its clear reflectiveness. Their sense perception of sight has the ability to see the big picture as well as the minute details. Its season is winter.

Ratna: Enriching Golden Yellow Energy

Ratna has the wisdom of equanimity with a sense of deep satisfaction and complete fulfillment. It exudes an enriching golden yellow color. People in this category are expansive, resourceful, enriching, and full of gravitas and potential. They appear powerful and impressive to others. They want their world to be substantial, established, and plentiful. They nest in an accumulation of immense richness and wealth, and take great delight in displaying it. They are expansive toward others, personally, emotionally, psychologically, and spiritually. They have a sense of equality toward all people and things, not preferring some experiences over others. They are neither personally close or distant. They are hospitable, generous, nurturing, and appreciative.

When neurotic, they have an underlying sense of self-pity, feeling unworthy and inadequate. They can be easily overwhelmed, making their life feel claustrophobic and suffocating. They are emotionally self-absorbed: needy, possessive, greedy, smug, and territorial. Never satisfied, they always want more and more. They feel separate from nourishment, resources, and richness. They mask that by becoming ostentatious, with a sense of entitlement, privilege, self-importance, smugness, pride, and arrogance. They fill the space, not allowing room for others, and are oppressive and over-indulgent. Everything seems overdone from the perspective of the other energies.

Ratna is associated with the element of earth because it includes everything in its expansive environment. The sense perceptions are taste, smell, and sensuous touch. Its season is fall, the time of harvesting the endless bounty of the earth.

Padma: Empathic Red Energy

Padma, glowing with the vibrance of red energy, has the wisdom of discriminating awareness, a finely tuned sensitivity to subtle experiences. They are highly intuitive in distinguishing between neurosis and confusion, ego-and non-ego. They are passionate, engaging, magnetizing, charismatic, and charming with a constant sense of invitation to a world of sense pleasures. Their aesthetic sense appreciates refined culture, beauty, and the arts. They embrace all the sensory pleasures and want the best the world can offer: excellent cuisine, the latest fashions, elegant furnishings, romantic music and poetry, flowering gardens, delicate scents, and the most rapturous environments. They listen deeply, speak from the heart, and have tremendous inquisitiveness and great compassion for others. They can also be romantic, flirtatious, and sexy, wanting to unite, merge with another. Padma is a lighter energy than ratna. Ratnas are settled in their own skin, powerful and impressive, whereas padmas seem a little too lightweight. Padma could feel as if they aren't taken seriously and may struggle to see themselves as established. They find ratna a little boring.

When neurotic, they are grasping, possessive, and overly emotional. They are preoccupied by desire and can cling obsessively to what gives them pleasure. Entranced by the play of seduction and manipulation, they constantly seek who and what they want in an indiscriminate way. They seem to prefer the game of seduction rather actually being with someone. They can be fantasy-oriented, narcissistic, have poor boundaries, and be codependent. They feel lonely, insignificant, and incomplete, so they magnetize others in order to seek confirmation and prove their own existence. They want to totally unite with a lover and are desperately afraid to let go. They fear they will lose any reason to live. Since they are totally dependent on another, they also hate them. When not engaged with others, they feel lonely, incomplete, inadequate, and insecure. Like a chameleon, they can change colors to meet any expectation from another.

Padma is associated with fire in its ability to both purify and destroy, with a promise of warmth that can also burn. The associated sense perception is hearing, in a larger sense of having resonance. The season is spring, when the world bursts into bloom and people fall in love.

Karma: Actively Engaging Green Energy

Karma has the wisdom of all accomplishing action for the benefit of others. It emits a green energy, swift and energetic like the wind. People are full of positive energy, confident, and act in timely and appropriate ways in synchronicity with the world. They are efficient, effective, and practical and so fulfill actions without hassles. Everything they do is done with the utmost skill and latest technology. They see the possibilities inherent in situations and automatically take the appropriate course.

When neurotic, they are restless and speedy. They are power-hungry, competitive, manipulative, and wanting to control and dominate. Filled with impatience, they try to accomplish all of their goals with a one-track mind as quickly as possible. They want to destroy anything that obstructs their forward-moving energy. Everything is something to fix or get done. They desire a uniform, controlled world. If something does not fit the scheme, they destroy it. Anyone not marching to orders is dismissed. They want to be top dog and demand respect and, in turn, have no respect for anyone who does not have their life together. They only want to associate with people who have utmost efficiency and take full responsibility. Then they become jealous of anyone who might get ahead, so they are perpetually filled with a fear of failure, performance anxiety, and paranoia. There is no sense of relaxation or going with the flow. It's all busy, busy, busy: endless work.

Karma is associated with air or wind with its forward moving force. The sense perception is functional touch, engaging muscles to perform an action. The season is summer, full of endless activity.

• • •

In short, the Five Wisdoms at their best are spaciousness, clarity, enrichment, feeling, and action. At their worst they are constriction, confusion, poverty, obsession, and overdrive. The most important thing to consider is that within buddha's ignorance is spaciousness; within vajra's anger is clarity; within ratna's arrogance is authentic pride; within padma's obsessive passion is compassion; within karma's jealousy is respect. When combined, some energies can become very intensified:

Vajra blue and karma green:
"I am right and I have to act on it."

Vajra blue and ratna yellow:
"I am right and need more territory."

Padma red and ratna yellow:
"I need you, I need you. I can't live without you."

Padma red and karma green:
"I am going to get what I desire."

Awareness of these energies can offer a perspective on all aspects of our life—particularly our relationships. We could find ourself asking, *why is it that one person brings out my intellectual curiosity and another my physical desire? Why do I feel at ease with one person and anxious with another? Why do I feel powerful in one situation but inhibited in another? What is the energetic relationship between people, these situations, and myself?*

To have an experiential sense, pick one of the energies just listed. Read the description of its constriction and feel it viscerally. Put yourself in that world. Then allow yourself to relax and feel open and spacious. Read the wisdom aspect of the energy. Feel it viscerally.

One of Trungpa Rinpoche's favorite slogans was, "Be who you are." My hit on this is, "Be the best of who you are." Others have said:

"The privilege of a lifetime is being who you are."

–Joseph Campbell

"The point is that our true nature is not some ideal that we have to live up to. It's who we are right now, and that's what we can make friends with and celebrate."

–Pema Chödrön

"Perhaps the biggest tragedy of our lives is that freedom is possible, yet we can pass our years trapped in the same old patterns."

–Tara Brach

And finally: "Be yourself, everybody else is taken."

–Oscar Wilde

If we become the best of who we are, we are naturally in our wisdom, which considers others. That is how we shine and that is how we serve. It's not some conventional idea of being religious and doing good. We serve by being. Here is a poem I wrote:

Just like a swelling ocean offers a wave,
and a spring plant offers a flower
So, we, from the fullness of our being,
offer the best within us.

CHAPTER 2

What Are Your
Wisdom Energies?

The enlightened expression of yourself is in accord with
your inherent nature…Working with the buddha families
[Five Wisdoms] we discover that we already have certain
qualities. According to the tantric perspective, we cannot
ignore them and we cannot reject them and try to be something else. We should work with our neuroses, relate with
them and experience them properly. They are the only potential we have, and when we begin to work with them, we
see that we can use them as stepping stones.

—Chögyam Trungpa Rinpoche

We Are Patterns of Energy In-formation

Some personality traits are dysfunctional or neurotic. Habitual patterns close us: we fixate, solidify, and believe
things to be true. When open, we are compassionate or
wise and our characteristics are experienced as five qualities of
intrinsic sanity. So, we can be stubborn, jealous, picky and
fussy, possessive, or aloof. Other times we can be charming,
easy-going, clear-minded, efficient, generous, or appreciative.
With some parts of ourself we have confidence and shine. With

23

other parts we feel stuck, perpetually falling on our face. Other parts we may habitually hide. We can develop a communication with all our energies to assess our strengths and appreciate who we are as well as acknowledge our weaknesses and make them our work points. We are a walking book filled with information about ourself. We are constantly in formation, in flux.

Our personality manifests in our physicality, thoughts, emotions, and expression. We radiate a particular energetic quality and engage in actions aligned with our energetic style. We *experience* the energy of our inner world through our thoughts, breathing, emotions, and felt sense. We experience the outer world through our sense perceptions. We *express* our energy through our body posture, the way we move, and how we dress; our facial expressions, physical sensations, and mannerisms; the tone and tempo of our voice and our word choices. We become an open book through our attitudes, decisions, actions, and how we relate to others.

We have the potential for all of the energies and yet, amazingly, are uniquely who we are. We have a pattern integrity. As a personality system we gain deep insights about who we are. The key to being our real self is self–awareness. Awareness begins to flood everything we think, feel, say, and do. We begin to recognize our deeply engrained habitual patterns.

We become fascinated. We all so want to know who we are: our personal mix of colors and how we manifest. We might say, "Got it: I must be green," or we could become totally confused and want someone else to tell us who we are—think padma here. So, to begin, it is "all about me." But why would we want to put ourself in a box labeled "green" or "red" or "blue"? Then we take the perspective that we are a mix of colors. Our sense of "me" just got bigger. The point here is to find a balance with all five and their infinite permutations. If we don't balance the energies, they explode or collapse.

Having our unique personality means that we see the world in a particular way. It can be truly hard to see that whatever we experience is from our own point of view. We are convinced that others must see it as we do. Like a fish in water, we are hardly aware that what we experience is our version. We might identify with others, whether it be nationality, religion, or profession, and feel that we are all swimming in the same water. We make assumptions that others are going to think and act according to our expectations, and we are shocked that they don't. We begin to see that we have been blind to people and situations more foreign to us. It is only through thoroughly experiencing the energies can we truly understand others.

Our Layered Self

We have a personal self that identifies with, and stays true to, our uniqueness. It includes both when we shine and when we get stuck. The problem is we often go around and around with this mantra: "I don't think much of myself, but it's all I think about." Actually that is our starting point. We work with our neuroses as our immediate access point.

We all have moments when we feel synchronized with ourself and our world. We experience a quality of openness and relaxation. We feel our own goodness and inner strength. At these times our concepts drop away. We are in the experience, in the groove, riding the energy of the moment. These are times when we shine and we are the best of who we are. At other times we can't seem to get out of our own way. We feel awkward at best, or gripped by strong emotions at worst. We feel stuck. We flip flop between these extremes of feeling good or bad about ourself.

How long can we punish ourself? Why do we need to con-
demn ourself all the time? How many times can we do that?
There comes a point where we have to treat ourself well.
We need to pull up our socks and celebrate life along with
the practice. Such celebration is close to the attainment of
enlightenment in one lifetime, actually.

–Chögyam Trungpa Rinpoche

Then we begin to see that we have a vast self where we
delve below the surface of our personality and align with a
greater consciousness, a deeper, more universal being. It gives
energy, power, and magnetism to our every endeavor. We allow our innate qualities to become our unique brand of brilliance! Underneath our individual stories, dramas, hopes, and
fears, we touch into a deeper peace, wisdom, kindness, strength,
and confidence. Confidence and loving kindness go together—
when confident, we are kind; when kind we are confident. Being more kind and loving to our vast self, we are more generous and open to others. So, then the world becomes kind and
filled with compassion as well.

Tension is who you think you should be. Relaxation is who
you are.

–Chinese proverb

So, there is a journey here. We learn to have some kind of
trust in our basic nature. We learn to believe in ourself by embodying a real sense of fearlessness, trust, and confidence. We
see that our style is not regarded as a mistake. We are who we
are. This inoculates us against the slings and arrows of others.
"Nobody can make you feel inferior without your consent," as
Eleanor Roosevelt famously said.

Our expression of wisdom can have many qualities:

- Relax and be to open our heart
- Relax and look to see clearly
- Relax and feel to have a visceral experience
- Relax and enjoy to feel vital
- Relax and do to be done

The Ups and Downs

Our energetic style intensifies in two ways: when our fixated thoughts become emotional upheavals and when life pushes our buttons. Inner and outer always work in tandem. "I am in a puddle on the floor because my lover left me and I just got fired." In this woe-is-me scenario, outer circumstances trigger an endless personal storyline of confusion and grief. Our energy can be stuck over a period of time, even a lifetime. This creates an imbalance in our psychophysical being. If we don't find a balance of energies in our life, one of our energies could explode or collapse. We could become psychologically and/or physically ill.

It is necessary to first work with the texture of the solidification. We could embrace whatever arises—the good, the bad, and the ugly—with an unconditional open heart. Befriending our stuck places is what turns our energy around from feeling constricted to feeling expansive. We do not have to discard what we think are our negative qualities as bad. In fact, by embracing them, we discover they are our best assets. When we appreciate both the sane and confused qualities of our experience, we discover our full spectrum of energies and have great liberty to be who we are!

So we don't reject our confusion—what a waste!—but recycle it into its wisdom aspect. There is a specific and reciprocal relationship between the neurosis and wisdom in each energy.

"Boy, he's so angry; wow he's so clear!" The key is that when we are self-referential, defending our mental fixations and a solidified sense of "I," we are in neurotic self-protecting ego. When we embody the wisdoms, with direct experience in the moment—what's happening is happening—we touch our wisdom.

Getting To Know Ourself

Knowing ourself, knowing our potential, is key to being able to interact more harmoniously with others and more effectively in what we do. Our multi-dimensional personality has five facets. You have the capacity to be:

1. Present in the moment
2. Insightful and think clearly
3. Resourceful and generous
4. Engaging and speak from your heart
5. Efficient in accomplishing your tasks

At different times in different circumstances, one or more of our energies is needed. Each has the ability to serve us. However, if we are locked into hours and hours of one energy day after day, we become energetically unbalanced and exhausted. How do we work with our mix?

> You see the absence of karma and decide that karma is the solution. But what if ratna is the solution? What if I need more nurturing to feel aligned enough to tap into karma? Or often padma is the solution. My passion gives me energy to take karma action. Vajra can do this too. If I can see the vision, I can take karma action.
>
> —Karuna Rockwell

To get to know ourself better, we can ask some questions:

- How do we envision ourself?
- What motivates us?
- How do we think, feel, and act in situations?
- How do we manage our emotions?
- Do our emotions get in the way or can we harness them to serve us?
- Can we balance our energies with all aspects of ourself engaged?
- Can we be fully who we are on the job?
- Are we able to bring our full attention to whatever we do?

Each of the energies has a different way of perceiving a situation. Let's take climate change. Buddha energy will be fairly indifferent: whatever happens happens. We get a lot of the vajra energy perspective from scientists who give us both the big picture and analyze the situation to its minutest detail. People with a dominance of ratna energy mostly care about the earth and the animals. This is very silly but I keep thinking a teenage girl with a dominant padma quality could say, "Great! I get to wear my summer clothes!" Karma people become activists.

The progression in our understanding of the Five Wisdoms goes like this: first it is all about me, then it is all about us, and finally it is all about all. It is like leaping into space where our perspective becomes transpersonal, non-self-referential, and vast. Seeing the interconnectedness of everyone and everything, the constantly moving, unceasing, dynamic, primal energy of the totality is transpersonal. The Five Wisdoms view offers a perspective of self-existing wisdom, not appropriated by any godhead or religion.

The Wisdom of the Five Wisdoms

During the many years that I have been living, teaching, and writing about the Five Wisdoms, I have been asked many times, "Why five? Isn't it just wisdom?" Ultimately this is true. The highest truth or wisdom is that there is nothing particular to hold onto; all is fleeting and impermanent. However, Tantric Buddhism speaks of wisdom as having five primary qualities which correspond to the elements. This is the kindergarten level: knowing colors and shapes. Ultimately there are infinite combinations pointing to the amazing diversity in people and life experience.

Ultimately the Five Wisdoms are a self-existing energy that is a positive life force. The good news is that this wisdom is our natural inheritance. It is a quality of wakefulness or sanity. It can be pointed out, recognized, and encouraged. It is close to us and we can experience it and touch into it all of the time. The genuine experience of wisdom is simple, direct, and sane. It is not theoretical, conceptual, or idealized. It is a deep root of basic goodness, primal in its pervasiveness and power. It is basic because it is primal. It is good because it is true. We can have a certain pride that basic sanity does exist in our state of being.

There are so many propensities and possibilities. Life gives us the experience we need, and we must make every experience meaningful.

Let's not mess this up!

CHAPTER 3

What Is Your Unique Mix of Colors?

We have a lot of curiosity about who we are. In fact, our energetic dimension is a complex system. It all comes down to how we desire and perceive the world. Our mix of colors defines our personality. However, though often thought of as a typology, the difference here is that we have all five energies with our unique personal mix. There are infinite combinations of patterns and characteristics, making everyone in the world unique.

Just think, there are as many combinations of the five energies as there are people in the world! As one ancient text poetically puts it, "...as many as the sands in ten Ganges rivers." Infinite.

We are born with certain energies, this is our karmic inheritance. We are also born into certain energies, like our family and culture. Some circumstances or situations, like our work, demand certain energies, so we learn some energies as we adapt to life. There is both our inherent nature and what we nurture and cultivate. The energies are also constantly shifting due to changing life situations and time of life. We are both predictable and unique; the world is both predictable and surprising. There is no such thing as a black-and-white world; everything is very colorful!

Defining ourself as one or another energy is a very two-dimensional approach and not very accurate. It solidifies and centralizes our sense of who we are. "I'm padma and want to be flirtatious in every situation," no matter how inappropriate it may be, or "I'm vajra so I always know I am right," which clearly makes everyone else wrong. By boxing ourself in, we miss the play of the totality. Though we could display one or two particularly clearly, the others are always at play. What is also true is that some energies might feel very foreign. We feel like a tourist. I have often felt like a tourist in ratna, "I have gone to Ratnaland!" My reaction often is, "There's no space!" At some point I discovered how much ratna there is in my own energetic make up.

Recognizing our style has to do with paying close attention to our habitual patterns and tendencies from day to day and moment to moment. It's a 24-hours-a-day lifetime practice. We watch how we are in different situations, when there are no external pressures and when there is a crisis. Do we get upset, go to the phone, and call one friend after another and tell our story? Or do we sit down and analyze the whole thing, writing it out to become clear? Or do we go into a hole and do not want to talk to anybody? These are deeply, deeply ingrained habitual patterns! It is also how we desire our world. Do we desire it hot? Do we desire it cool? Do we desire it many colored, rich, and exciting or sparse, peaceful, and calm? Do we desire spicy or comfort food? Do we insist on clarity in every situation, not being able to stand confusion? Do we want decisions to be made right now, not being able to tolerate uncertainty? When we find ourself asking these questions, we need to pay attention to the flickering interests, and how we desire the world to be.

Knowing our mix of energies is extremely helpful. We could think of them as parts or facets of our personality, whether in their wisdom or neurosis. Our lives will be more harmonious if we have all of the wisdoms available to us. This allows us to draw on them and know what is the most needed or effective in a situation.

The wisdom of buddha provides a spaciousness so that each of the energies can also shine. Dominantly vajra, Clark also has a soft clarity. Ratna Gabriella has a tremendous graciousness. Padma Felicity enjoys the pleasures of life with her friends in a gentle way. Karma Steve knows when to act and when not to. When the neurosis of buddha energy combines with these four they all manifest their neurotic side more extremely.

The wisdom of vajra provides clarity; it's neurosis creates indignant anger. The wisdom of ratna grounds and nourishes; it's neurosis creates a poverty mentality. The wisdom of padma brings enjoyment into our life; it's neurosis creates emotional confusion. The wisdom of karma insures that what needs to be done will be done; it's neurosis leads to confrontation.

Dominant, Enhancement, and Mask

Our *dominant* energy, or basic nature, quality, or style, has to do with a sense of familiarity. We will recognize it and feel at home. We have always known ourself to be this way, since childhood. It feels primal, deeply ingrained, as naked as the day we were born. As a normal neurotic person, our dominant has both intelligent and confused aspects. It might not be where we are most comfortable, feels most pleasant, or we find most interesting. But it's what we seem to know best. It's what we identify with. We might show our dominant energy more fully or be more of a blend, so it's not always easy to detect it. Sometimes it's submerged or hidden. Others might see it in us before we do. Sometimes we are the last to know who we are.

As we start to identify with an energy, or two, as our dominant(s), we begin to deepen our experience of it. Friendliness and curiosity toward the dominant starts the process of freeing it from its shackles of neurosis. It also creates a sense of potentiality for other energies to become more available to us. We become more sophisticated about the whole process, becoming connoisseurs of our confusion and familiar with our wisdom. We begin to see many more possibilities within us, our full pallet of colors. We being to relate more to the totality of our world, allowing more permissible experiences.

Next to consider are *exits*. These are psychological shifts of energy from our dominant energy. An exit can either be an enhancement, which we have cultivated, or a mask or persona, which we take on to be more accepted. Exits can change as our situation changes. For instance, when I was a creative artist, performer, and single, I had a lot of padma energy. When I got married and had a family, and all the etcetera that goes with that, it brought out more of my ratna. Certainly, going from being an artist to an administrator brought out more karma. Teaching and writing have brought out the clarity of vajra.

An *enhancement* energy as an exit is, by definition, an expression of our sanity. It is an energy with which we have learned to express ourself: the way we dress, an adornment of who we are, our skill set. Perhaps we have admired it in others or see how useful it is. Perhaps we see it in our culture or family. We feel comfortable in it, so we often express ourself that way. It can be very helpful. Others might think it is our basic nature because they see it in us first.

To fully manifest our enhancement, we could emphasize it, develop it, make it into a style or way to relate to the world. It could change as our life situation changes. For instance, if we are very padma but have a job that requires a lot of karma energy, we could cultivate karma energy. We can also use an enhancement energy like an antidote to save ourself from a painful situation. If we are in an emotional upheaval, we might want to do something active, like clean the house or play soccer. We begin to have more sense of being able to switch gears—whatever the situation demands, we can do it. We are not just in one energy to meet every situation.

A *mask* energy arises based on confusion. There is always a level of discomfort because we do it as a pretense. We fake it. We pretend to be something because we feel we should, that we are expected to relate to the world in a more acceptable style. Perhaps we are at a company party and want to appear likable or are in front of a classroom and want to appear that we have the answer. But, somehow, we feel out of sync with ourself. It can lead to mental stress and/or physical illness because we are not being who we are. Interestingly, the same energy could be both an enhancement and a mask: we could manifest either sanity or confusion depending on situations. It is also possible that someone does not have a mask.

There is a lot of sanity in relating to our enhancement. We are attracted to it so want to experience it. The mask is more complicated—we take it on, but are not at ease doing so. Generally, we are not aware of these categorizations and learning them takes time. So, we go on a journey to deepen our friendship with our basic energy and see the skillfulness of the enhancement. Confusion is inevitable.

When I was first introduced to the Five Wisdoms I thought, OK, I got this... And then I was confused for years. Now, after some 40 years, my personal mix is more evident to me. Interestingly, my mix is more balanced. I am practicing what I preach and incorporating, "the daily diet of five."

Another possibility is called complementary. We often choose an energy that complements ours in our friends or partners. It can ventilate our style or even puncture our solidity. It basically provides another reference point. It can be like taking a vacation from who we are. So, we might gravitate toward a person who is quite different from us. If we are an overly serious kind of person, we might delight in a friend who just likes having fun.

Ultimately, our enhancement becomes integrated into who we are. Our mask falls away when we feel more comfortable exposing ourself in a genuine way. Simply put, when we enjoy our energies, they dawn as wisdoms. Then we respond with the combination of wisdoms that are needed in the moment. We can become embodied, colorful, and dynamic in attuning to our world and responding to what is needed in an appropriate and timely way.

When we trust our basic nature and have confidence in it, we relax. Then we permit all aspects of ourself to shine through rather than being stuck in one set of characteristics. We put ourself in a bind if we continually desire to be like someone else. Admiring another is fine; thinking you have to be them is self-destructive.

The Dynamic Play of the Five Wisdoms

When we start to see the lively, powerful, and potent dance of the energies, we see that there are limitless ways they play off of each other. How the energies combine is a never-ending exploration. There are so many possibilities in our mix of colors. Someone's anger could be a threat. Another person's intelligence could be inspiring for us but could create jealousy in another.

Most importantly, as I wrote in *Natural Brilliance*, "The buddha energy is the foundation one; it accommodates the others. It has an affinity to the energetic state we experience in meditation, but exaggerates it. When the wisdom of buddha permeates the other four, their wisdom arises. However, any energy overly intensified becomes stuck buddha. There is nowhere else to go: we zone out. So buddha energy is the fulcrum: experiencing its wisdom liberates the others; engulfed in its stupor, we experience the neurosis of the others."

The qualities of spaciousness, clarity, and warmth are the essence of buddha, vajra, and padma wisdom respectively. In their stuck aspect they are denial, aggression, and passion. That we can be open and closed, clear and critical, and warm and cold are pretty familiar to us. Ratna and karma are more stable than vajra and padma and they have a relationship with each other. Vajra becomes karma, "I see clearly what needs to be done and I am going to make it happen." Padma becomes ratna, playful courting moves into a stable marriage.

With each energy, there could be more relationship to either the neurosis or the sanity. It is not uncommon to feel that you have the neuroses of all of them! Bad news? Good news? Actually, it is neither. It's just your energy. The most basic instruction is not to solidify who we think we are, but just stay with our awareness. Let the recognition of ourselves or others arise with a sudden insight.

Let's look at how the energies feed off of each other and create a neurotic cycle. First there's buddha's ignorance and immobility; that starts to wake up to vajr's criticalness, sharpness, and harshness. Then there is ratna's pride and sense of territoriality; that is furthered by padma's obsessive desire; wanting to protect that at all costs is karma's need for control and underlying paranoia.

That was the bad news.

The good news is the wisdom-oriented cycle. There is buddha's openness and sense of all accommodating space. There is vajra's inquisitiveness and understanding. Ratna brings in possibility, enriching the situation. Padma brings in appreciation of detail, refinement, and discrimination. Then karma makes it happen. This is a wonderful cycle for the creation of anything, from a work of art to the creation of a society.

We could also think of ourself as having layers. Our true nature is at a core level. We feel totally open and have unconditional confidence. Then there is a layer of emotional reactivity, particularly when we are uncertain of our ground. We are locked into our version of reality, triggered by what others say and do, and move into our defensive routines. This is the layer of the ego. Our actions are the third layer. In any given situation our experience is always a combination of these different layers.

Some styles are more acceptable than other styles in our culture and family. For instance, in Latin American or southern European cultures, being emotional is quite accepted. Northern countries, and I am generalizing here, tend to be cooler in nature. If we are in an extremely efficient, capable, and organized family, but we are really just a padma sweetheart, it could be that our padma never gets acknowledged in our family of origin or in our marriage. So, we cover it over with karma and padma becomes submerged where it festers as neurosis. Our true self has not been allowed to see the light of day. One day there might be a volcanic eruption of this energy and we have an affair. Sound familiar?

Our emotions are very immediate and available so we can become aware of how they create certain patterns and sequences. In a given situation, one emotion could trigger another one. A common progression could go through passion, aggression, and ignorance. Once I was listening to music I love. At first there was such passion and sense of longing and connecting. Then they went on a little too long, and I start to get critical and angry. Finally, I just tuned out.

Very common in our world is that intensified vajra, sharp and direct, becomes karma, wanting to move into action. As well, padma's seduction can lead to ratna's indulgence in that. Passion can lead to either greed or jealousy. A familiar example is how padma dominates a new relationship as we court and flirt, and then ratna is more present with home and family. So we begin to see how these energies work situationally.

Karma, manifesting as speed, and ratna, manifesting as earth, are like opposite forces. They are the strongest ones in their expression, very definite. Vajra can be clear without being pushy and padma can express a genuine passion, so both allow more space for others. Vajra and karma are the masculine energies associated with insistence on being right, competitiveness, and power. Padma and ratna are the feminine energies associated with engaging emotionally, attracting others, and creating enjoyable situations. Buddha is neutral and is not gender specific.

Mental activity is vajra energy, which is more masculine. Embodied energy, like ratna and padma, is more feminine. When we are just in our heads, we don't integrate sensuality and sexuality. An image I use is that water and wind (the elements of vajra and karma) can snuff out fire (the element of padma). It looks like burn out. Wind could also increase the vital energy of fire.

There are many more examples of the dynamic play of the energies in chapter 4 of my book *Natural Brilliance*. We could definitely say the possibilities are infinite.

Instruction for Noticing the Five Energies

From Nem Bajra, a Five Wisdoms Training graduate

Buddha Energy

- I breathe in and I breathe out...
- Let go of any specific agenda, just be aware of the surrounding.
- Notice the space in the room, the vast and boundless hazy sky, and the stillness of things.
- Reflect upon the environment and space in your office, where people come and go, work together and all wonderful things happening in your everyday work.

Vajra Energy

- Seeing. I see...
- Notice the structure of house with pillars and beams, the window frames, the distinct shapes of houses in the distance, and the shapes of the nearby hills.
- Reflect upon your vision and mission, organizational structure, management principles, infrastructure, and policies that allow you to conduct your business effectively.

Ratna Energy

- Touching. I sense...
- Notice the richness of fruits and vegetables, the nutritious wheat bread, the earth that you walk upon, and the abundance of trees and plants in the garden.
- Reflect upon your resources including people, equipment, and money that enable you to carry out your projects. And how you appreciate revenues, materials and labor provided by customers, partners and suppliers.

Padma Energy

- Hearing. I hear...
- Notice the kindness and caring of people in the room, listening to their stories of joy and challenges, and being heard by everyone.
- Reflect upon people at work, dialogues, teamwork, social events, client relationships, etc.

Karma Energy

- I walk, I sit, I stand, I do…
- Notice birds flying, wind blowing, walking along the garden.
- Reflect upon operations at work, production, delivery, project management, sports events, etc.

Let s Go for the Rainbow

Ultimately, we want to be able to manifest all five energies in their wisdom. We might want to nail it down, but when we take the perspective that we are a mix of colors, our sense of "me" gets bigger. We have the potential for an infinite combination of energies. Embracing all of the energies is a more complete picture of who we are. Every facet of our personality is connected to every other facet. We can recognize their distinctiveness and also understand their relationships, how they work together, the sense of layering, bleeding, or merging of colors. Ultimately, we see that all facets are of one thing, like a prism, rainbow, or kaleidoscope.

CHAPTER 4

Becoming Who You Are

We do not have to be ashamed of what we are. As sentient beings we have wonderful backgrounds. These backgrounds may not be particularly enlightened or peaceful or intelligent. Nevertheless, we have soil good enough to cultivate; we can plant anything in it.

–Chögyam Trungpa Rinpoche

You can think of the spiritual practice as a kind of spiritual re-parenting...you're offering yourself the two qualities that make up good parenting: understanding–seeing yourself for who you truly are–and relating to what you see with unconditional love.

–Tara Brach

An interesting twist of life is that though we became who we are at birth it takes a lifetime to fully inherit who we are. Somehow that first innocence of childhood, that fundamental goodness, is perpetually challenged. Throughout our lives we are as if continually re-creating ourself to meet what life has to offer us. The good news is that by instilling goodness in ourself, we can create a psychological and physical sense of well-being.

Where We Find Ourself

If we stop to reflect about what we really want, without a doubt we would say we want to be happy, or fulfilled, or, free from the oppression we feel about our lives.

However, too often we have a black and white, good and bad, view of the world. We think we have to change ourself, to be better somehow. We want to transform into something else. We want to turn away from the so-called bad and turn toward what we think of as good. This indeed becomes a battle. We struggle with the parts of ourself that we don't like, and the more we struggle, the tighter we get. The tightness itself becomes another reason to think we are, somehow, bad. We could also want to change the world so we get politically involved. There are endless "wrongs" that we want to set "right." We think the solution is "out there."

Habitually, we think of something external that will give us happiness or fulfillment. Our world is delightful and draws us out to enjoy it, but this gets tricky because it is a powerful seduction. We dream of more money, a better car or house, or a vacation. We are also perpetual shoppers. If we are ill, we look for this cure to this ailment and that healing modality for that pain. Even in the spiritual realm, we are seduced by the brilliance of great spiritual teachers and traditions, but never commit to one. We become more entertained with more adventures. We stay in the marketplace and never come home. But our desire for external objects of gratification will never be sated. Our wanting will never end. Sought after this way, happiness will always elude us. Fundamentally our dissatisfaction with life has little to do with externals.

Perhaps we need to pay attention to the wanter, the desirous one. At some point the shopping has to stop and we have to allow ourself to be fully immersed in working with ourself. We need to connect to the core of who we are, the fullness of who we are.

We have to cook. But how do we start? The biggest obstacle to us finding our way is self-deception. Ignorance. Denial. We refuse to see that our deeply engrained habits are undermining our being. I often get out of balance myself and note that I don't take my own words to heart. As many times as I have been told that I need to take more breaks when working at my computer so as not to grow concrete bricks on my shoulders, I forget. A sneaky little reminder enters my mind-stream, yet I go on clicking away. How stupid can we get even when we know better? Very stupid.

At the same time, we have to stop judging ourself. For me, two words that work better than good and bad, and the conflicting states of mind aroused by them, are wholesome and unwholesome. Simply put, wholesome means that which promotes mental and physical well-being and unwholesome is that which is harmful to us. What we each choose to do to promote health is different. How we perpetually sabotage our well-being is also different. Some of us need to find ways to relax, others might need to rouse more energy. So, we need to be careful in selecting that which helps to bring us into balance.

Fortunately, we can go deeper. Perhaps we have noticed that we feel our best when we are truly relaxed and content for no real reason at all. We have felt the best of buddha energy, a sense of timelessness and spaciousness. Warmth and clarity could have arisen spontaneously. Yes, we might say it was because we were on a vacation far away from the worries of our daily life. But in doing so, we miss the point. We need to acknowledge that these qualities of being exist within us.

So how can we be nourished from within without going to that tropical isle of our dreams? We could come home, come home to ourself. As my daughter said to me one day, "When I feel lonely, I find that who I miss most is myself." Rather than always focusing outward, we can cultivate ways of just being with ourself. We can find a sense of spaciousness, relaxation, and warmth within us, wherever we are, whatever we are doing. This is something we all long for, yet it seems elusive. As a seven-year-old, my daughter sometimes played having a tea party with me. She liked to make up the names of the teas. One afternoon I could hardly contain myself with laughter as she offered me "Peace and Quiet" tea. She understood what I most wanted.

There are two factors to our primary struggle: the outer and inner equation. We take great delight in mastering our external world, having the best technology, the most efficiency, and more possibilities. Anything we want to know is a few clicks away. How seductive is that? Moreover, there is an exponential growth of material goods. We know more, own more, and accomplish more. To take advantage of every opportunity, we move through our lives with great speed. We pile meeting on meeting, task on task. External demands are out of proportion to what we can handle. We can't remember things as they become overwhelming. Preoccupied by what came before and what happens next, we are not in the present moment. We revisit decisions, because we can't remember we made them before. We are confused as to how to prioritize the day, not knowing what to accept and reject. The dis-ease of stress is a daily occurrence.

> If we wish to pick flowers from a tree, we must first cultivate the roots and trunk, which means that we must work with our fears, frustrations, disappointments, and irritations, the painful aspects of life. We must see the truth of suffering, the reality of dissatisfaction. We cannot ignore it and attempt to examine only the glorious, pleasurable aspects of life. If one searches for a promised land, a Treasure Island, then the search only leads to more pain.
>
> –Chögyam Trungpa Rinpoche

Practicing Being Ourselves

Magic is the power within oneself. You have enough strength, exertion and energy to view things as they are, personally, properly, and directly. You have the chance to experience the brightness of life and the haziness of life, which is also a source of power. The fantastically sharp-edged quality of life can be experienced personally and directly. There is a powerful sense of perception available to you.

–Chögyam Trungpa Rinpoche

Unfortunately, we tend to have a negative preoccupation with ourself. We become full of ourself in a critical way. We have times of elation and times of despair. We flip between extremes of feeling good or bad about ourself. We seem to be ignorant about what fundamentally makes us happy. We are self-absorbed rather than self-aware. It's as if there is a part of us that is committed to keeping us unhappy.

To turn this around, we could just stop. Discover what is triggering us. Is it work? Relationships? Basic survival? Is our response on automatic, deepening the rut of our same old ways of going about things? Or can we undercut the juggernaut of our habitual patterns? Can we simply be with the experience rather than react or try to fix it? If we accept pain without the confusion of fear, we can listen to its message and respond with clarity.

It seems that there is no other way than to work through the natural situation of daily existence. Hope, fear, pain, pleasure, misery, bliss: these dichotomies constantly go on. In order to transcend them, we have to use them as stepping stones, without relying on heretical ideas that enlightenment could be achieved by external means. Something has to develop within ourself.

–Chögyam Trungpa Rinpoche

Change can only come from deep personal work. There are propensities and possibilities: being aware of our propensity to behave in certain ways and the possibility to open to new ways of being. This equates with the Buddhist perspective that transcendental knowledge cannot be achieved by logical means; we have to cultivate it within ourself. We can empower ourself, our life, with basic principles and core practices. We can find balance between inward turning and outward going. What we arrive at is that our true nature is not some ideal that we have to live up to. It's who we are right now, and that's what we can make friends with and celebrate.

Take note of these 5 points:

- Look at yourself with total honesty, cutting through self-deception
- Stop sabotaging what you want most, your happiness
- Create positive attitudes
- Have good intentions and cultivate actions that support them
- Trust your innate intelligence

In this way, we can steer ourself toward a more wholesome way of being. The more we do this, the more we are capable of doing it.

The Doubt and Confidence Equation

Self-aggression, our inner critic, and self-doubt are pervasive in our society. A doubting mind is based on fear. We believe our story line and go around and around with our favorite top tunes. Being triggered by external events and people reinforces our internal sense of doubt in ourself. It's like we are ingrained with a sense of original sin or basic badness.

We are haunted by a need to accomplish, a get-ahead mentality. We are driven by deadlines, bottom lines, and goals. A sense of failure is close behind. The voices of parents, teachers, peers, and the church buzz around us like mosquitos. Then they become internalized. We live with a sense of basic badness, shame, guilt. It makes us feel unworthy, not good enough, and that we don't measure up. We have made the inner critic very powerful. But it doesn't have to be this way. We can get on equal footing with our critical mind. No one can make us feel bad unless we consent to it.

Confidence is the potency of our own being, with our myriad of colors. When we overcome self-doubt, we tap into our natural power or strength. It is based on loving ourself and feeling worthy. We cultivate an authentic presence, powerfully in the present full of spaciousness, clarity, and warmth. This transcends dark versus light. We practice rousing and riding our confidence.

Brilliance overpowers doubt. It is a state of confidence that is unwavering and needs no reference point. There is no room for doubt. It is gentle because fear does not arise. It is strong because it is resourceful. It trusts in the heart so it is joyous and has humor. Then we open to the self-existing dynamic energy of phenomenon. It is golden, brilliant, luminous, sacred, and, most of all, colorful. We can experience the endless display of our world. We know this before we can articulate it.

When we actually lean into doubt, it can open to vastness. My favorite slogan is, "When in doubt go to Buddha." There is intelligence in doing nothing.

Radical Acceptance

When the fabric of my marriage was tearing at the seams, I knew the world I had known would no longer be. I was confused and distraught. I was in a therapy session with Virginia Hilliker, a person who I consider the grand dame of Contemplative Psychotherapy. I was going on and on about how confused

I was about the ending of my marriage. Finally, she smiled and looked at me and said, "You aren't confused. You just don't accept." Her words hit me like a lightning bolt that penetrated the darkness of my confusion. Yowie! That was a moment of deep insight! Virginia had a masterful way of performing a therapeutic intervention. It was always done with a smile so it had a sense of loving kindness as she cut to the heart of the matter. Spinning circles around myself trying to "figure it out" was getting me nowhere. I had to surrender to the situation as it was. Acceptance is seeing things as they are. And letting them be. Without reactivity.

> Radical acceptance is the willingness to experience ourself and our life as it is. A moment of radical acceptance is a moment of genuine freedom… Nothing is wrong—whatever is just "Real life."…On this sacred path of radical acceptance, rather than striving for perfection, we discover how to love ourself into wholeness.
>
> —Tara Brach

So, we can be bitter and resentful, or be in the silent awareness of things as they are. We can resist or accept what is. When we resist, there is a hardening, an inner contraction of negativity. When we accept, we expand, yield internally, and surrender.

A primary delusion that we carry around is that we are in control. Instead, we could accept that today will be what it is, let go of what was yesterday, and have faith in what will be tomorrow. When we have learned to accept things as they are, our life gets easier. We will still make mistakes, fail, and sometimes have a rough ride. Accepting something doesn't necessarily mean liking it. It means we have stopped trying to manipulate it. We could simply let go and move on to discover what is next.

Denying or ignoring the truth of the moment creates tremendous confusion for us. We become weak, a victim of our circumstance. When we accept, we are strong. When we take full responsibility for something, we empower ourself to be able to change anything.

When we are confused and full of doubt, we have likely failed to accept things as they are. We have forgotten that what happens, happens. Everything has its intelligence, its brilliance. Our endless effort to protect self is our one enormous folly. No self, no problem. So, aligning with our wisdom, our goodness, the best of who we are in the moment, time and time again, is the mark of a warrior. We can always be armed with the best within us. We can lead from within.

Fundamentally, there is only one error, one mistake we make: we forget that we are inherently good, wise, and loving. We don't appreciate this simple yet profound truth of our existence. Our experience of it is also magical and inspirational, beyond concept. It opens our heart. There is a sense of perpetual warmth toward ourself and others. The times when our heart truly opens and we feel raw, tender, or perhaps sad in a sweet sad way, we have come to the depths of our being. We can cultivate these moments of tender heart and gentleness.

The Kaleidoscope of Who We Are

The message of the Five Wisdoms is that who we are has many subtleties. Like an ever-shifting kaleidoscope, we manifest different energies in different situations. Our personal self has to do with our personality. It gets very caught up with the triumvirate of me, myself, and I. This self is ego's hard wiring: the mental models that propel us through our day. Then there is a rich juicy layer of thoughts and emotions where there is always a lot going on. We get triggered by what others say and do, become reactive, and move into defensive routines. Our vast self is where we delve below the surface of our personality to a deeper, more universal being. It is the essential nature of our very core, unchanging and basically good. Our authenticity is sourced from this basic goodness. The good news is that hard wiring is inseparable from our unique strengths, values, and vision. Our innate qualities can become our unique brand of wisdom. This gives energy, power, and magnetism to our every endeavor. Underneath our individual stories, dramas, hopes, and fears, we can touch into the deeper peace, wisdom, kindness, strength, and confidence that is already there.

> When you find that you are a genuine person, you begin to feel good and solid. Beyond that, more than solid, more than real, you realize that you have guts of some kind. When you see yourself genuinely, you find a very large space there, which is unconditional and contains ventilation and breathing space. When you have seen yourself fully, you begin to feel unconditionally good. At the same time, you being to acknowledge the existence of greater wisdom.
>
> –Chögyam Trungpa Rinpoche

Our basic nature is generic. There is a sense of equality in all beings. The Five Wisdoms point to the diversity in people, places, and situations. We have a kinship with others in the basic goodness of our humanity and yet we are all uniquely ourself. We are uniquely who we are and have our very special way to shine and a particular way to get stuck. Being authentic unmasks who we are; we discover we can be who we are with confidence. Living in our busy often chaotic world, it is easy to lose our authenticity. However, if we think of those who we most admire, they seem to come from deeper values. Personal authenticity is the catalyst for the wisdoms to shine. I have found that living in and visiting other cultures gives us a sense of kinship with others.

The wonder of the diversity in our world never ceases to amaze me. No matter what our circumstances, we can touch our inner wisdom. I am reminded of Etty Hillesum who, as she walked the barbed-wire fence of the concentration camp by moonlight, reflected on how wonderful the world is. So, this is possible. It has been done before and will be done again. We can light the torch of wisdom to illuminate the darkness of suffering and confusion. We can rouse a wholehearted intention to work with ourself and others to create a better world. Even my tango teachers agree and often tell me they are "creating a better world, one tango at a time."

As the events of the world take their shifts and turns, holding our deepest values can be our guiding light to keep us on course. From the perspective of the Five Wisdoms, this lies in discovering the wisdom at the heart of confusion, a wisdom that responds to the energy of the moment with openness, clarity, and warmth.

> We must be willing to be completely ordinary people, which means accepting ourself as we are without trying to become greater, purer, more spiritual, more insightful. If we can accept our imperfections as they are, quite ordinarily, then we can use them as part of the path. But if we try to get rid of our imperfections, then they will be enemies, obstacles on the road to our "self-improvement."
>
> –Chögyam Trungpa Rinpoche

Everyone has their very unique journey. Everyone has their own potential or capacity to gain higher realization, as every fruit has its potential to be ripe. How much we realize our wisdom depends on our level of being ripened.

CHAPTER 5

Wherever You Go
There THEY Are

If you can afford to be what you are, then that automatically means that you could receive others as your guests. Then the ground your guests are treading on is safe ground, so nobody is going to fall through the floor. What you are is a sound, well-built house, your own house, and people could be welcome in it. That makes people more comfortable and welcome, so they don't have to put up their portion of resistance anymore. It is mutual understanding.

–Chögyam Trungpa Rinpoche

We live in a world full of people. We are social beings. Most of us relate to and communicate with others every day. All of our relationships effect who we are. Yet we often don't have a clue as to how to foster genuine relationships and have meaningful communication. Whether in our personal sphere, in the public arena of work relationships, or on a global scale across cultures and religions, we need to discover how best to relate and communicate. This is our challenge. As Trungpa Rinpoche said, "People are our business." Societal norms keep us locked into stereotypical roles. Caught up in our differences, we create a barrier between ourselves and others. Opening to others is difficult and thus rare, but how rare does it have to be? It just creates layer on layer of *in*authenticity.

As if we didn't have enough to deal with in our own mix of energies, there is the constant challenge of how we relate to others. Everywhere we go, there they are. And we have reactions, whether positive or negative, to everyone in our lives. There also seems to be a mystery underlying our relationships. Why are they both predictable and surprising? Why are we awkward or at ease, tense or friendly, with different people? Why do some people seem aggressive and others engaging? Why does one person bring out our intellectual curiosity and another our physical desire? Why do we become triggered by some people and inspired by others? Why do we feel powerful in one situation but inhibited and frustrated in another? Needless to say, the mix of colors gets more confusing when we open to others' energies. Whose movie are we in?

> In inviting sentient beings as guests, the bodhisattva, the practitioner in the Mahayāna, has a constant sense of the impermanence of the relationship—the guest is going to leave. So we view this as an opportune time, and there is constant appreciation. Our guests come. We entertain them and relate with them. Afterward, the guests thank us, we say good-bye, and we go back to running our home. There is a sense of the preciousness and the impermanence of the relationship, a sense of that relationship being extremely special. Our guest may be our husband, our wife, or our child—everybody is the guest of everybody.
>
> –Chögyam Trungpa Rinpoche

The Five Wisdoms system has great insight into human dynamics. When we understand energy, we understand the dynamics of relationships. By having an experiential sense of both the confusion and sanity of each energy, we can read the energy of others. With a constant inward and outward oscillation of awareness, we can recognize their sanity and align with it and we can see where they get stuck and have compassion.

Most of us take our relationships for granted. We assume that our boss James, or our neighbor Molly, or our student Steven, is going to meet our expectations of how a boss or neighbor or student should think and act. Too often we are surprised to find that it is not so. Misunderstandings lead to conflicts, which lead to a frozen atmosphere.

Communication comes to a standstill. We would rather just get the job done or go on with life day after day and not deal with them. However, when we give our relationships attention, they will go more smoothly. Everything we do will feel supported by that relationship.

> ...business modeling is for the most part trivial, but the problems are often intractable. You know, Joe hates Sally's guts, and they don't talk, and haven't for years, and they need to work together to succeed. It is a huge gap, but not one that can be solved intellectually.
>
> –Fred Kofman

Here are some dynamics in relationships. If two karma people are in a space and they are speeding around each other, sparks fly because there's so much friction from the amount of movement. If a padma and a vajra person are together, the padma person is full of intensity, heat, and emotion and the vajra person is impatient with all of the drama and becomes judgmental. A buddha person just spaces out.

We could look at the patterns of how our energies resist or merge with another.

Here is a classic example of how one energy can affect another. Imagine that padma Felicity and vajra Clark are in a relationship. She is attracted to his sense of strength and clarity.

He is attracted to her bubbly personality, and how she is always expressing herself. At best, the relationship is very complementary. However, they get polarized when they go into their neurosis. He gets impatient with her needing to relate with everything emotionally and she feels constantly judged by him. She wants more engagement: he prefers to be unto himself. When they soften and merge, they become open to each other's full palette of colors and a subtle dance takes place. By relating to someone openly in this way, we are actually relating with their style of enlightenment.

Cultivating good relationships takes practice. For instance—and I can't say this enough—when we look at someone's faults, instead of seeing them as a weakness, we can have compassion for them. Whether we are someone with a difficult family life, have a conflictual work situation, are a therapist or teacher, or hold a leadership position, the same principles apply. Primarily we need the intention to make our relationships a priority. Conscious relationships can be a vehicle for essential change, a creative and dynamic way of working with others. They bring out the best qualities in each person and enhance communication.

In marriages, increasingly "until death do us part" has been replaced by "I want out of here." What is happening? Why is this so pervasive? Why are we continually surprised at this phenomenon when it is so common? Most importantly, how can we cope with the inexpressibly deep distress that is caused by partners splitting up? Perhaps the institution of marriage has been a disservice to many. It is not a given that two people are going to be on the same path, same wavelength, or same spiritual orientation as they move through life. Some people are naturally more consciously evolving and the status quo of their relationship is no longer satisfying. In these times of rapid change and endless possibility the couple has insurmountable exterior forces which can erode the status quo of their relationship. This is not to say that there aren't many people who have found fulfillment in marriage. It is just to point to the fact that because our world has so many opportunities, we are not all going to branch out in the same direction.

Authentic Relationships

What we need for an authentic relationship, based on the six paramitas, a traditional teaching on relating:

1. **Motivation:** making others a priority

2. **Generosity of spirit:** offering the best of ourself

3. **Discipline:** bringing work with ourself into working with others

4. **Patience:** it takes time

5. **Exertion:** sticking with it

6. **Understanding:** holding the view of working with self and others

My son Julian was having trouble with a work colleague. I said, "If you think that working this out is a distraction, it will never resolve itself. If you make working out your differences a priority, then things will go well." Later he commented, "This is the most important business advice you ever gave me."

Interestingly, having good relationships starts with having a good relationship with ourself. Sitting meditation, which we will explore in Chapters 9 and 10, is the most fundamental discipline of looking at ourself without judgment. It is the time proven method to honestly face ourself. We become more aware of our thoughts, feelings, and actions in how we interact with and affect others. Working with ourself becomes a powerful tool for working with others. It requires that we know ourself very well, so we can be a clear channel. The more we work with ourself, the more spontaneous we are in opening to others. The more we know ourself, the more we can know others. There is an oscillation between self and other. It is a potent combination of a personal and interpersonal path. It can be of enormous help to others and makes relationships a very lively journey.

The essence here is that we give another the best of who we are. It means being in the moment with someone, whatever they bring to us. We are open to whatever arises and are not thrown off by the unpredictable. Some of us panic when confronted by an unfamiliar situation. We just want to fix it. This takes us away from the moment. Instead, we could stay with it. Then we can offer a helping hand. It might not be heard or it might be the wrong time for someone to hear it. Later, they might come up with something completely appropriate. Their intelligence is at play too.

Cultivating Genuine Relationships

Cultivating authentic relationships requires that we develop certain skills. There are four steps to deepen our understanding of interpersonal process. These steps hold the essence of a contemplative approach to working with others:

1. **Authentic presence** is open and receptive and lets go of seeing only our own side.

2. **Energetic exchange** is being able to pick up on another's energetic tone or quality, the felt sense of another.

3. **Unbiased perception** allows us to see another, enter their world, and see things their way.

4. **Effective action**, or engaging effectively, involves spontaneously knowing what to say or do.

The inseparability of these four, enhanced by the Five Wisdoms qualities embodied in ourself, is very powerful. When we are present, we intuitively tune into others and see their energies clearly. Then we know how to respond. The commitment to working in this way can be a big leap. It is a willingness to take on confusing situations. It can be immensely rewarding and mutually beneficial. Our relationships can be more authentic as we speak not only from our mind but our heart. It allows us to be more effective in the world.

At the same time, we can sabotage our efforts to connect with someone: our ratna neediness can overwhelm another; our padma manipulation can turn off a prospective partner; our vajra having to be right and our karma controlling can get very old in a work relationship. We continually need to ask ourself whether we are being fully who we are in each moment? Are others? Or are we just picking their brain? Or wanting to get the job done? Or being aroused without connection?

We seek complementary energy in the friends and partners we choose. They tend to pull us out of our dominant energy, provide another reference point, give us a vacation from our internal dialogue, and ventilate the whole situation. Because of this, we might gravitate toward a person with a very different style. They could point out things and puncture our neurosis but also provoke, threaten, and irritate us. There are classic examples of this, like an intellectual dominantly vajra man marrying a very seductive padma woman. However, when we care more about how another sees us than we do about ourself, we put our worth in their eyes. This can lead to disaster.

Let's delve more deeply into the four steps.

1. Authentic Presence

Cultivating an ability to be present is key to being with others. When fully present, we are synchronized with ourself and we are more wakeful and gentle. Simply being present and having an unconditional positive regard for someone is very powerful. We hold the space for others, we are immovable in our care for them. It is intrinsically compassionate—open, warm, and friendly—a gift from the heart. There is a dignity in compassion that does not let it get mushy. The essence is sharing our being, the best of who we are. Because it is a shared experience, everyone benefits. It is not pity or feeling sorry for someone but shows a willingness to really connect. Even if we did nothing else but be present in our relationships, they would improve remarkably.

One day I was having a hard time and my daughter heard me crying. She came into my bedroom and just sat on the bed with me, resting her hand on mine. She said nothing and neither did I. The storm cleared and we said a few things to each other. It was only later that I realized her simple presence was all that I needed.

With the help of sitting meditation, we learn to continually come back to a sense of spaciousness. We come to the present moment over and over again by shedding our protective defenses. Our fixed way of being makes us more sure of our ourself, but also more closed. Therefore, openness can sometimes make us more confused. Slowly, we develop trust and confidence to be open. It has a fearless quality. We allow ourself to feel and trust in the intelligence in the situation.

Our sense of spaciousness invites others to be present in a spacious way. There is a gradual shift of allegiance from the content—agendas, business, task at hand—to the process of being with someone. Our openness transmits a sense of well-being. Each moment, each day, when we drop our own agenda, we make ourself available to others. First we empty, then we engage. As the process deepens, our sense of being with a person deepens.

2. Energetic Exchange

Energetic exchange is sharing energy that is unobstructed, without interpretation, concepts, or projections. It is commonly referred to as empathy, emotional resonance, or sympathetic vibration. The power of working with energy is that it is intuitive. We spontaneously know how to be and what to do. We tune into ourself and enter a state of energetic oscillation with another. We sense the emotional atmosphere. Whatever energy is in the room colors our mind. It happens naturally, whether we are aware of it or not, in all relationships. We tune into the tone or quality of a person and develop a somatic response to them. We "catch" the feel of another person. Our most vivid experience of this is when we are in love, open with a strong intention of relating, but it also could be an intellectual meeting of minds.

The basic premise is that we can't relate with depth if there is not shared experience. Exchange opens us to that possibility. It has an effect beyond what is obvious. When we drop our own story line and put ourself in someone's shoes, we break down the barrier between self and other. Energetic exchange is like an electric current that transcends dualism. We get in touch with our permeable nature and the distinction between self and other gets blurred in a positive sense. We merge—their confusion becomes our confusion; their joy becomes our joy. Because it is a shared experience, the exchange goes in both directions, like a warm hug, so is mutually healing. We enter a world of interconnectedness. It is egoless, non-dual, not one not two. Whatever is happening is happening. We can let go of our struggle and relax. We can take a "big mind" attitude and have a basic trust in our sanity that is always available.

The main obstacle to exchange is our self-protective concern with our own needs. We habitually create a fortress of self-defense. We armor ourself and feel separate. We may even feel like we are open, but the chances that we are not seeing them for who they are, but only our version of them, is high. We can't enter their world unless we are somewhat free of our own self-absorption. One day, while walking my eight-year-old daughter to school, I listened as she was jabbering away about this and that. I kept silent. Then she turned to me and said, "You don't seem very chattative today. What's the matter?" I told her I was preoccupied. She has continued to be a very sensitive barometer to how present I am.

Projections and expectations confuse communication. We don't know if it is their story or our story that we find ourself in. The closer we are to them (primary partner, work colleague, etc.), the more reactivity we will experience. This leads to very solid armoring on both sides and we become polarized, stuck in a negative exchange. We could become enmeshed, and in a sense start living each other's lives. This happens. Perhaps someone has an illness or is aging and another person feels the need to take care of them. For the 12 years after my stepmother died, I took care of my father's affairs. At times, it definitely felt that I was leading his life as much as mine. I am sure this is familiar to many.

We also have our biases and predisposed views, the filters through which we see the world. We have definite ideas of what is acceptable or permissible. We have our excuses for not opening, our strategies of avoidance. Our biggest obstacle is fear, a perpetual feeling that someone or something is threatening. We can work with our fear by becoming aware of how we get triggered. Then we are not caught by surprise. When we are able to re-engage, we give our relationships a chance.

Most relationships, at some point or other, become confusing. Great! It is an opportunity to work with our own and another's confusion. Our own stuckness will arise in relating to others so it is a tremendous opportunity to work on ourself. We can cut through our resistance to what is happening and dissolve our habitual patterns of avoidance. Our awareness begins to undermine our strategies of avoidance. We can just stay with whatever is happening, ride it out. We habitually close down when we find the situation unworkable. When we stay with what is awkward or painful, we come alive.

We all have boundaries, our armoring. We have different ones depending on both our style and life circumstances. We create defenses because we feel vulnerable and have wounds. If our life circumstance has been difficult in some way, the wounds penetrate deeply and we become even more defensive. These wounds are like little time bombs in our makeup. If the situation triggers them, we put up our boundary.

We do not always have a choice with whom we relate. In families, the synergistic setup of the triggers and the defenses become deeply, deeply ingrained by constant daily repetition of the same patterns of behavior. We could have clashes in styles. We then pass those same propensities into the next generation, and the next. We go for what is familiar. What we can learn from this is the importance of working on ourself first. Yet to work with deeply ingrained propensities takes a long time.

We might find that someone's stuckness is too much for us to handle. But most importantly we work with our stuckness, not theirs. No one can make us feel like a victim, we do it to ourself. We might need to come to certain agreements and set boundaries. Giving the relationship more space can be the most helpful thing to do. When we have more distance, we can relax and see their stuckness as just energy. Ultimately, it might be most skillful to bow out of the relationship without blame. We could see it as a perfect storm, a coming together of intense energy. But we need to recognize that it is not the place we want to live.

In relating to people, we sometimes attempt to conceal the split between self and other, covering up or glossing over separateness or differences to eliminate discomfort. Ultimately this creates confusion because we are not seeing who we are in relationship to each other. We could simply acknowledge that we are both different and connected. We are both separate and unified.

Here are some ways we block exchange to keep our distance:

Buddha: We just feel separate, not involved, alone, spaced out.

Vajra: We judge, criticize, interpret, analyze, feel intolerant, rigid, superior.

Ratna: We feel overwhelmed, inadequate, not good enough, arrogant.

Padma: We are emotionally self-absorbed, another's pain makes us irritable.

Karma: We are speedy, competitive, no time for someone, get impatient.

With exchange, we touch people at human level and relate to the fullness of another, instead of our version of them. It is mutually healing and nurturing and can be delightful and joyous. While this is the hallmark of intimate relationships, we can also love anyone unconditionally. Great healers do not discriminate as to who they like or don't like.

Exchange is the very key to healthy relationships but it does not mean losing oneself in another. For instance, if someone is crazily acting out, we are able to see it for what it is: intensified energy. There is a sense of connection yet we feel grounded and hold our seat. We could also have a tendency to avoid the intensity and close off. So, we need to gauge our ability to tolerate what is coming up. In fact, the more intensity in our interaction with another, the more there is the capacity for intimacy. This is why a relationship like a marriage, if a conscious one, is a powerful learning experience.

We need a sense of touch-and-go. Touching is connecting fully but then we need to let go. Otherwise, we become enmeshed, trapped. We might think we are being compassionate, but we are just caught in their suffering. This is "idiot compassion," as Trungpa Rinpoche coined it. We might do this merely in order to confirm ourself. When we practice touch-and-go we create openness.

3. Unbiased Perception, Clear Seeing, and Insight

Presence and exchange are very powerful, but they need the intelligence of clear seeing. They work together, joining mind and heart, intellect and intuition. Clear seeing enables us to see someone more accurately. An insight about them seems to come from nowhere, like an aha moment. It pops up in the midst of our oceans of rambling thoughts like an island of clarity. It is a moment of wakefulness or spontaneous flash. We are suddenly free from the "figuring out" capacity of mind, analyzing and interpreting. When we have insight into someone or a situation, we experience it as tangible. It can be almost a physical sensation of "clicking in."

Presence, exchange, and clear seeing allow for accurate communication. When we open to the atmosphere of a situation and specific highlights within it, we are aware not only of what people are saying, but also their energy. Their actual words or smile represent a small fraction of their communication. We could read between the lines, interpreting what they don't say. Their storyline could be a smoke screen. Staying with this draws the covert out of the overt, the unknown out of the known. It allows them to reveal the heart of the matter, the meaning at a deeper level. In this way we penetrate and reveal situations.

Clear seeing enables us to see another person as a full human being, rather than someone as a set of problems or with an opposing opinion. We cut through any sense of one-upmanship and our tendency to hold fast to our idea of what is right. We can also cut through an itch-scratch mentality toward problems, which is a defensive response like jumping in to fix it.

When we relate in a human way rather than problem-oriented way, we get to the point of the immediacy of human contact. It's important to be in the moment, in the now, not the history. Our history of problems is endless. We are better off supporting another's true self, not who we would like them to be. Otherwise, we end up with a false relationship. It takes a lot of bravery to let go of who we think we are and who we think the other person is.

Projection is the primary obstacle to clear seeing. We all carry around our version of reality. Absorbed in our version, we project it onto others and see people and situations in terms of our interpretations. In any relationship there are four people: our personal self, the other person, our version of them, and their version of us. We often relate to our version rather than seeing them for who they are. We then have expectations of them and emotional reactions when things don't go our way. We create a world in which projections are bouncing all over the place and they become very convincing and solid. We create an environment that is heavy and intense. We see that it is polluted with red or green or blue projections.

Clear seeing is quite rare. Sometimes, when it does happen, it is so fleeting that we hardly notice it. But when we do, it is a meaningful moment, a moment when we feel completely touched by someone. Something comes into focus in a heartfelt way. Those moments have a wakeful quality and resonate over time. It can be heartbreakingly touching.

When giving mediation instruction or working with a client or student, I often get tears in my eyes...and they do as well. In this moment, we have truly "met" each other.

4. Knowing What To Do

Presence, exchange, and clear seeing lay the groundwork for open and meaningful communication. Our ability to be helpful to others is trusting our innate intelligence and is not so much based on having theories, techniques, and systems. The latter can reduce anxiety but could obscure what is really helpful. As well, anxiety might be a necessary learning ground. Our actions are continually informed by a sense of openness and compassion, a space for natural intelligence to arise. We cultivate an open mind rather than having a set of beliefs. It is a willingness to experience whatever arises, staying with the uncertainty and not knowing the outcome. We can relate to the particular situation and feel it, rather than impose our beliefs as the only right way. Great teachers, healers, and leaders have dazzling successes because of their presence and intuition.

Authentic or genuine relationships share a common ground of experience, so what we say and do arises out of that. Being helpful happens spontaneously in response to open communication. An essential change takes place, a genuine experience that is simple, direct, and sane. There is a union of spontaneous presence and innate intelligence. We could intervene to move the process forward but there is no need to convince someone with logic. The intelligence becomes self-evident. Everyone looks honestly at what is happening without trying to change it. If we try to change the situation, it is not appreciating it. When we appreciate it, we connect with the intelligence present.

When we take on the task of consciously relating to others, we enter another person's life. As well, they enter ours. When with someone, we might first see their confusion. Seeing the intelligence in their confusion, from the Five Wisdoms perspective, we align with that. We don't try to solve the confusion in a logical way. We have insight in sensing the energy of the situation and letting it be as it is without appropriating, rejecting, or ignoring it.

When we experience our sanity, we can absorb another's confusion and draw out their sanity. We could help to bring out their best, support their true self, not who we would like them to be. We help them to uncover a sense of well-being, see that distressing emotions are not an enemy, and recognize that a particular situation is workable.

Rather than being critical of their weaknesses, we could support their strengths. We could encourage people to be less critical of themselves and appreciate their own good qualities. Connecting to their goodness and intelligence is more important than giving them solutions for battling their problems. Instead, we could encourage them to connect with what they feel passionate about. Working with the Five Wisdoms enhances this.

We can also encourage people to let go of what is no longer working for them or show them how to look at a situation differently. We could point out how they are obstructing their own good intentions. We could make people aware that they have possibilities and options and that they don't have to feel stuck. They could experience a sense of relief at being able to let go of something. They could experience a sense of making a fresh start. Ultimately, we could inspire someone to be fully who they are. We could model that life is a learning journey and encourage them to create a wholesome, creative life.

Our primary obstacles to genuine communication and our ability to be helpful arise from either having too much enthusiasm, too much aggression, or too much simple-mindedness. Generally, we are unaware of these tendencies in ourself. When we are too enthusiastic, we get into trying to rescue someone or take over the situation. We see ourself as the savior. Taking an aggressive stance means that we want to find the quick fix and change someone or something. Simple-mindedness is withdrawing into a cloud of denial. So, again, working within ourself is key to communication.

· · ·

The process of developing genuine relationships has many ups and downs. When we can gain familiarity with these four aspects, we can cycle through them continually, whether in a few moments or in broad strokes over years. We can continually re-engage, feel the particular situation, and communicate. In so doing, our relationships will be more creative and appropriate. By staying open to situations, we transmit a sense of confidence and ease. We might think that this kind of relationship would drain our energy. In fact, it recharges us.

A big part of my trainings is in relational dynamics. In a small group we do an interactive practice called the Five Modes Presentations, as described in my book *Natural Brilliance*. They are an effective way to really enter someone's world.

We look at their:

- **Body:** the outer or physical world of people, places, and situations
- **Speech:** the inner or energetic world of emotions and subtle energy
- **Mind:** the hidden or private world of ideas and mental models
- **Quality:** the dominant quality of expression
- **Action:** the activity that emerges from the quality

A commitment to working on our relationships is a big leap. It is the cornerstone of Buddhism. It is such a big leap that we take a vow to hold to that commitment—the vow of a bodhisattva. With the courage to look at ourself without blinders, we see others more clearly. Integrating personal practices and interpersonal work with others brings great joy. We use relating as a mutually healing and empowering tool. This is all we really have to offer others.

> I've learned that people will forget what you said, people will forget what you did, but people will never forget how you made them feel.
>
> —Maya Angelou

PART II

Where
We Get In
Trouble

CHAPTER 6

Ego Is the Culprit

Ego has extended itself so far that it begins to lose track of the boundary of its territory…The size of its empire cannot be conceived or imagined. Since it includes everything, it cannot be defined as this or that…This is the highest level of concentration and achievement that confused, samsaric mind can attain.

—Chögyam Trungpa Rinpoche

Now that we have seen how we create a sense of separate self, let's take a closer look at the masterpiece that is our ego. It is the creator of a solidified sense of self, samsara (the cycle of conditioned existence), and the whole catastrophe. It's all about self-identification and separation from others. This sense of a self as an autonomous entity is the culprit. For example, we use the terms "ego-centered," or "ego-maniac." Its sole purpose is to protect us from what we perceive as "other." Our ego defends our basic needs, unfulfilled desires, and dissatisfaction. It is involuntary, repetitive, and persistently thinking about me and my story. An egoic mind has a sense of self in every thought, emotion, and action. It is only interested in what is workable from the ego's point of view. Facts are neutral, but the content of ego is different for each of us because we perceive the world differently. We distort facts in the service of ego. We are convinced that, "I know who I am and this is the way the world is."

The structure of how ego creates and maintains itself is the same for everyone. It is what keeps ego percolating. If we are not aware of this we solidify. When we become aware, it's not ego but an open mind. Ego, when recognized, weakens. We can learn to observe it, go beyond it, and smile or laugh when we confront it.

Putting others down is a great way to maintain our ego. Faultfinding and complaining strengthen the self. Resentment, bitterness, indignation, and taking offense add more energy. Reactivity becomes highly charged. Grievances and long-standing discontent sees to no other purpose than ego. Ego/self feels right and therefore superior.

Our self could feel trapped in its solidity, but since other is a threat, we gravitate toward what feels secure. The more other is sensed as a threat, the more we are stuck, frozen, heavy, and numb. Since this is a precarious slippery slope, full of wishful thinking, the struggle can be intense. In the endless looping of thoughts to secure ourself, we let ourself be bound. We make ourself stupid.

So, we create a boundary, the walls of our fortress, our castle. We are simultaneously the king or queen and major general. We spend a tremendous amount of energy creating and maintaining our boundary. It's as if we were dropped in the ocean and were trying to push away the water to stay dry. However, we begin to see our boundaries as the walls of our prison. It is a totally claustrophobic, unpredictable, chaotic environment in all aspects of our lives: psychological, relational, social, and political.

An aspect of ego is that it has a watcher. The watcher keeps track of what we find acceptable or not. Most significantly, in wanting security and permanence, we deliberately ignore our innate wisdom and methodically create confusion. We keep a confused mind alive by being focused on survival, entertainment, and our prejudiced views. We think we can win at ego's game, as it always holds promises. Thus, our confusion is intentional and it effectively boycotts wisdom. We do our best not to give birth to our enlightened mind because it involves too much surrender and is too terrifying.

> We create our security by putting things into categories, naming them, by using relative terms to identify their inter-relationships, how they fit together. And this security brings temporary happiness and comfort. There is no attempt to deal with projections as exciting and fluid situations at all; instead the world is seen as being absolutely solid and stiff. Everything is frozen movement, frozen space, solidified. We see the colors as they are, but somehow they are plastic colors rather than rainbow colors. This solid quality is the dualistic barrier.
>
> —Chögyam Trungpa Rinpoche

From the perspective of the five energies we could say, respectively, that what is threatening could feel too empty, too sharp, too overbearing, too seductive, or too active. In fear we try to avoid it, in anger we want to destroy it, and in passion we want to possess it.

There is no choice but to start where we are, at ground zero, and slowly unravel the entrapment of our ego. We begin to see through our hang-ups and deceptions. We begin to see that the fundamental obstacle to being able to access our wisdom is ego. It is what binds us to acting in habitual ways without vision. Our ego accumulates outer reference points and then provides us with inner credentialing, "I am a teacher, my students love me, and I am getting a promotion." However, when we go from reference point to reference point, we create a small world. Our reference points ground us but they also imprison us. If we are unaware of this, we take the thinker to be who we are. We need to drop our reference points to allow our mind to expand.

Ego has a sense of self-absorption that, in turn, creates a sense of self-importance. We are so proud of the triumvirate of me, myself, and I. On the other hand, it's often not that we think so much of ourself but rather that we think badly of ourself. "I am not good enough." "I don't have what it takes." So we could be full of ourself, but full of ourself in a negative way.

Our ego has a strong commitment to keeping ourself happy. The machinations of our mind is constantly manipulating our world to conform to how we want our world. It is as if we are all addicts and our wanting is unending. Our basic needs and unfulfilled desires are constant. We have a perpetual sense of dissatisfaction and anxiety. Moreover, there is an ignorance about where happiness really lies. We might be able to identify the causes and conditions of our unhappiness, but we don't know what to do about it.

Ego is very clever indeed. When we can't have the world the way we want it, we rely on numerous distractions to protect ourself from our discontent. Our mind wanders in search of the next juicy bit of phenomena. The internet, for example, is constantly taking us down some rabbit hole or another. Have you ever searched on Google for one thing and then found endless distractions that capture you? How about a new dress? A new gadget? Sound familiar?

> Distractions are everywhere, all the time...We literally screen off our actual world, with all its ruggedness and rawness...It is easy to think the relentless external stimuli are the problem, but what we are surrounded by are just phenomena, nothing more. The objects of our world are just there, innocently, just being what they are...When we think in terms of distractions, we look outward and blame external conditions for our jumpiness. When we think in terms of wandering mind, we look inward for the source of our problem. We take responsibility.
>
> –Judith Lief

Ego is perpetually in relationship to other people, whether to confirm itself or be convinced that other is either the friend or the enemy. When someone confirms us, our ego puffs up. We could get in a habit of ingratiating ourself to others to keep that warm flow of energy coming toward us—think padma energy here. When we feel threatened, our ego is under attack, we become highly reactive, and retaliate. We could indulge in a perpetual stream of faultfinding, complaining, and blaming, being resentful, bitter, indignant, aggressive, or offended. This strengthens the ego. There is a conviction in our version of things. This is vajra energy.

Let's look at facts, consensus reality, and how thoughts arise. Facts are neutral: the sun is shining. We could leave it at that but quickly our mind goes to, "You promised me you would work with me in the garden when the sun came out." Or, "I really need to drop everything and go work on my tan." Our thoughts are tricky because they get absconded by ego— there are facts and then we have our take on them. There is much subtlety in how we each perceive our world. We need a great deal of awareness to distinguish between pure perception and our overlay on reality. We need to determine whether our thoughts are in the service of our ego or seeing things simply as they are.

> ...[obstacles] come from indulging oneself with good experiences and traumatizing oneself over bad ones. In either case it's a question of being duped by one's own thinking...the problematic character of the experience is created by one's own way of thinking. The experience itself does not create any problem...[the problem] is your own conceptual bias. If you cling to the good and dislike the bad experiences, these are your own conceptual doing and will cause trouble.
>
> —Khenpo Tsültrim Gyamtso Rinpoche

No Ego: No Problem

Sounds simple, right? But ego is tenacious and has such a sophisticated way of maintaining itself. Our familiar habits are so ingrained that we go into our defense more easily than going into a situation with openness. Why, oh why, do we do this? Because, with the collapse of ego, everything with which we identify, all of our reference points are gone. What a scary thought! How can we exist without them? So, as we saw, fear arises from an open, primordial space and we sabotage our innate capacity for awakened mind.

In the following exchange, we see Chögyam Trungpa as he responds to a student's question:

Student: How do you give up grasping, or step out of it?

Chögyam Trungpa: Well, you can't just give up grasping just like that. Automatically, you are aware of yourself giving up grasping, which means you are grasping for nongrasping. So it seems that the ultimate and obvious thing is that one has to give up the person who is grasping.

Student: How do you do that?

Chögyam Trungpa: By not doing anything—meditating.

• • •

As human beings we have the potential to disentangle ourself from old habits... We have the capacity to wake up and live consciously, but, you may have noticed, we also have a strong inclination to stay asleep. It's as if we are always at a crossroad, continuously choosing which way to go. Moment by moment, we can choose to go toward further clarity and happiness or toward confusion and pain.

–Pema Chödrön

Aside from our ingrained ways of being, we also deal with a juggernaut of external circumstances seemingly endlessly coming toward us. Our to-do list could be getting out of control. Our relationships could be getting strained. We could have major life events pile up and feel overwhelmed. In all of these situations, my favorite slogan is, "When in doubt, go to buddha." Pause. Do nothing. We can disarm ourself rather than go into battle. Not impulsively reacting is an effective way of getting beyond ego's predicament. We can just take a moment, take a breath.

It is not uncommon to be continually hijacked by someone's negative energy. If someone is angry at us, we could take a moment and ask ourself, "How much of this is about them and how much is it about me? How are they coloring their world? How am I?" We can do this without turning them into an enemy or feeling bad about ourself. They can be who they are and we can be who we are. The best protection is non-reaction. Letting go has greater power than hanging on.

Ego relies on a lack of awareness. When we see through the machinations of our constricted ego, our ego weakens and our mind opens. Instead of being caught in our ego, we open to an awakened mind. As well, when the egoic aspect of our mind relaxes, our sense perceptions come alive. We are just being and sensing. The problem is not that we don't have sanity, but that we are not open to it.

Ego is spiritually unconscious. It is much too concerned with the preservation of ourself to care about anything else. So we could think of egolessness as an invitation. When we begin to look beyond the reality that ego creates, we see that it is not just empty and nonexistent. We begin to realize that beyond egohood, there is a tremendous aliveness, vitality, strength, and energy. This aliveness and energy is luminous and bright, and it contains tremendous wisdom.

Duality, the split between self and other, made a bad name for itself by creating ego. However, there is a superior understanding of dualism. Ultimately there is no problem with duality. It's no longer a dirty word. If we see it as a problem, we misunderstand this view. Yes, there is definitely dualism: self and other. But though things appear, they are also ultimately, fundamentally, not there. The world could be seen like a dream. So it has a more romantic sense, a lightness, a sense of freedom. This is getting in touch with our true nature. Throughout this journey, we will also see that ego is not a problem, as the best of who we are is egoless.

> We have lost our unity with our true nature. We have lost the realization of who we are and that is the greatest failure there is. Nothing else is really a tragedy or a real serious failure in comparison with the failure of losing our unity with our true nature. This has already happened to all of us from the very beginning and that is why it is impossible to really fail again. Any subsequent failure is just an idea. "Oh, I am losing my job. I failed. I didn't pass my test. I failed again. My relationship is falling apart. I failed again. My meditation is filled with turbulence. I failed. I wasn't able to live the life that I fantasized. I am not able to live according to my ideal standards. I failed." These are all concepts.
>
> –Anam Thubten

It's also helpful to reflect that on our deathbed all of our reference points are meaningless. We can't take all that we hold so dear with us. Period. End of story. Our body gives us a very graphic picture: when our body weakens it moves to a formless dimension, a deep process that passes all understanding. Practicing letting go is the ultimate way to prepare for death. And it gives us new life.

This is the picture I prefer: In the middle of the river, with the shoreline out of view, the raft begins to disintegrate. We find ourself with absolutely nothing to hold on to. From our conventional standpoint, this is scary and dangerous. However, one small shift of perspective will tell us that having nothing to hold on to is liberating. We could have faith that we won't drown. Holding on to nothing means we can relax with this fluid, dynamic world.

–Pema Chödrön

Spinning Mind and Still Mind

When our head is restless and spinning, we are in a state of confusion. When we have a still, peaceful mind, we are awake.

Observe the interplay of restlessness and peace throughout the day.

CHAPTER 7

How We Get Stuck

We don't exist as one whole being, one whole entity at all.
We are a collective. We are a collection of lots of things,
and all of those entities are uncertain whether that entity
exists or not...So there is no sense of being, really, fundamentally. It's purely a dream we try to put together.

–Chögyam Trungpa Rinpoche

Buddhism, in some ways, is as much a psychology as a
religion. It is an extremely sophisticated understanding
of the nature of mind and how it works, based on experience. The four noble truths, which we will go into more ex-
tensively in Chapter 16, give an overview of Buddhist
psychology. To focus on the origins of suffering we study Five
Psychophysical Aspects, traditionally known as skandhas. To
focus on the suffering and confusion we experience, we study
the Six Intensified Realities, traditionally known as the six
realms. We realize the cessation of suffering when we become
relaxed, open, and at peace. The path is working with ourself
to come to that realization.

The Four Noble Truths of Buddhist Psychology

1. The truth of suffering
2. The truth of the origin or cause of suffering
3. The truth of the cessation of suffering
4. The truth of the path that leads from suffering to cessation of suffering

Five Psychophysical Aspects

As Buddhist psychology is more interested in the process of mind than content, we study how the mind functions. This process is the same for everyone, and the content has many variables, primarily based on our energetic make-up and life circumstance.

The Five Psychophysical Aspects—traditionally called skandhas—are a description of the *origin* of neurotic mind, how we develop and maintain ego. Note that the understanding of the word ego described here is different from the Western psychological understanding. These aspects show how we create a self; an "I" as a solid, separate entity. They show the structure and process in our never-ending struggle to maintain our sense of self. Because our existence is radically impermanent, we have a basic insecurity. We try to *maintain* the illusion of substantiality, continuity, and relative autonomy. In studying the aspects, we see how we create, confirm, and maintain solidity.

Therefore, the five aspects refute the idea of a substantial self. Instead, the five aspects are a collection of tendencies and events labeled "I." Each of the five aspects is distinctive yet depends on the others; they build on each other but also refer back and recycle. When we see how we become solidified, we then see how we can unravel the solidification.

The primary agenda of ego is the preservation of a self as a separate entity. Things are the way they are because our ego wants them to be that way. We lose track of the fact that our ego created the situation. We feel safe in the small mind of ego. We maintain a personally biased, self-referential point of view. We treasure the triumvirate of me, myself, and I.

Because ego wants what is workable for ego, the process of solidifying ego is intentional, methodical, and deliberate. We depend on reference points, something to hang on to, to prove we exist—and we so want to indulge in our favorite neurotic patterns. Instinctually, we use work and entertainment as survival tactics to avoid the unknown. We put up active resistance at the edge of what we find permissible. This can be very vivid in times of crisis and transition.

Ultimately, we desire permanence, security, eternity, and to believe in something. We create a seemingly solidified world to feel secure. But it's a slippery situation, full of wishful thinking. We do not accept the transitory nature of things. We ignore self-existing wisdom and take a blind, deaf, and dumb approach. It's hard to catch ourself being ourself. It requires lots of awareness of the minute particulars of our existence. Finally, we could see the five aspects are neutral: if we don't grasp, they become wisdoms. In fact, we don't have to achieve egolessness at all. We are egoless, because our wisdom is innate.

Open Primordial Space

Our fundamental state of mind is open, spacious, and free from confusion. This self-existing primordial intelligence is basically good, boundless, and brilliant. It does not depend on relative situations: it is unconditional. Relative, conditioned situations arise from it. In this state we are "at one" with whatever is happening, we are going with the flow of an unceasing play of energy. We might glimpse it in situations when our mind clears, like waking up from sleep and not knowing where we are. This state also has a quality of uncertainty, bewilderment—where, what, who. And that can generate fear.

Let's delve more deeply into the Five Psychophysical Aspects.

1. Freeze/Split (related to the buddha energy)

Traditional Name: form, ignorance

This is an instinctual, subconscious, automatic reaction to anything we identify as threatening or fearful. We are triggered and we panic. We suddenly feel the need to protect ourself and we can become self-conscious. Our personal self is now in opposition to whatever is "out there," or the non-self. We deliberately ignore open, fluid, intelligent space, attempting to shield ourself from the fear of insubstantial openness. Separating ourself does not feel right, yet we prefer it to the non-specific discomfort of open space.

2. Uncertainty/Feeling (related to the ratna energy)

Traditional Name: feeling, intuitive intelligence

Next, we begin to have a semi-conscious awareness of our existence at a subtle level. It is experienced as bodily sensations, a felt sense, in reaction to something happening "out there," some "other." We send out tentacles to explore the texture of "other." We want to feel concrete things to reassure ourself that we exist: "If I can feel that out there, then I must be here." There is great uncertainty about our relationship to other: is it friendly, hostile, or indifferent? Pleasant, unpleasant, or neutral? Our basic question is, "Is this comfortable or not?" It is like a baby feeling hunger or a wet diaper.

3. Perceiving/Reacting (related to the padma energy)

Traditional Name: perception, impulse

Our reaction to the felt sense establishes a further separa-tion between self and other. We recognize, discriminate, and compare, like a child exploring their world. We form an atti-tude—welcoming, defending, or indifferent—about "other." We might have feelings of attraction, hunger, grasping, or wanting to possess or consume. We may feel revulsion, rejec-tion, warding off, or wanting to eliminate. Or we may feel in-difference, numbing, avoidance, pretending it does not exist. It is a constant effort, trying to figure out how to maintain ourself in relationship to other.

4. Concepts/Intellect (related to the karma energy)

Traditional Name: mental formations

This is where intellect comes into play. It labels and names. It defines, categorizes, and forms opinions to further justify and solidify a separate self. This is beyond the subliminal reactivity of the first three; it's more sophisticated. Intellect finalizes the sense of separation. "I" is the product of intellect. Using a vast memory bank of personal data, we bring together disorganized and scattered experiences and knit together the past, present, and a possible future. We confirm ourself by clinging to our personal storyline as justification for who we are. Mostly, we experience our mind as this fourth aspect.

5. Solidified Chatter (related to the vajra energy)

Traditional Name: consciousness

We develop a "watcher" that combines and maintains the first four: 1) freeze/split, 2) uncertainty/feeling, 3) perceiv-ing/reacting, 4) concepts/intellect. There is an ongoing flow of mental chatter and discursive thought which elaborates, gains momentum, and fills in a storyline. It is uncontrollable and illogical. It holds everything together and adds to the data base. It has a cohesive quality like an undergrowth, cement, or glue. The watcher reports back to the central headquarters of ego, which is self-absorbed and self-serving. It is a highly restricted awareness, deciding what to include and what to exclude. It fixates on what creates self and excludes or ignores what is not useful, creating tunnel vision. It feels convinced that it knows what's what.

Summary of the Five Psychophysical Aspects

These aspects go from heavier to lighter. The buddha energy is the fundamental space. Feeling, related to ratna energy, is the heaviest, slow to experience as it puts its tentacles or antenna out to perceive what's happening. Impulse, related to the padma energy, is sharp and quick to seduce the world and communicate with it. It is lighter than the previous two. Concept or formations, related to the karma energy, is very active and efficient. Consciousness, related to the vajra energy, it's all about intelligence and intellect.

Note that the first three are subconscious, automatic, and mostly felt as simultaneous. Four and five are conceptual.

1. We **panic** and **recoil**.
2. We **sense** other in relationship to self as positive, negative, or neutral.
3. We **react** by liking, disliking, or not caring.
4. We **solidify** with our concepts.
5. We **maintain** our sense of separate self.

Projections Into Intensified Realities

Now that we have a solid sense of self, we project our version on the world. We are convinced it is the way things are. Our projections confirm we exist so we can get on with our trips, locked into one or more Intensified Realities. Most confusingly, projections perpetuate themselves: we project and then a projection bounces back at us. We create whole worlds of bouncing projections.

Things are the way they are because *we* want them to be that way. Simply put, we create our projections and in turn those projections confirm our existence: the projector and projections validate each other. This is how we color our world. This gets accentuated when something divergent to our view confronts us. We forget that we actually created our limiting view. It creates a gigantic delusion. Round and round we go. We create environmental pollution and hazardous waste. It is almost inspiring that the limited mind of ego could be so clever.

Summary

- Creating our "self," we play god.

- Projecting our version, we become director of our own movie.

- Creating Intensified Realities, we star in it.

How to Practice With the Five Aspects

Awareness of the process of the solidification of ego makes it more transparent. We can catch ourself being ourself and begin to see how we get entrenched in the solidification process. Catching the first freeze is best, but it takes considerable self-awareness. It's a moment of subliminal intuition to close or open. But at first, we are more likely to experience a full-blown intensified reality.

Awareness of each aspect could look like this:

1. What triggers the freeze, the split? What is your experience of the panic? How do you close off?

2. What does the uncertainty feel like? What are your bodily sensations? How is your intuitive intelligence feeling out the situation?

3. What do you perceive is happening? What is your impulsive reaction? What are the subtle feelings of attraction, revulsion, or indifference?

4. How do you name what is happening? How do you interpret, categorize, and form an opinion? What kind of thoughts and emotions are being generated?

5. How do you maintain your intuitive feelings, your impulsive reactions and your opinions and emotions? What is your mental chatter saying that weaves together your storylines and justifications?

At what point does the storyline feel solid? What Intensified Reality—as we will explore below—are you in?

The Five Aspects and Therapeutic Modalities

The Five Psychophysical Aspects correspond to specific Western therapeutic modalities. Here are some examples:

1. Freeze/Split

These therapies re-train a person so they are not triggered by a traumatic event.

- Eye Movement Desensitization and Reprocessing (EMDR)
- Irene Lyon's Healing Trauma

2. Uncertainty/Feeling

These are body-centered modalities using the somatic, felt sense.

- Dr. Peter A. Levine's Somatic Experiencing
- Ron Kurtz's Hakomi Method, mindfulness-centered somatic psychotherapy
- Pat Ogden's Sensorimotor Psychotherapy

3. Perceiving/Reacting

- Environmental Therapy, working with staying in contact with the world
- Contemplative Psychotherapy

4. Intellect and 5. Solidified Chatter

- Most talk psychotherapy. This modality misses the root cause (first split) and body-related (psychosomatic) aspect. It re-organizes cognition but not experience.

Six Intensified Realities

Traditional Name: six realms

The psychophysical aspects are like jump-starting a car. Projections are like gaining speed. Intensified realities are like going for the ride. We create a solid sense of self and then we project our version onto the world: "This is the way I see the world so this is how it really is." This is the birth of the psychological styles of the Intensified Realities which are the neurotic versions of the Five Wisdoms. We can experience all of the realities, but we are usually firmly rooted in one or two. We can travel from one state of pain to another. Confusion and suffering become a familiar ground to occupy us. We think it is a safe haven but it's actually a prison.

Our deeply engrained, self-absorbed, habitual patterns are a closed system of self-aggrandizement entrenching us in a cycle of confused existence. Our solidified self maintains itself at a microscopic, instantaneous level in the minute particulars of our habitual tendencies. Our internal scripts make our life manageable and safe. We manipulate each situation to fit or further validate our version of existence. We are keenly conscious of maintaining a self: ego always keeps the engine running at a low idle. Then finally, we run out of gas. We get stressed, exhausted, and sick.

We perpetuate the illusion of permanence and maintain our story lines to ensure something is happening. We feel certain we can win at the game we created and are willing to struggle as long as there are promises. Because of this, we alternate between hope and fear. Our emotions are the peak experiences of Intensified Realities, colored and reinforced by conceptual explanations and rationalizations. The most extreme solidification, most divorced from things as they are, is psychosis. It's an intelligence gone wild.

There is a need for clarification between our ordinary human life and the intensification of the desire reality, which is one of the six. Our everyday reality is about passion, a passion for life, but the desired reality is an intensified, exaggerated, extreme case of fixated passion. It creates chaos in relation to passion. In our ordinary life we function intelligently, make choices, work, study, and meditate. Ordinary life also has more gaps, the possibility for openness, and thus the potential to change our situation.

But how do we know if we are in an intensified reality?

1. There is a tenacity of certain preoccupations. It's all about "how I am doing" in securing or entertaining ourself.

2. It feels real. We are convinced that this is the way things are. We simply can't understand people in another reality.

3. When others try to get us out of our preoccupation, they can't—and neither can we. The prospect of opening to another reality is irritating because it's so uncertain. We are afraid to give up the security of the known.

The Six Intensified Realities

Absorption Reality

Traditional Name: the God Realm
*This is a neurotic aspect of Buddha energy: ignorance tinged with desire

We close off from the world to dwell in extremely pleasurable mental and physical states. We are attracted to altered states of consciousness induced by spiritual practices and drugs. We want this to go on forever, so we make great effort to maintain our bubble. Many understand this to be the primary point of spirituality. This reality is not painful in itself, but there is pain in the fear that it will not last. So we fear the highs because the fall will be so great.

Survival Reality

Traditional Name: the Animal Realm
*This is a neurotic aspect of Buddha energy: ignorance

We want our world to be familiar, so we create situations to conform to our expectations. We trap ourself in continual, self-contained, self-justifying rounds of activity, which gives us a sense of security. We don't like changes or surprises. Cut off from the outside world, we become introverted and shut down. We want to be left alone and we put up a permanent do-not-disturb sign. We are numb to experience and play blind, deaf, and dumb. We seek oblivion, ignoring what goes on around us. It is a kind of stupidity that narrows our perspective and sees no alternatives. There is a stubborn, serious quality that is deadly honest, has no sense of humor, and is perpetually uncertain about one's existence.

Aggression Reality

Traditional Name: the Hell Realm
*This is the neurotic aspect of Vajra energy: anger, hatred

Hot Hell

We live in a world of aggression and see the world as a field of combat. We sense threat, so we arm ourself with aggression, magnifying the striking potential of others out of all proportion. We want to strike first, as the best form of defense. We want to destroy the object of aggression using physical, intellectual, and emotional weaponry which could be direct and brutal. We feel justified in seeking vengeance, which feeds our anger and resentment, and so we lash out. As the cycle of justification and aggression builds on itself, we are in a perpetual state of hatred. Aggression permeates the space and becomes claustrophobic. We lose track of who is hating whom and do not know if we are the oppressor or the victim. We also don't know whether we are trying to destroy something or achieve something by destroying it.

Cold Hell

Our aggression turns inward into debilitating self-criticism and self-hate. We become frozen and our blood runs cold. We feel imprisoned. There can seem to be no way out but suicide, complete annihilation.

Hunger Reality

Traditional Name: the Hungry Ghost Realm
*This is the neurotic aspect of Ratna energy: greed and pride

We have a pervasive sense of poverty mentality, fundamentally feeling that we are poor, hungry, and needy. Whatever it is we desire, we never have enough. We are perpetually concerned with our substantiality, so we are obsessed with wanting more to take in and consume. We lose track of what we have and are preoccupied with expanding, becoming rich. Everything is regarded as something to possess. We build an empire and cultivate power: status, fame, dominion. We are fiercely territorial, hoard our possessions, and display our wealth. We are impenetrably self-centered with a puffed-up pride.

Desire Reality

Traditional Name: the Human Realm
*This is the neurotic aspect of Padma energy: fixated passion

We perpetually grasp at the intensity of pleasurable situations, clinging to pleasure provided by people, places, things, and ideas. We have an obsessive passion or irresistible craving to join with another. We feel an acute sense of separation from anything pleasurable, so we find union as quickly as possible. We could indiscriminately join with whatever is exciting and alive. To be loved and accepted by those we want to attract, we become a chameleon, wanting to be who they want us to be. Continual comparison with others creates jealousy. When our love object is not around, we feel a sense of loss, utter desolation. And though we long to connect, we do not feel confident enough to attract someone and fear rejection. We could become desperate, feeling that life is not worth living.

We are constantly manipulating to get what we want and we push away what we don't want. Because we want the best, we are obsessively discriminating: selective, fussy, and picky. Choices are extremely confusing, so we end up in a traffic jam of discursive thought. We are critical of anyone or anything we don't perceive as the best. We are prone to imagination, nostalgia, and fantasy. We are uncertain as to what is real and what is unreal. We don't know who we are or why we are here.

Ambition Reality

Traditional Name: the Jealous God Realm
*This is the neurotic aspect of Karma energy: jealousy and defensiveness

We perpetually compete to accomplish something higher, greater, better. We compare ourself to others and are jealous of their accomplishments. When successful, we lord it over others. We are driven because of the underlying paranoia that we will not succeed. We are highly energetic, continually moving, hyperactive, tense, and agitated. We speed about trying to achieve everything at once. We cannot prioritize, so we just do the thing in front of us, or go in circles. It's better to keep busy than to do nothing. We are locked into increased control, concentration, efficiency, and accuracy.

We are resolute, never faltering in our vigilance to keep everything under surveillance, watching all of the hidden corners to avoid any threat. We are suspicious and distrustful of everyone and everything, never knowing who will trick or betray us. If someone tries to help us, we see them as oppressive or infiltrating. If they don't, we see them as selfish. If they give us alternatives, we feel they are playing games. We are very direct and willing to fight. Because we could become obsessed over the possibility of hidden plots, our defenses could be complex and indirect, like war strategies. Yet as ambitiously as we strive forward, we are prone to self-doubt.

● ● ●

The whole trajectory of moving from the first freeze, through the other Psychophysical Aspects, projections, and Intensified Realities can be tremendously helpful in regulating how we are in the world.

CHAPTER 8

The Trauma Pandemic and the Nervous System

You are the sky, everything else, it's just the weather.

—Pema Chödrön

A s a young girl, Cheryl was continually chastised by her mother who even spoke ill of her to friends when she was present. Jason was from a split home and became aggressive when his mother moved across the country. Beth's parents split up when she was very young and her mother died when she was eight years old. There was no emotional support from her father and stepmother. Bill knew from a young age that he was gay and had feelings that he could not express because he felt it was taboo. So, he bottled up his sensitive feelings and the shame surrounding them. Lucien lived in a spiritual commune when he was growing up. His parents were very involved in the community and had little time for him. He always felt somewhat lost.

Cheryl, Jason, Beth, Bill, and Lucien all carried their childhood stories into their adult lives. We know these people. Their stories are so commonplace that we often shrug them off. But for them, childhood included real trauma and left them scarred. Not because of horrendous physical or sexual abuse, but because their primary care givers were either neglectful or overly critical, and not necessarily out of mal-intent. The therapeutic profession has a name for early childhood trauma: Complex Post-Traumatic Stress Disorder (C-PTSD).

There is a hidden epidemic. Millions of children never get the loving care that would give them a sense of well-being and confidence. Unfortunately, parent education is practically non-existent in most communities. People can live with their stories of early childhood trauma for their entire lives. In many cases the wounding goes back many generations and, if not addressed, is passed on to future generations. We all have had adverse situations in our lives. It's not even the trauma; it's our reaction to it. Some of us are devastated, others get stronger. My sister spent the last 20 years of her life in depression; I became successful in my career.

We could be more aware of signs of trauma in family and friends. When someone is easily triggered, overly reactive, or shut down, we could sense that there is a story behind their behaviors. In many cases, such people become extremely bright and well-functioning, often overachievers. In other cases, they live with a perpetual sense of self-doubt and dislike of themselves. Most tragically, unresolved emotions can trigger chronic physical illness, which is rampant in our day and age. Millions now suffer from auto-immune diseases for which the Western medical world offers little help.

As a body-centered life coach and personal development trainer, I encounter people like this all of the time. As a Buddhist teacher and meditation instructor, I see our Buddhist centers attract such people. In a search of peace, people seek refuge in spiritual communities. A person could start to use the dharma to cover up or subvert deep, unprocessed issues—particularly in the areas of intimacy and sexuality. It has been termed "spiritual bypassing." Someone could present as a very accomplished practitioner, even a teacher, but be a babe in the woods when it comes to personal matters.

Meditation can backfire. When someone who is chronically

stressed tries to do mindfulness practice, their mind may be racing so much that it becomes impossible. It can be like putting a time bomb on a meditation cushion. In a practice program participants could, when intensified, isolate themselves or even have psychotic breaks. Generally, staff do not have the training or skills to deal with extreme mental states. It's not in their job description.

We are fortunate that neuroscience and body-based therapists are offering new insights into the whys and wherefores of this epidemic. Neuroscience has become indispensable in unearthing how we get traumatized and what we can do about it. Stephen Porges has introduced the polyvagal theory. Bessel van der Kolk has been a beacon of insight into trauma. Pat Ogden's work, Sensorimotor Psychotherapy, and Peter Levine's work, Somatic Experiencing, emphasize somatic processing. Irene Lyon's work on healing trauma is beautifully clear and to the point.

The Autonomic Nervous System

The nervous system is a superhighway of nerve cells, residing primarily in the skin, along which impulses are in constant motion. It consists of the sympathetic and parasympathetic nervous systems which are a balancing of focus and relaxation. We are attentive and then we rest. The sympathetic is the arousal system, constantly operating in a healthy range. It wakes us up. The parasympathetic vagus nerve controls the throat, thorax, vocal cords, tongue, lungs, as well as hearing in the middle ear.

Biologically we are wired to look for threat: physically when our survival might be at risk and psychologically, when we fear, for instance, rejection or abandonment. We ask, "What bad thing might happen to me?" We fear saying and doing something so we are not rejected. Neuroception is a term used to describe how neural circuits distinguish, without our conscious awareness, whether situations and people are safe or dangerous. As noted, Buddhist psychology sees it this way: there is a sense of threat, which leads to fear, which leads to splitting off from a free-flowing, harmonious relationship into a world of defensive armoring. The resultant solidified sense of self is ego. Trauma creates rigidity, tension, oversensitivity, shutdown, confusion, overwhelm, and an endless array of hyperactive behaviors.

People can deal with a highly vigilant state of chronic anxiety all their lives. It can be exhausting. If they are continually surrounded by the triggering stressor, there is seemingly no way out. Even when not triggered, they are trapped in anxiety because their mind continually spins out the traumatizing story. It's interesting to note that animals don't experience this because their cognitive functioning does not come into play.

Three responses to threat have been clearly documented: fight, flight, and freeze. This is where a person's disposition or style comes into play. When some people feel threatened, they want to fight. Others flee when the stress is too much to handle, and remain very intensified. A child who is not able to fight or flee will shut down. A person can be stuck "on" (sympathetic: fight, flight, freeze). If they can't fight or flee, there is increasing nervous-system activity. When there is no effective defense, they shut down.

There are several ways we could look at the threats that lead to trauma or emotional intensification. Shock trauma, which we usually think of as a trauma, comes from verbal, physical, or sexual abuse, natural disasters such as war and accidents, or major illnesses and injuries. Childhood trauma has to do with attachment to primary caregivers. Secure attachment is created in a nurturing environment. Anxious or deregulated attachment results when there is neglect: caregivers are both there and not there in a seemingly unpredictable way—at least to a small child. Avoidant attachment comes about when the child has to be self-protective due to parental aggression. Finally, the accumulated stress of living in our modern world can itself create trauma.

A significant fact about trauma is that it is not the incident or ongoing situation itself, but the reaction to it. Irene Lyon uses the analogy of a car accident. After a minor accident, Gretchen is fine, returns to her life, and functions normally. Penny, however, has continual anxiety, becomes cautious, and doesn't want to drive. She develops symptoms such as sore muscles, digestive problems, and insomnia. She could become psychologically disabled for life. There are also amazing stories of people who are able to overcome their distress after experiencing extreme situations.

Irene Lyon has another helpful analogy to illustrate how some people have more capacity to handle stress than others. In this analogy, a swimming pool represents our stress-handling capacity and beach balls in the pool represent our stress or trauma. Being stressed is like having too many beach balls in our pool or having a pool too small to hold them. To create a healthy system, we need to either let go of some balls or create a larger pool.

Stephan Porges' polyvagal theory describes the functioning of the sympathetic and parasympathetic nervous systems in order to show how we respond to and recover from stress. In the normal functioning of the nervous system, the sympathetic nervous system responds to a stressful situation. Then the parasympathetic nervous system calms us down. The cycle of arousal and calming down is a biological must, but it is designed to happen in a short period of time. In extreme situations, our sympathetic nervous system reaches a peak and the parasympathetic is unable to bring us down. We stay in a heightened state of arousal. This deregulates the nervous system because the energy cannot be discharged in a timely manner. It has a hard time letting go.

Daniel Siegel provides a beautiful illustration of how this

happens. Hold your hand with the fingers wrapped around your thumb. Suddenly point the fingers straight up; this represents the sympathetic nervous system reacting to a traumatic situation. To illustrate how the parasympathetic calms us down, let your fingers relax and fold back over your thumb. If the parasympathetic is not able to reach the height of the sympathetic peak—symbolizing chronic stress—the fingers stay straight up.

In Bessel van der Kolk's seminal work, *The Body Keeps the Score,* he emphasizes again and again that the physiological stress response is more accurate than the intellect. Emotions are stored and locked in our body. When triggered, they go off like little time bombs.

Fear, the Root Cause

According to Buddhism, fear is at the very root of ego and samsara. Much of our suffering is caused by fear. It is the primary tone of a separate self. When we are anxious or afraid, a physiological response gets triggered. Our hearts start pounding, our bodies secrete stress chemicals, digestion shuts down, and blood flows to our arms and legs so we can fight or run away. Over time, this physiological response wears out the body.

> Fear is not a trivial matter. In many ways, it restricts our lives; it imprisons us...the gasoline in the vehicle of ego is fear. Ego thrives on fear, so unless we figure out the problem of fear, we will never understand or embody any sense of egolessness or selflessness...This undercurrent of fear lurks behind a lot of our habits. It is why it is so hard to just sit still...We have to keep ourself distracted at some fundamental level. We have to keep our momentum going.
>
> —Judith Lief

There is a seduction in fear. It could become addictive. We love its intensity. We would rather watch films with violence and evil and horror than those based on love and goodness and caring. Even love stories and romantic comedies are based on hope and fear. Movies, novels, and documentaries that are based on love and goodness and caring are inspirational. They bring out the best within us.

Then there is the dynamic duo of hope and fear. We live in a realm of desire. There are so many things we want, some for our basic survival and many others for our entertainment. Our desires create hope. We so much want what is pleasurable, whether it is all-night partying or becoming an well-informed person. Right on the heels of hope, we have fear. We fear we won't get what we want and will get what we don't want. This dynamic duo of hope and fear keeps us spinning and creates much of our suffering.

> Everything we run away from, everything we deny, denigrate, or despise, serves to defeat us in the end. What seems nasty, painful, evil, can become a source of beauty, joy and strength, if faced with an open mind. Every moment is a golden one for him who has the vision to recognize it.
>
> –Henry Miller

Fearlessness

How do we overcome the contraction of fear? Escape from that fearful tornado?

Fearlessness!

Whereas fear takes us away from the present moment, fearlessness brings us into the now. The choice is always ours. Do we get caught in story lines about the past and projections into the future? Or do we stay present with what is happening right here now? Now is the only answer. The past has dissolved and the future has not yet happened. Now and now and now. Being in the now is an act of fearlessness.

The situations of fear that exist in our lives provide us with stepping stones to step over fear. In order to be fearless, first we need to enter the fear. We shouldn't cast it out. Instead, it should be regarded as a starting point, the kindling to build a big fire of fearlessness. We have to make friends with it. We discover that fear has a sense of panic but insight is also right there. Ultimately, staying with fear is tuning into insight and spontaneous skillfulness.

Fearlessness is accepting and embracing whatever there is. We develop loving-kindness as a direct antidote to fear. Our benevolence is the protection that renders it impotent. The more fearlessness evolves, the more available and vulnerable we become. We find sadness and gentleness are part of fearlessness. There is both joy and sadness, like mixing sweet and sour together. With this potent mix, we develop resiliency, an ability to maintain our capacity for high stress.

Neuroplasticity: Rewiring and Healing the Nervous System

The good news is that there are things we can do about trauma. Every experience changes our neural networks, the most fundamental change being in our heart and brain. We can actually choose our experiences to change the software that prints our body. In fact, there is no such thing as hardwiring. Neuroplasticity is the capacity of the brain, nervous system, and entire human organism to change, grow, and adapt. This kind of fundamental transformation comes from our internal state, how we interact with others, and our environment. In simple terms, we can switch from our reptilian brain, which looks out for our survival needs, to our mammalian or cognitive brain, which can make decisions and also has a nurturing and loving aspect.

In order to operate at a higher level of cognition, we need to feel safe. Our capacity for neuroception—how neural circuits distinguish whether situations or people are safe, dangerous, or life threatening—is how we determine this. Fundamentally we cannot learn, be creative, and love without feeling safe. An environment that creates safety and trust allows the neurological change in ourself. It activates our pre-fontal zone where it builds more synaptic connections. This is why providing children with love and care is crucial. Every child has six basic needs according to psychotherapist Jay Earley:

1. Safety – Being safe from harm or abuse
2. Belonging – Being cared for and loved
3. Autonomy – Support for personal power
4. Self-esteem – Being seen and valued
5. Stability – Stable family life and consistent parental relationship
6. Understanding – Understanding ourself and the world

The Vagus Nerve

The vagus nerve gives us a very useful tool to heal. It is the longest nerve in the body, originating in the brain and passing around the digestive system, liver, spleen, pancreas, heart, and lungs. Vagal tone regulates the sympathetic and parasympathetic systems, and in particular activates the parasympathetic. It is measured by tracking our heart-rate and breathing rate. When we breathe in because we are engaged and inspired, our heart-rate speeds up. It slows down when we breathe out, let go, or are just being. The longer there is between our inhalation heart-rate and our exhalation heart-rate, the higher our vagal tone.

High vagal tone improves the function of many body systems: better blood sugar regulation, reduced risk of stroke and cardiovascular disease, lower blood pressure, improved digestion, and reduced migraines. Amazingly, it detects pathogenic and non-pathogenic organisms in the gut microbiome, which have an effect on our mood, stress levels, and overall inflammation. Then it initiates a response to modulate inflammation. It is associated with having more stress resilience, so our body can relax faster after stress.

Low vagal tone is associated with cardiovascular conditions and strokes, depression, diabetes, chronic fatigue syndrome, cognitive impairment, and much higher rates of inflammatory conditions including autoimmune diseases (rheumatoid arthritis, inflammatory bowel, endometriosis, thyroid conditions, lupus, and more).

Ways to Increase Vagal Tone

The implications of the following simple and basic practices on our overall health are far-reaching. We can greatly influence inflammation and our immune system. When we are aware of being overly aroused, we can take measures to calm ourself in a non-conceptual way. Our breathing can change and we can soften.

Here are some ways to tone the vagus nerve and come into parasympathetic:

1. Meditation and yoga naturally bring the body into harmony with slow, rhythmic breathing from the diaphragm rather than from the top of the lungs.

2. Humming, chanting, and singing stimulate the vagus nerve because it is in proximity to the vocal cords.

3. Loving kindness meditation promotes feelings of goodwill toward ourself and others.

4. Washing our face with cold water.

5. In the shower, alternating cold and hot water, for as long as you can stand the cold.

6. Balancing the gut microbiome. The presence of healthy bacteria in the gut creates a positive feedback loop through the vagus nerve.

7. Touch, whether touching ourself or being touched by another, as with a massage or Reiki.

8. Maitri shawl practice is wrapping ourself in a shawl or blanket, like a mother holding a child.

9. Some genres of music are quintessential to embracing the para-sympathetic.

10. Free-flowing dancing allow us to express ourself with a sense of energetic release.

We can create a relationship with our wounds by simply sitting and feeling the energy within us and resonate with it, speak to it, and make friends with it. We could silence our critic and fall in love with the parts of ourself we like the least. This approach would probably need the help of a therapist.

Finally, and most significantly, the Five Wisdoms postures work very specifically with the sympathetic and parasympathetic nervous system. On the one hand, they arouse our neurotic habitual stuck patterns. On the other hand, through repeated practice, they create a flow of energy through our psychophysical being and bring us into the parasympathetic. The postures will be discussed in Chapter 25.

PART III

Turning It Around With Somatic Intelligence

CHAPTER 9

The Path of Meditation

Learning, from a non-ego point of view, is based on opening one's heart and discovering a natural sense of discipline.
Discipline in this case means attuning ourself to our inherent purity. We don't have to borrow anything from outside
ourself or mimic anybody. We are naturally pure and intelligent. We may already have some idea or experience of
that, but we also need to go further in opening ourself.

–Chögyam Trungpa Rinpoche

L et's go back to the beginning. Our suffering and confusion run deep. The demand for sanity to relieve us from
our confusion is the beginning point. What moved the
Buddha to sit beneath the bodhi tree more than 2500 years ago
was to confront his confusion and find its source. He discovered the path to awakening, to liberation.

Meditation

The practice of meditation is a time-proven way to come to
a sense of basic being, just being, awake being. It is being present. It is a very sophisticated understanding of mind, the indispensable basis to look inquisitively and honestly at who we

are. Most of our suffering is caused by running away from psychological pain and unwanted experiences. The juxtaposition of pain and the possibility of relief from pain, is the basic motivation to put us on the path of practice.

When we let go of our inner struggles with me, myself and I, we have glimpses of spaciousness, a cessation of our inner turmoil. Acknowledging our confusion and agitation, rather than trying to hide it, might be the first time we actually see who we are. Through practice, we befriend ourself and integrate and balance our energies. We work with both our inner thoughts and emotions and the outer circumstances of people, places, and situations.

Mindlessness keeps us from being present. We get lost in thought. We are preoccupied. We are caught in habits and activities that dull us out. We indulge in obsessing or fantasizing or become blank or foggy. We are too lazy or too busy and become either a couch potato or a speed runner. If we are interrupted when in a state of mindlessness, we are irritated.

The rational mind has an enormous potential to understand ourself and our world. Most of the time we have cognitive explanations for everything—either one concept or another will deliver the answer. The basic point is that thoughts are merely a finger pointing to the moon saying, "Look here." They could be inspiring, but ultimately do not go very deep. To get to a deeper place we need to drop our concepts and become embodied. The direct experience of our awake being is more potent, more expedient, and leads to realizing wisdom.

We have two minds: moving mind and still mind. Moving mind works on the surface skimming along thought after thought, noting feeling after feeling. This wandering mind finds endless distractions. It often takes us for a roller coaster ride. There is no depth. Stillness is like a rock. We are totally present. In meditation and throughout our day, we can begin to observe when we are restless and when at peace. We could even find that it is not as much about quieting our thoughts as seeing their transparency. Then they have no hold on us. Our mind abides peacefully when we let it be.

"Coming home, coming home to ourself," is a metaphor to just be, the most effective way to find a sense of inner peace and happiness. Why? Because all qualities that are ultimately fulfilling are within us. Our quest can lead us on a long journey, but coming home is the ultimate place to be. We can learn from this simple story of a boy who wants to meet his father. His mother takes the child out their front door and goes on a long journey with him through the mountains. In the end they come in the back door of the house. There, the son finally meets his father.

Meditation is a way of looking at what is, not spiritual bypassing, which is ignoring life's harder truths, or spiritual materialism, which is being attached to transcendent states of consciousness. It is not relying on an external savior or doctrine. Our grand attempts to cover up our pain begin to unravel. The simplicity of the technique exposes us completely. It's like walking on stage, under the spotlight, naked. A heightened awareness allows us to contact the deepest parts of ourself, making it impossible to escape from ourself. Instead of rejecting or denying difficult thoughts, feelings, and physical sensations, facing them is a more efficacious. We are right there, looking at our naked self, moment after moment. We become aware of our restless body, erratic breath patterns, and overly active mind. We can be up-to-date with our state of mind. The discipline is a crystal-clear mirror.

We give up our ambition for high spiritual attainment and work with the nitty-gritty of who we are, a continual process of unfolding ourself to ourself. We come to realize that happiness, calm, and peace are not the goal but a byproduct. It could find it disappointing to see that we actually have a lot of work to do on ourself but there is no spiritual path that is going to save us. We need to commit to working with ourself. We have no choice. I have to say, and it is a sad truth, that even many spiritual teachers have not done this deep work with themselves.

We have a fear of facing ourself. That is the obstacle. Experiencing the innermost core of our existence is very embarrassing to a lot of people. A lot of people turn to something that they hope will liberate them without their having to face themselves. That is impossible. We can't do that. We have to be honest with ourself. We have to see our gut, our excrement, our most undesirable parts. We have to see them. That is the foundation of warriorship, basically speaking. Whatever is there, we have to face it, we have to look at it, study it, work with it and practice meditation with it.

–Chögyam Trungpa Rinpoche

Discipline

On a regular basis, it is necessary to press the refresh button of our being. We can do this in the formal practice of meditation as well as throughout our day. Mindfulness can happen anytime anywhere: showering, brushing our teeth, traveling. Each time we come back to ourself it's like saying, "Welcome home!" These short moments of self-awareness bring us back home. We do not necessarily have to do long practice sessions but just dip into practice mind many times a day. We could pause and go in or just feel it as a supportive backdrop to the chaos.

Within us is an energy-potential as real as uranium. When we settle into just being with ourself, for even a few moments, we find our potency. When we come to a sense of center, synchronized with ourself, we touch into our vital energy. We recharge. If we do not have time to do that on a regular basis, we are running out of gas through the day, through the weeks, the months, the years. Having a daily practice discipline that benefits mind and body seems essential.

A daily-practice discipline takes a great deal of investment to reap its rewards. The thought of doing something repeatedly does not feel very attractive and doing "nothing" for a period of time is even less desirable. Just sitting and breathing might be the best thing for us, but it is hard to commit to it. For discipline to work, we need it to come from inspiration rather than a should. Taking on a daily practice is somewhat antithetical to what seems natural. It is not so surprising, then, that the child going to school for the first time, when asked by his mother how it was, says, "It was fine, but I have to go back tomorrow." For those who say they don't have time to practice, I say, "When you don't have time to practice, practice all the time."

> Don't say you don't have enough time. You have exactly the same number of hours per day that were given to Helen Keller, Pasteur, Michelangelo, Mother Teresa, Leonardo da Vinci, Thomas Jefferson, and Albert Einstein.
>
> —H. Jackson Brown

We see tremendous commitment in those who take up sports or an art form. We are awed by their prowess and find them inspiring. Martha Graham, a woman of grand style who was a major contributor to the development of modern dance over seven decades, talks about practice.

> Practice means to perform, over and over again in the face of all obstacles, some act of vision, of faith, of desire. Practice is a means of inviting the perfection desired. I believe that we learn by practice. Whether it means to learn to dance by practicing dancing or to learn to live by practicing living, the principles are the same. In each, it is the performance of a dedicated precise set of acts, physical or intellectual, from which comes a sense of achievement, a sense

of one's being, a satisfaction of spirit. One becomes, in some way, an athlete of God.

–Martha Graham

I feel fortunate to have learned the rewards of discipline early in life, as a dancer. To perfect a turn, a jump, or a movement ending up on your partner's shoulder, we have to do it many, many times. It takes strong motivation and diligence. Once we get it, it is effortless and we do it with ease.

I first started meditating at the height of my professional dance career. Though as a professional dancer and the director of my company, I showed confidence, capability, and creativity, inside I knew things were not quite right. I was driven by elation and despair. As many of us did in the 1960s, I was seeking a spiritual path, though I was hardly aware of it at the time.

Meditating uprooted most of my conceptions about life, dancing, and art. The injunction was: don't do something, just sit there. It was the most challenging thing I had ever tried to do. Naturally active, outgoing, and creative, the sheer act of sitting still confounded me. The very idea of taking an hour out in the day to just sit seemed inconceivable. The one thing that made sense to me, as a dancer, is that I understood discipline.

Then I became addicted, a meditation junkie. I needed my daily fix. I also realized that talking and reading about it would only go so far. I had to do it. So, I sat. Over the years I have come to make the practice of sitting meditation my source of strength and basic intelligence. Traveling with my daughter several years ago, I would periodically say to her, "I'm going in." It began to be my code phrase for loosening the tentacles of the outside world and going to my center.

Many of us shirk getting into discipline. It's because we have not been penetrated by it sufficiently to reap its rewards. In contrast, we could see our practice as ultimate nourishment, a cradle of loving kindness. If we practice wholeheartedly, practice will permeate our life. Most importantly, we don't meditate and then flop. We pay attention to every detail of our life so it has meaning for us. Our life does not have to be the same old same old. We begin to experience a tender heart full of joy, wakefulness, and sanity.

Pain, Resistance, Possibility, and Motivation

The particular predicament we find ourself in is that we are propelled by desire. The more we desire something, someone, the more "real" he/she/it seems to be. "I want that, because I can't live without it." If we do not get what we want, we are full of complaints and feel wronged or unworthy. Whatever we are attached to, that is what binds us. It is our downfall. Like Winnie the Pooh who gets stuck in the hole because he desires the honey inside that hole, we become similarly trapped by our desires. In short, we are victims of our own mind.

As helpful as meditation is, there are many obstacles we might face. For some, the taming effect of sitting still and cutting thoughts could be experienced as a kind of lobotomy. It is an outrage to the creative mind, to the industrious person. Resistance can be a major obstacle. Trying to bring meditation into our life can also perpetuate a black and white, good and bad, world-view. Our radar as to what is right and wrong becomes heightened: we long for an open state of mind and beat ourself up when we feel constricted. We feel we are being good when we practice, and bad when we don't. We experience a heightened self-consciousness. We can't act because we are afraid of exposing our neurosis, so we shut down. I call this contemplative constipation. When I first considered therapy in my life, I had a similar attitude. My thoughts were, "What will I ever use for creative juice, if I get rid of my neurosis?"

Over time we experience subtle shifts, signs of progress. We feel more settled, tame, and have more insights spontaneously arising about ourself and situation. The progression of settling is traditionally described metaphorically as a waterfall cascading down a cliff, a smoothly flowing river, and a great unmoving ocean. We develop a sense of stability. We are not separate from the technique but become the technique. We are more open, and full of warmth. There is tremendous appreciation for the moment we are in, whether joyful or painful.

No doubt our world is complex and we have many ways of coping with it. Some love the challenge and become Type A personalities. Some are overwhelmed and withdraw. Some become dependent on others. We have a tendency to trust complexity: complicated answers, complicated logic. Meditation is a way of simplifying the logical mind which attempts to fixate, hold on, grasp, and take things to be definite and solid. It is the very simplicity of meditating that is disarming. There is nothing complex about the present moment.

Following a Path

We arrive on the path of meditation because we have a vague feeling that something is not quite right. We feel somewhat embarrassed about the pain, chaos, and confusion we find ourself in, so we hide behind our coping strategies. We think our pain and confusion is secret but we all have it, so it is very public. We have tried to maintain the fiction that we are not suffering, that we are OK, but it is not working.

Getting on the path is committing to exposing what is there as well as beginning to taste another way of being. That in turn makes us more curious as to what this path has to offer. It is helpful to commit to an authentic way of working with ourself. There are many who have gone before us who, by trial and error, have discovered wise and skillful methods to bring out the best in human beings. Hearing inspiring teachings can make us feel wonderful, but our inspiration fades unless we continually work on ourself. We could see our whole life in terms of a journey of awareness.

For most of us, much of the time, we would rather go with the habitual flow of life that is not too demanding. We are so caught in the mundane tasks of life that we feel we have no time for anything else. We are too lazy to wake up. We forget what feels good. Perhaps we are embarrassed about who we are, so we shrink from our own goodness, the best of ourself. We would rather keep up a good facade. Desiring comfort is human and not a problem; when it is substituted for a spiritual life, we might be missing something more fulfilling.

Understanding the skillful means of meditation gives us an understanding of any discipline. In synchronizing our body, breath, and mind, we connect with our intrinsic health, and our sanity. There is a reciprocal relationship between them: we develop conscious mind, conscious breathing, and conscious body. This is fundamentally true whether playing the violin or doing the dishes—as opposed to working out on a treadmill machine and reading the news at the same time.

At some point, the focus of my creative work shifted from performing choreographed work to improvisation. It seemed more natural to let things arise in the moment of performance rather than a product created in the past. I adopt the same approach in my work with others. I write so people have an understanding of the material. When engaged with people, I work with whatever arises. I value and appreciate both. What intrigues me is the difference in mind set from which each arises: one involves precision, the other open awareness.

Meditation cultivates a warm heart, a sharp intellect, openness, and inquisitiveness. There is a constant play between being, awareness, and intelligence. The result is that we are thoroughly processed and whatever occurs is workable. We begin to experience the sanity of our basic being. Awareness in our everyday life becomes pervasive. Simple irritations become transparent, and unexpected disturbances that upset our comfort and security become opportunities to practice. We see things as they are and accept them as they are. When we see our solidity is not so solid, we see phenomenon is not so solid either. We taste the very ephemeral, fleeting quality of all we experience.

I advocate breaks. Not for coffee, gossip, or whining, but to sit and come back to basic being and recharge. A break could be a short moment of self-awareness that brings us "back home." We could just sit and breathe deeply. It could be in the middle of a meeting or sitting at our desk or pausing in the middle of house cleaning. These breaks rest the mind so it has a chance to work to the best of its ability.

> The whole idea of meditation is to develop an entirely different way of dealing with things, where you have no purpose at all. In fact, meditation is dealing with the question of whether or not there is such a thing as purpose. One is not on the way somewhere. Or rather, one is on the way and is also at the destination, at the same time.
>
> –Chögyam Trungpa Rinpoche

We all need guidance in cultivating the capacity to work with a practice discipline and the inevitable personal process that arises from it. A meditation instructor or spiritual guide helps the practitioner to undo the blind momentum of our habitual patterns. A guide helps to clarify where we are and how the path could unfold.

When we come home, come to stillness, our heart opens. We give our heart space to feel itself. It awakens a gentleness, so we begin to accept ourself as we are, and relate to our imperfections as part of the path. We cultivate a non-judgmental friendliness to our experience. Rather than perpetually acting on our desires we stay with our heart and feel its fullness. We allow our heart-hearth to embrace ourself and others.

In having experienced the poignancy of our own journey and have less anxiety about ourself, we are more open to others. Dissolving our fixation on self allows us to open up to others. The more we have tasted our own stuck places, the more we are able to meet others in their stuck places. The more intimate we are with ourself, the more universal our understanding of others becomes. We transcend the particulars of people to go to the core of humanity.

CHAPTER 10

The Practice of Meditation

To begin with, the main point of meditation is that we need to get to know ourself: our minds, our behavior, our being. You see, we think we know ourself, but actually we don't. There are all sorts of undiscovered areas of our thoughts and actions. What we find in ourself might be quite astounding.

–Chögyam Trungpa Rinpoche

M editation is not an activity, it is a state of mind. It is not a self-improvement technique, but the fundamental discipline of coming to ground zero, the timeless present. We learn to trust our heart in the present moment. It has a tangible sense of just being, where we drop agendas, credentials, and ambitions. It is not about psychological processing and is not even spiritual. Rather, it has a simplicity that leaves us with nothing to hold onto and nowhere to go. We do less so we can observe more. We discover the profundity of our being by just being, at one with just being in non-being. Ultimately, meditation is a labor of love. Our attentiveness toward ourself is a form of self-love.

Meditation is the most radical thing we could do. We just do the technique without any ideas about it in a very direct, almost stupid, way. It is designed to disrupt our habit. Doing nothing is the most direct way of un-sticking our stuckness. We say no to body's habitual tendency to move, overly active speech patterns, and wildness of mind. We are not feeding or reinforcing our trips. However, though opening to the unconditioned can create a sense of non-duality, it can also be unsettling. It is a totally uncompromising approach.

Space, the Final Frontier

The inspiration of space, whether our own open spaciousness or the mystery of the cosmos, has created wonder in human beings since beginningless time. It draws us forward on the path and, in some sense, all of our practices have to do with a sense space. We become acutely aware of a sense of contrast: me and my confusion here, spaciousness and clarity out there. We are stuck; space is salvation. "Give me some space," is really code for, "I want some sanity here." The polarity between confusion, constriction, and claustrophobia versus spaciousness, openness, and sanity creates a constant struggle. We go through continual patterns of opening and closing, always asking ourself how much to open and how much to protect ourself. No space and open space become the common thread of our practice. Sadly, we create a black and white world of good and bad.

Initially, the contrast between what's in here and what's out there becomes heightened. Time and again, the seduction of our neurosis sabotages our well-being. It is pretty normal to feel more neurotic when we first start sitting. Yet confusion is good because it invites further questioning. Dissolving our fixation on this allows us to open to that. We see phenomenon is not so solid either. We mix our mind with space and go beyond this and that. Relaxing the boundary of self, we are included in a larger world. We are in a self-existing reality with no one to be aware. It has a stabilizing effect.

No doubt we have gravitated toward meditation to seek this sense of spaciousness or calmness, qualities conventionally known as the fruit of meditating. There is a sense that there is more space around our thoughts and we move through the world with more equanimity. Space is a good thing. At some point we realize that we don't have to make a journey to space. We realize that space is everywhere. But empty space leaves us in no-man's land and is not an accurate picture of reality from either the Tantric or quantum perspective.

We long for space but are afraid of it. In mindfulness practice there is a sense of being tamed by space. But we also enter a world of discomfort. Space can be scary. It's the unknown, the groundless. It can be terrifying and threatening because it is so undefined. It's a tricky relationship.

Here is how space looks with our different practices, the last three of which we will explore later:

no space	fixation
space between	gap
space within	mindfulness
space around	awareness
space within and around	mindfulness/awareness
take in no space, send out space	tonglen
space as full emptiness	mandala perspective
inseparability of space and confusion	co-emergent wisdom

Lets Take Our Seat

As enhancement and support for our practice, we could as-sign a particular place in our home to create a contemplative container. It becomes our retreat place where we withdraw from the vicissitudes of life and feel protected in our practice. It could be inviting with candles and incense. We could feel we come home to the best part of ourself. Making time early in the day for just being changes the quality of the day and affirms what is primary for us. Our contemplative container helps to arouse a sense of intention and inspiration.

To begin a session, first we could take note of how we feel without judgment: tired? speedy? emotional? Then we arouse strong motivation: "I am sitting here with the sole intention of stabilizing my mind." The technique of meditation works with mindfulness and awareness of our body, breath, and mind. They are the primary aspects of who we are, so being very at-tentive to them is key. We sit on a cushion or chair in an upright posture, legs crossed if on a cushion, and feet firmly on the floor if in a chair. Our hands rest on our thighs. Our gaze is relaxed and slightly lowered so we don't become distracted. Our breath is the focus of our meditation. We breathe easily allowing our breath to go in and out without trying to change it in any way. Every time we are aware of mental activity, we acknowledge it by saying "thinking" to ourself.

We embody the technique: grounded in our body and at-tentive to our breath. We continually come back to basic being, this breathing body. The simpler the technique, the less danger there is of sidetracks. The technique says, "Sit, just sit. Be here right now." It is intentionally blunt and bold. It boycotts our ego, cutting through our endless mental chatter and dramas be-cause it is so straightforward.

We could find this hard to take, insulting in fact. But we could also see it as a powerful tool. Impulses and desires are neutralized as we sit in stillness, following our breath and acknowledging our thoughts without getting caught up in them. This is in contrast to relating to thoughts obsessively, when they become powerful. The fundamental instruction, as Tibetan Buddhist nun Pema Chödrön puts it, is, "Stay, stay, stay." But we find that our mind is very slippery. Are we just being as an expression of wakefulness or are we mindless, pre-occupied, or half asleep? So, again and again, we come back to a deliberate attentiveness to our body, breath, and mind.

Two things become obvious. On the one hand, emotional upheavals seem to become more exaggerated, more flagrant. We feel more crazy than ever. It is not that we are, but practice exposes our neurosis. On the other hand, we could experience a taming quality in our being. The technique allows both space for things to arise as well as a way to work with them. It acts like a lightning rod, grounding overly volatile energy in the simplicity of just being here. Through continued practice, we cultivate a dispassionate attitude to our endless dramas and we experience a simple sense of being.

> The sitting practice of meditation allows a sense of solidness, a sense of slowness, and the possibility of watching one's mind operating all the time. You become aware that you have been missing a lot of things in your life. You have been too busy to look for them or see them and appreciate them. As you begin to meditate, you become more perceptive. Your mind becomes clearer, like an immaculate microscope lens.
>
> –Chögyam Trungpa Rinpoche

We work with the extremes of tight and loose. If we become too tight, we will rebound and want to flop. If we are too loose, we can become wild and chaotic. We can monitor ourself. If there is bumpy terrain, we tighten our seatbelt; if it's too tight, we can relax it.

Inevitably we experience hot and cool boredom. Hot boredom is like being locked in a padded cell. We are miserable, irritated, and just want out of there. We have resistance to getting totally, properly bored. Slowly, from the taming process of mindfulness, we begin to experience the spacious and relaxed quality of cool boredom. We begin to appreciate the subtleties of boredom. We could even long for it. Actually, a sign of accomplishment is how bored we can get! It is a deepening sense of well-being.

> Boredom is important because boredom is anti-credential, anti-entertainment, and as we develop greater psychological sophistication, we begin to appreciate such boredom. It becomes cool and refreshing, like a mountain river. That very real and genuine boredom, or "cool boredom," plays an extremely important role. In fact, we could quite simply say that the barometer of our accomplishment in meditation practice is how much boredom we create for ourself. Cool boredom is rather light boredom: it has its uneasy quality, but at the same time it is not a big deal. Cool boredom is like what mountains experience. With cool boredom, thought processes become less entertaining—they become transparent. Cool boredom is hopelessness at its most absolute level.

> —Chögyam Trungpa Rinpoche

Sitting Meditation

Generally, we have a dissonance with our body as it feels solid and constricted, especially when in pain. Our mind wants to be in control and doesn't want to listen to the body. When the mind's discursiveness quiets, correspondently our body's agitation settles. When we are mindful of our body, we have a sense of just being in embodied awareness. We focus not only on our breathing, but also our body. So, sitting in the upright posture, doing nothing—seemingly wasting our time—is the most beneficial thing we can do. When we relax, it creates a kind of innocence in us and we became naïve again. The tantric rationale to just sit is that innate, natural wisdom of the body comes into balance naturally in the upright posture. Our body is a highly intelligent teacher, always communicating with us.

The synchronization of body, breath, and mind is ultimate healthiness, an expression of well-being. Practice is purifying. A new sense of self comes into being: we feel more grounded, rested, open. The embodiment that comes from meditation is the secret to sanity. It gives us a sense of the power of the body to transform our mind. The pliancy and suppleness of mind and body brings joy.

Good posture is inseparable from wakeful mind. Trungpa Rinpoche called it physiologically marinating oneself in dharma which allows the psychological aspect of bare attention. We tend to forget this, but it is a psychophysical and psycho-sensual practice.

We demonstrate our aspiration to be awake through good posture. If depressed, we can pick ourself up. If drowsy, we can wake ourself up. If distracted, we become present. Sense of being has to do with being on the spot: one point, one dot, one stroke. It is a total sense of being powerfully present. We are synchronized with ourself and our surroundings. We sit in a powerfully present body, feeling an affinity with earth and embraced by space.

Meditative Posture Images

1. Sit like the Buddha
The Buddha is an example of good posture, a physical expression of basic goodness.

2. Connect heaven, earth, and human
We join the spaciousness of heaven and good mother earth in our posture.

3. Sit like a tree
We grow roots, have an upright posture like a trunk, float our head like leafy branches.

4. Sit like a breathing rock
We could have an immovable quality yet alive and breathing.

5. Sit like a mountain
Thoughts and emotions pass by like shifts in the weather.

6. Sit like an ocean
Thoughts and emotions are like waves which never disturb the ocean's depths.

7. The body has form but is empty
When our discursiveness mind quiets and our agitated body settles, there is space.

Sitting Meditation and Breath

Breathing, as an expression of being right here. It is the technique universally used to bring us into the present moment. Allowing our tongue to float in the mouth is a detail that is helpful. When we are sitting and breathing, we are mixing our breath and space. We are also mixing our awareness with space. Our state of mind is reflected in our breathing. Following the breath brings us into the present moment. We are a breathing body. The body says wake up and relax. In meditation we bring together our body, our breath, and our mind.

The reference point in shamatha [mindfulness] is the breath. The traditional recommendation of the lineage of meditators that developed in the Kagyü-Nyingma tradition is based on the idea of mixing mind and breath. This means you should be with the breath; you *are* the breath. Your breath goes out and you go out. Your breath dissolves into the atmosphere and you dissolve into the atmosphere. Then you just let go completely. You even forget meditation practice at that point. You just let go. There is a gap. Then naturally, automatically, physiologically, you breathe in. Let that be the gap. Then you breathe out again. Out, dissolve, gap. Go out again, dissolve, there's a gap. Go out, dissolve, there's a gap. You continue to proceed in that way.

–Chögyam Trungpa Rinpoche

We could experience breathing like this:

In-breath	Out-breath
solidity of being	sense of being
struggle, panicked	relaxation, well-being, survival
this	that
heavy headed	spacious, lightness
demanding	free
body discomfort	easily aligned with body
sense perceptions distorted	letting sense perceptions be

The Five Wisdoms are present in sitting meditation:

1. The presence, receptiveness, and affinity with space of buddha energy
2. The dependability of the earth's support of ratna energy
3. The clarity of mind of vajra energy
4. The open heart of padma energy
5. The can-do attitude of karma energy

The Four Foundations of Mindfulness

The four foundations of mindfulness demonstrate precision in meditation and help to navigate our practice. Each has an intelligent alertness to bring us back to mindfulness. They are concerned with the process, rather than the contents, of mind.

They relate to the three aspects of meditation technique: our posture is mindfulness of body, our breathing is mindfulness of aliveness, labeling our thoughts is mindfulness of effort, and just being is mindfulness of mind.

1. Mindfulness of Body: embodied body

Mindfulness of body is the basic foundation of our discipline. We are grounded and connected to the earth, like a breathing rock. Our body rests on the meditation cushion and mind rests on the body. We need to make a distinction between true body and psychosomatic body. True body is being settled with nowhere to go. Our thoughts have a settled quality. When we sit, we really sit. It requires trust. Psychosomatic body is having ideas about our bodies. We could be anxious, depressed, nervous, or in pain. We perch or slump rather than fully sit. We are not touching our true body. In our practice we flicker between psychosomatic body and true body.

2. Mindfulness of Aliveness: our psychophysical barometer

Mindfulness of aliveness is being awake to experience rather than having a sense of austerity about our practice. We are aware of our breathing and our sense perceptions. We touch in and let go. It makes our meditation very personal and intimate. We develop confidence that we can tune into this state of mind spontaneously without having to capture and hold it. We have both a sense of well-being as well as a subtle anxiety about our survival. In this case, survival mentality is not coming from ego, but an ingrained instinct to touch into our life force.

3. Mindfulness of Effort: the jerk of awareness

Ordinary effort is where we struggle and push toward a goal. It's heavy-handed, striving, ambitious, and speedy. It arises from a sense of inadequacy. We become solemn, dutiful, and narrow-minded. Having no joy or appreciation stagnates our practice. Right effort is based on confidence and trust in ourself and a commitment to discipline. It is an innate ability of mind, a sudden jerk of awareness, to come back to the present. It is a fast and instinctual built-in mechanism. We don't go through a process, we just come back. Right effort is effortless. It's like a lover's attentiveness toward their lover or a hunter's attentiveness toward their prey.

4. Mindfulness of Mind: just being

This is the practice of bare attention, just being. It's beyond working with a technique. It's the ability of mind to be one-pointed, on the dot. The watcher falls away. We are alert, awake, and totally up-to-date in the moment. Being simple, present, and precise slows down the fickleness of mind jumping back-and-forth. So, there is a sense of both accuracy and sense of freedom.

Summary of Practice

The four foundations in meditation

In summary, the body establishes ground. Aliveness opens us to being sensate. Effort is effortless coming back. Mind is moment-to-moment awareness, bare attention.

Fine-Tuning Our Understanding of Mindfulness and Awareness

Mindfulness is the ability to bring our attention to the present moment and not be distracted. Being in the present moment—the only moment—stabilizes the mind. We are not jumping from one distraction to another, nor are we engrossed in our thoughts or emotions. Instead, we are attentive to what we are doing in the moment that we are doing it. A stabilized mind brings our mind and body together in the precision of moment-to-moment experience. We bring one-pointed attention to whatever we are doing. Now, now, now. Look, look, look. Stay, stay, stay. It is a very precise way of working with the mind.

The taming or settling aspect of meditation through acknowledging our thoughts and coming back to our breath is essential to begin our practice. By stopping the speed of our thoughts, we see our them arise, dwell, and dissolve. We can let go of all we fabricate. We see thought patterns as simple phenomenon, mere occurrence. Complications become transparent. There is a natural resting. We experience the well-being of body like a mountain, the well-being of breath like a gentle breeze, and the well-being of mind like an ocean without waves. Mindfulness develops precision, stability, clarity, and a warm heart. Its value as a pacifying and stress-reducing process is unparalleled.

> In the practice of meditation, the way to be daring, the way to leap, is to disown your thoughts, to step beyond your hope and fear, the ups and downs of your thinking process. You can just be, just let yourself be, without holding on to the constant reference points that mind manufactures. You do not have to get rid of your thoughts. They are a natural process; they are fine; let them be as well. But let yourself go out with the breath, let it dissolve. See what happens. When you let yourself go in that way, you develop trust in the strength of your being and trust in your ability to open and extend yourself to others. You realize that you are rich and resourceful enough to give selflessly to others, and as well, you find that you have tremendous willingness to do so.

> –Chögyam Trungpa Rinpoche

There are issues that could arise. 1) Strict mindfulness becomes too goal oriented. We think we had a good meditation session or a bad meditation session which creates a good girl/bad girl approach. It's very black and white. 2) It's tiresome. It takes too much effort so we avoid our practice. 3) It could lead to dullness and a non-thought bias. 4) It has a propensity for spiritual materialism as we could get attached to a blissful state.

The transition from mindfulness to awareness is slow and subtle. As the mind settles into unconditional, cool boredom and relaxes, it creates the space to expand into panoramic awareness. In the beginning, we have glimpses of openness rather than being aware all of the time. The precision is carried over but there is more of a sense of freedom. The environment becomes part of our meditation. We go from nothing happening—and that's just fine—to becoming aware of whatever is happening in our environment. With stillness of mind, the activity of mind can be seen more clearly. There is a simultaneity of stillness and intelligence. Stillness is simple and precise which allows spaciousness and intelligence to arise.

Mindfulness has a sense of being dutiful; awareness is more romantic. Too much mindfulness leads to dullness. Too much awareness leads to agitation. With awareness, thoughts become no big deal, just part of the environment. There is a lighter touch. It's like flying kite. We hold on tightly (mindfulness) yet there is a sense of freedom (awareness). If we don't hold, the kite goes wild. If we hold too tight, the kite won't see the sky.

With awareness, there is a stillness in which thoughts and sense perceptions are included without being a distraction from nowness. We clearly see what is happening with an uncontrived knowingness. We are open to what's here, so the next situation arises out of that naturally. Awareness is "going with the flow." We welcome all circumstances and aren't thrown off by them. Instead of experiencing projections as solid and frozen, we experience them as exciting and fluid. We find the world to be more vivid and alive yet see its fundamental insubstantiality. We gain trust that, in letting things be, we allow them to unfold in their own way. As well, we know what to do, can act in the moment, and then let it go.

My experience is that when I bring my mind to stillness and hold my seat, whatever happens, I will not get upset. In contrast, if I become speedy and caught up in a situation, flying all over the place, I react negatively to the circumstances. Awareness allows us to see things clearly and position ourself wisely in relationship to them. We become more aware of our mistakes and so learn from them. We discover ever-greater confidence and humility. We move into a more conscious way of living.

We could view mindfulness as a candle burning undisturbed and awareness as the flame of true knowledge, a clarity that burns through the confusion of ego. The steadier the flame, the more brilliantly the true nature is illuminated. Another image is that of a glass of water with dirt in it. When stirred, it is confusion. When settled it is mindfulness. Clear water is awareness. A third image is that we are at a carnival holding a teaspoon full of water. We walk through the crowd with mindfulness so we don't spill the water, and are also aware of all that is around us.

The discipline of meditation develops intuition and intellect. The more the discipline, the more the intuition. Discipline and intuition slowly produce intellect, like rubbing two sticks together to get a spark. Intellect is seeing things clearly with greater depth and precision. We could have a sudden openness when insight arises like a flash. We see what is appropriate without question or doubt.

The Distinctions Between Mindfulness and Awareness

The Fruition of Our Practice

Mindfulness	Awareness
stillness	insight
being present	include the environment
"this" oriented	"that" oriented
on the dot	open to occurrences
letting go	letting be

In Practice

Mindfulness	Awareness
reference point of body, speech, & mind	reference point of space
introverted	more expansive
the gaze is lowered	the gaze is raised
non-conceptual	non-conceptual and conceptual
resting	resting and discriminating
cutting thoughts	sharpening intellect
mind stays	mind is with whatever is happening
committed to precision	letting the world come to you
goal oriented, sense of expectation	no goal, no journey necessary

Possible Experiences

Mindfulness	Awareness
very literal	somewhat romantic
self-contained	more adventurous
serious, solemn	light, sense of humor, joy
non-thought	thoughts are part of the environment
sense consciousnesses are subdued	sense consciousnesses are adornments
subtle expectation	expanded confidence
candle undisturbed by wind	flame that burns fuel of conceptual ego
gentleness, maitri	compassion
self-conscious	less self-conscious
attachment to good and bad	discriminate without bias

Result

Mindfulness	Awareness
peace	liberation
simplify life	engage fully in life
relaxation	ease in relating with world
confidence	intelligence, door of wisdom

The fruition of mindfulness and awareness is resting relaxed in a natural state, beyond a technique. There is a sense of panoramic awareness as well as an appreciation of detail. It is like being in touch with the depth of the ocean and waves at the same time. We are able to open to a greater world. The times we experience ourself as wakeful, spacious, clear, accommodating, and inquisitive, we feel at our best. It allows us to take delight in the world around us. We see there is nowhere to go. We rest in space. This is unconditional presence, unconditional wakefulness. There is an emphasis on pleasure, a transcendental sybaritic attitude which is not indulging. It is simply not seeing the world as hostile. This is Tantra.

CHAPTER 11

Your Primal Being: Elemental Embodiment

But true magic is the magic of *reality,* as it is: the earth of earth, the water of water—communicating with the elements so that in some sense, they become one with you. When you develop bravery, you make a connection with the elemental quality of existence. Bravery begins to heighten your existence, that is, to bring out the brilliant and genuine qualities of your environment and your being. So you begin to contact the magic of reality—which is already there in some sense. You actually can attract the power and strength and the primordial wisdom.

–Chögyam Trungpa Rinpoche

Embodied Elements

The elements make up the phenomenal world and are the material aspect of all things and processes. Elemental processes create the universe, sustain it, and ultimately destroy it. Our most primal aspect is that we are made of the elements: earth, water, fire, air, and space. Our bodies are of the same ingredients as the environment, no different from rocks, trees, and the ocean. There is a dynamic play of the elements as in the weather, the seasons, and all-natural phenomenon. The dynamism of the five elements underlies the complexities of all that exists.

We began by looking at the Five Wisdoms in terms of personality and psychology. Primal being is not about *who* we are, which is more psychological, but *what* we are, which is more physical, elemental. The elements are primordial, self-existing both internally and externally. They are unconditional, not caused by circumstances. They are the basis of medicine and psychology, have capacities to purify and heal, can connect us to the sacred, and are often used in ritual ways by the world's religious and shamanistic traditions.

The elements are more primal than our psychological development as bodily experience precedes psychology. They are psychophysical and are the constituents of every physical, sensual, mental, and spiritual phenomena. They are correlated with character, temperaments, body types, thinking styles, emotions, colors, tastes, and illness. They are continually functioning within us at subtle level: moving, balancing, and harmonizing. Water washes away and fire burns to purify; earth stabilizes and air or wind provides movement.

The outer world is obvious to all, but we rarely take in its elemental nature. When we do, a whole dimension of reality opens to us. It can lead to a deeper understanding of ourself and our relationship to the world, having a positive effect on the quality of our our bodies and our lives. Natural settings nourish us. We love vacations and outings in nature. We take in the essence of our surroundings: the earthiness of earth, the waterness of water, the fireness of fire. We enjoy the rich soil of a garden, the freshness of oceans, rivers, and lakes, the warmth of sun and fire, the invigorating mountain air, the relaxation of wide-open spaces, and the peacefulness of the vast sky.

The elements of our body work harmoniously together to keep us alive. They work to pump blood, digest food, and fire neurons. They can be healing, refreshing, and wonderfully enjoyable. When we are spacious and relaxed, the elements are in energetic harmony, function naturally, and we have a sense of well-being. We are in balance and we feel good. When the balance is lost, we fall prey to illness and death. Fully meeting an element is energizing, joyful.

We can pay attention to the elements on a day-to-day basis using common sense. They affect us on an instinctive level—when we are deprived of an element, we yearn for it and respond. When we are hungry, we bring in the nourishing, sustaining energy of earth by eating. When we are thirsty, we drink water which gives us a sense of life energy, pure and fluid. When our energy is stirred up, windy, and groundless, we ground and come back to earth. When feeling sad and lonely, we rekindle the fire within us. When lethargic, wind moves us into action.

The presence and action of the four elements in our body corresponds to the energetic qualities of the Five Wisdoms.

Earth is connected to ratna and has a sense of solidity, steadiness, substantiality, tangibility, weight, density, and roughness. Earth maintains us. It is the material basis of our life. As Mother Earth, it nourishes us. That we can walk in this world is thanks to the earth element. It is present in our body as skin, flesh, and bones, and in the world as plants, stones, and trees. We have a sense of being grounded: our weight, mass, substance, fleshiness. We have a form, a shape, with boundaries: top, bottom, front, back.

Water is associated with vajra. We experience the binding together, fluidity, and cohesion of water. Water is the source of life. About 60% of our body is water, so we are as if floating in an immense river of life energy. We have a sense of flow, circulation of the blood and the lymph system, a moistness of the body.

The *fire* element is associated with padma and has tremendous vitality and radiance. It preserves our body and is connected to our heart, our passion. Love is our life force, so we keep our fire well-lit and cared for. We have a sense of temperature, heat, electrical currents, and sparks of energy.

Air is the breath of life associated with karma. Breath is everywhere, within and without. It props up the body and is responsible for its movement and activity. We enjoy breathing when we tune into a gentle respiratory rhythm. We have a sense of the continual quality of the micro movements of the breath.

Space is associated with buddha and accommodates the other four. Without spaciousness the other four would be overly constricted. Our experience is a sense of consciousness, a fundamental kind of awake-ness, knowing we exist, are here, and have a body.

In short, here are their physical properties: earth is solidity, water is fluidity and cohesion, fire is temperature, air is motion, and space accommodates the other four.

The elements have the capacity to purify, balance, and heal. Control over the inner elements and the outer elements is a central part of Tantric practice. The natural world is seen to be sacred and alive with beings and forces both visible and invisible. A conscious relationship with the elements changes our perspectives about our relationship to the natural world. It is, in a tantric sense, key to spiritual practice.

We can experience the elements on three levels:

1. mental

2. psychophysical

3. outer manifestation

For example, if we slow down to observe ourself in performing an arm gesture, we see that we first have an intention of mind (mental), then a bodily intimation or impulse as in chi, prana, or energy (psychophysical), and finally the gesture itself (outer phenomenal).

From a Tantric perspective, the elements can be seen as a creation story. The process or creation goes from the least tangible to the most tangible: first there is an inkling of existence and then either a seed syllable, from the Buddhist view, or chemical compound, from the scientific perspective. Then there is the first elemental sound. That becomes light, and in turn, light becomes heat or energy. Lastly, energy becomes elemental and manifests as form. Physics is also recognizing the meeting of the psychological and the physical worlds. This is a spiritual way of looking at how things evolve into a manifest form.

Working with elements in our body is also a skillful way to practice letting go, dissolving, and dying. We come into being through the coming together of the elements. We die through the dissolving of the elements. We don't even have to be fearful of death as we are already a part of the elements. In dying we experience our earth body becoming heavy and merging with Mother Earth, then the fluidity of water, then the heat of fire, and then air/wind, going every which way in our body and out into space. All dissolves into space. Dissolving this body at death is the most intense experience of life. It also has the potential to liberate, finally free of this cumbersome elemental body.

Embodying the Elements and Emotions

We have seen how we get stuck from a psychological viewpoint. The Five Psychophysical Aspects and the Six Intensified Realities *explain* the emotions. In contrast, understanding emotions through the elements is a more *embodied* experience.

Due to our habitual ego-driven patterns, the elements become unbalanced, either by overuse or neglect. The lack of balance can be due to illness, agitation, dullness, or distraction. If they become increasingly unbalanced, we experience mental and physical symptoms. We could feel more and more anxious and vulnerable and become more and more self-referential, trying to protect ourself. Then we could use intensified emotions as a defense. This is the relationship between the physical elements and our psychology, our emotions.

Whether affected at a physical or emotional level, we experience elemental imbalance. It is a psychophysical situation, so it's circular: elemental imbalance affects our emotions and emotions affect elemental imbalance. So, the elements are another way to see how we get stuck and how we can shine. Our awareness of the presence and action of elements in our body can lead to balance and deeper understanding of ourself. We begin to see how they affect us on an instinctive level. For instance, having too much of one element can lead to illness, agitation, dullness, or distraction. When deprived of an element, we yearn for it.

. . .

The following practice shows us the profundity of how the elements can affect us. We will have more sensitivity to when our elements are in or out of balance and enable us to come into more energetic harmony. For the element/emotion you want to focus on, first read the six phases below. Get a sense of each phase and its particular quality. Then sit with eyes closed, bringing your attention to your whole body, allowing it to settle. Stay with your breathing. Fill your body on the inhale, and slowly let it go on the exhale. Then, experientially, go through each of the six phases.

Space/Buddha

1. **The space element functions naturally and there is a sense of well-being.** Space is the most fundamental or primal element, vast and pervasive. We feel open, accommodating, spacious, and expansive. Our body feels as if it were boundless, a sense that the inner space of our body and outer space merge. We are at one with all things. We enjoy spacious, peaceful, and blissful qualities.

2. **The space element creates instability due to habitual patterns.** With too much space, we feel disoriented, lost, disjointed, disconnected, out of touch, ungrounded, and unable to prioritize. With too little space, we are closed down and solid. We feel blocked and become dysfunctional.

3. **The space element creates increasing psychophysical instability and self-concern.** Whether two spacious or too solidified, we start to feel a pervasive anxiety and vulnerability.

4. **Intensified emotions arise as a defense, to cope.** We dwell in ignorance and denial. We go blind, deaf, and dumb. "I am bewildered, lost."

5. **Come into balance by embodying the space element fully.** We bring a sense of space into our body energetically. We fill every cell of our body with space, expanding from the inside out. We become spacious, relaxed, and warm. We feel fulfilled, balanced, and in energetic harmony. This is the primal space of self-existing spaciousness.

6. **Experience the intrinsic wisdom of space in simple actions.** We experience spaciousness when we sit or stand in stillness by completely dropping any impulse to move. We are still without any reason to be still. We feel nourished by space. Stand and then step forward with an open gesture, being fully present. Visualize white light on the top and back of the head and make the elemental sound, "AH."

Water/Vajra

1. **The water element functions naturally and there is a sense of well-being.** Our body is around 60% water. It is filled with an immense river of life energy, a source of life. We feel the pervasive sense of flow and fluidity. Water binds together, makes things cohesive. We can let our mind and body settle like a still pool with a sense of ease and deep comfort with ourself. We enjoy calm, clear, pure, and fluid qualities.

2. **The water element creates instability due to habitual patterns.** Too much water brings a sense of turbulence and agitation. If we neglect our water element, we become frozen and rigid.

3. **The water element creates increasing psychophysical instability and self-concern.** Whether agitated or frozen, we feel continually anxious and vulnerable. We lack a sense of well-being, are out of tune with ourself, and are unaware of emotions.

4. **Intensified emotions as a defense, to cope.** We flip into hot or cold anger as a justification and a defense. We arm ourself with aggression and either lash out or attack ourself with self-hate. "I'm right; you're wrong."

5. **Come into balance by embodying the water element fully.**
   We bring water into our body energetically. We become an immense river of life energy, self-existing clarity, and purity. We feel fulfilled, balanced, and in energetic harmony.

6. **Experience the intrinsic wisdom of water in simple actions.** To experience the water element, we first stand in stillness. Then we bend down to scoop up imaginary water with our hands, raise it, and pour it over ourself to cleanse and purify. Experience brilliant blue light like a laser beam from the third eye in the forehead and make the elemental sound, "EE."

Earth/Ratna

1. **The earth element functions naturally and there is a sense of well-being.** The earth element is the material basis of life and the most tangible of the elements. We walk on this world thanks to the earth element. We feel the earth's solidity, strength, roughness, tangibility, weight, and density in the earthiness of stones, trees, and plants. We feel the element of earth in our bones, flesh, tissues, and skin. With the earth element, we feel grounded, stable, connected, at home in our body. We enjoy the qualities of fullness, comfort, and joy.

2. **The earth element creates instability due to habitual patterns.** If we have too much earth element, we become indulgent, stagnant, and heavy. If we neglect earth, we become insubstantial, hollow, hungry.

3. **The earth element creates increasing psychophysical instability and self-concern.** Whether we have too much or too little earth element, we feel continually anxious and vulnerable. If we have too much, we feel lazy, unable to move,

insensitive, depressed, and have a tendency to oversleep. If we have too little, we feel ungrounded, unstable, dissatisfied, disconnected, and are always wanting more.

4. **Intensified emotions as a defense, to cope.** We experience a deep-seated sense of poverty and lack of self-worth, that we are not good enough. We may feel empty, hollow, insubstantial, and insignificant. "I'm worthless." To counter that, we defend ourself with puffed-up pride.

5. **Come into balance by embodying the earth element fully.** We bringing the earth element into our body energetically. We feel fulfilled, balanced, and in energetic harmony. We feel spacious, relaxed, and warm. We are deeply satisfied and fulfilled, and have no need for anything more. We become self-existing equanimity.

6. **Experience the intrinsic wisdom of earth in simple actions.** To experience the earth element, first stand in stillness. Then make slow, grounded movements. Tune into how the body is part of nature's body. With a golden yellow light in our belly, make an offering gesture and make the elemental sound, "UH."

Fire/Padma

1. **The fire element functions naturally and there is a sense of well-being.** The fire element is the vitality of life, the passion and warmth of life. We keep the fire well-lit and cared for in our heart hearth. Fire makes us creative, energetic, enthusiastic, and inspired. It also has power to transform and to heal, preserving our body and giving us a radiant glow. It makes us good-humored, warm, blissful, and joyful. We enjoy its vibrant, vital qualities.

2. **The fire element creates instability due to habitual patterns.** With too much fire element, we become overly outgoing, constantly expressive and wanting to connect. If we neglect fire, we feel isolated and desolate.

3. **The fire element creates increasing psychophysical instability and self-concern.** We feel continually anxious and vulnerable. If we have too much fire, we feel agitated, restless, and unstable. We are quickly irritated and have a perpetual discursiveness of mind. If we have too little fire, we lack energy, vitality, enjoyment; we are uninspired.

4. **Intensified emotions as a defense, to cope.** We desire the heat of intensity. We pursue anything that offers pleasure, whether real or fantasized. If the fire goes out, we feel desolate, isolated, and lonely. The world is an emotional desert. The spark of life has gone out and life is not worth living. "I want to love and be loved."

5. **Come into balance by embodying the fire element fully.** We bring the fire element into our body energetically. We feel the fire of life, the vitality of warmth, connection, and engagement. We feel fulfilled, balanced, and in energetic harmony. We become self-existing passion.

6. **Experience the intrinsic wisdom of fire in simple actions.** To experience the fire element, first stand in stillness. Allow the inner fire to arise within our body and express itself in expressive movement. Circulate red light through the communication centers—the heart, throat, and genitals—and make the elemental sound, "EH."

Air or Wind/Karma

1. **The wind element functions naturally and there is a sense of well-being.** The wind element is the breath of life. It is everywhere, within and without. It is fresh, penetrating, transformative, flexible, and communicative. It cleanses the emotional, mental, and spiritual body. Air props up the body and is responsible for its activity. Enjoy the feel of our respiratory rhythm. Breathe in all the air we need, and breathe out and let go all that we don't need. Be aware of the lightness and the strength of wind in our body. Enjoy the quality of potential action.

2. **The wind element creates instability due to habitual patterns.** Too much wind element makes us speedy and without direction. If it is neglected, we are immobilized.

3. **The wind element creates increasing psychophysical instability and self-concern.** We feel continually anxious and vulnerable. If we have too much, we have trouble sticking to things, procrastinate, and lack any satisfaction in where we are and what we do. We are readily tossed about by external influences. With too little wind, we can't act.

4. **Intensified emotions as a defense, to cope.** We have a groundless anxiety, an underlying paranoia, feeling suspicious and uncertain. We sense a lurking threat of the sinister unknown, as if the world is out to get us, or undermine us. But it is unpredictable. We defend ourself with jealousy if anyone who gets ahead of us. "I have to be in control."

5. **Come into balance by embodying the wind element fully.** We bring the wind element into our body energetically. The winds find their natural place and direction in our body

and we have a sense of well-being. We feel fulfilled, balanced, and in energetic harmony. We become self-existing accomplishment where everything is already accomplished.

6. **Experience the intrinsic wisdom of wind in simple actions.** To experience the element of wind, we need to be active. Play with these possibilities:

    1. Pick a spot in the room and run fast to the chosen spot.

    2. Pick a spot in the room and walk slowly, purposefully, to the chosen spot.

    3. Pick a spot in the room and run fast, using a slow mind, to the chosen spot.

    4. Run in frenetic way, with no goal other than to be haphazard.

    5. Pick a spot in the room and run to the chosen spot with ease of movement and ease of mind.

    Once the movement(s) are completed, stand and visualize green light in our limbs and make the elemental sound, "O."

* * *

Making the connection between an element and an emotion is a profound experience. With practice, it can be a useful tool to regulate ourself when we feel unbalanced.

CHAPTER 12

Becoming Sensational

In Buddhist Tantra, a lot of reference is made to the idea that pleasure is the way, pleasure is the path. This means indulgence in the sense perceptions by a basic awakened mind...Things are seen clearly and precisely as they are. One does not have to remind oneself to be in the state of awareness. The sense objects themselves are the reminder. They come to you, they provide you with awareness. This makes awareness an ongoing process. Continuity in this sense does not need to be sought but just is. Nobody has to take on the duty of bringing the sun up and making it set. The sun just rises and sets. There is no organization in the universe that is responsible for that, that has to make sure that the sun rises and sets on time. It just happens by itself. That is the nature of the continuity of Tantra that we have been talking about. Discovering this is discovering the body.

–Chögyam Trungpa Rinpoche

The world is alive, aware, and it is speaking to us, communicating with us. There is always some kind of message taking place. We are in an energetically reciprocal relationship with it. All phenomena radiate energy and we meet phenomena through our senses. Our sense perceptions allow us to make a direct relationship to our environment in a non-conceptual, non-psychological, non-emotional way. Great spiritual teachers have infinite energy because they are plugged into the world. As for me, a solitary retreat is the best time of my year. It is such an elemental experience, a time to invite magic.

> Look. This is your world! You can't not look. There is no other world. This is your world; it is your feast. You inherited this; you inherited these eyeballs; you inherited this world of color. Look at the greatness of the whole thing. Look! Don't hesitate—look! Open your eyes. Don't blink, and look, look–look further.
>
> –Chögyam Trungpa Rinpoche

> Look deep into nature and then you will understand everything better.
>
> –Albert Einstein

It may sound simple, and we might assume that we connect to our senses all of the time, but mostly we take them for granted and go about our life on automatic. We also usually act on the world, rather than receive it. Opening the doors of perception could feel nourishing because we let life touch us, rather than trying to control or manipulate it to please us. When we truly connect to our sense perceptions, it is a sensational experience. They may lead us into a world we only thought we knew.

Our sense perceptions are our antenna or bridge to the world, an intermediary between our inner consciousness and the outer world. They are fields of awareness which include our sense organs or faculties (eyes, ears, nose, tongue, skin), sense fields (seeing, hearing, smelling, tasting, touching), and sense objects (a tree, a song, a rose, food, a touch). Our senses include our mind, a sixth sense. Together, they are our potentialities to experience the five energies in the world.

There is an experiential intensity to each sense. Seeing gives us the most sense of separateness, the most sense of duality (I and other). It is very hard to get out of dualism. Hearing has more of a sense of surround-sound. With hearing, we are in it. Sound allows us to merge with it. It can enter us and we want to move, to dance. Smell and taste are experienced very viscerally, internally. Touch could be either I/other or felt from the inside. Touch is very deeply visceral. Seeing is the most dominant sense perception. There is a bias toward it and it has come to mean "knowing." However, we have the ability to "know" or experience through all our senses. For example, we experience touch with our body. Skin is our biggest senses perception organ and is crucial to navigating our world.

Just being, and being in silence, is not so much a restriction as an opening to cultivate pure, direct perception. Our sense perceptions invite us into the present moment to be open and attentive. Our mind naturally expands. But a few seconds after nowness our thinking mind butts in with a subtle picking and choosing, a sense of positive, negative, or neutral, and we form opinions. With pure perception, we connect to an object—look, listen, smell, taste, feel—and be fully there, waking up to the whole world from that one perception, be it sight or sound or touch.

There is a kind of exuberant energy that comes with the perception. We experience it as though we are it. We become almost indivisible, a direct communication without anything in-between. There is no watcher because we are completely involved, already there. We are aware without putting anything into it. The world may seem brilliant, luminous, glowing, and radiating. There is a sense of enriching presence, a feeling of deep appreciation. When we tune into the world by fully experiencing our sense perceptions, we experience it as powerful and magical.

In Tantric Buddhism working with sense perceptions is a path toward awakening, a vehicle for profound experience. Understanding perception is key to understanding reality. We can perceive the world without language, spontaneously. Rather than an inferential understanding gained through knowledge, we gain wisdom through direct experience. Book learning is a barrier between ourself and phenomenon. Seeing the nature of reality is more direct, and so more potent. The sacred path is not about words and books. The profundity of sense perceptions is that they are profoundly good. Our inherent ability to sense, to have simple, enlivened relationship to our world, is like a gift, a blessing.

The world becomes sacred when we truly see, hear, taste. Pleasurable or distasteful, intense or subtle, when we open without judgment, we can have a sense of equality to all experience. When we openly accept what is, we rest in equanimity. This is a gateway to wisdom, a way we can feel wholesome, joyful, and have tremendous appreciation. We feel thankful, blessed. We could experience not only a sense of composure but a sense of wakefulness and delight. This kind of awakening cultivates gentleness and confidence. Living life fully means being here.

There are limitless fields of sense perceptions; the world is limited by us. Some people and some cultures are more tantric or shamanistic by nature in their ability to connect to the phenomenal world through their senses and the felt experience of energy. They tune into the self-existing magic of the phenomenal world. This kind of awareness engenders enormous health and strength, a sense of wholesomeness.

If the doors of perception were cleansed, man would see things as they are, infinitely.

—William Blake

However magical, working with the senses is also a down-to-earth experience. The profound gets more simple, more immediate. Different spaces, environments, or situations have different psychological effects on us. We can't necessarily change those effects, but we can stop resisting them. For instance, loud city sounds—drilling through cement, the roar of trucks, the call of sirens—can be potent and penetrating when we stay open to them. Heightening our sense perceptions allows us to connect with the power and potential in the world. So, we are continuously falling in love with the world, experiencing its fullness, power, and magic. When connected to the phenomenal world, auspicious coincidence happens naturally.

We could even experience pain very directly without it being a threat. I had a very vivid experiences of this while lying in bed for weeks on end with a fractured pelvis. Rather than reacting to the pain, becoming a victim of it, I simply observed it. It was still my pain but it didn't take over. I became very curious as the pain became more intense at times and other times subsided. Sometimes I became one with it, and let myself be engulfed by it. Then there was nothing to resist or fight.

In Ursula le Guin's Earthsea Cycle, part of the training of a wizard is to name everything. The premise here is that by naming things we know them. Naming in this sense is not mere labeling, but knowing their essence. A thing and its word are very provocative, poetic, like mantra.

Practicing With Sense Perceptions

To open to our senses, we need to settle our self-justifying spinning mind. As we have seen, we are constantly commenting on how we are doing, like an ever-vigilant watcher assuring that we are in our comfort zone. This is ego performing its job. Our tenacious ego mind justifies our existence and keeps us feeling safe.

By relaxing the mind, you can reconnect with that primordial, original ground, which is completely pure and simple. Out of that, through the medium of your perceptions, you can discover magic, or drala [wisdom energy]. You actually can connect your own intrinsic wisdom with a sense of greater wisdom or vision beyond you.

–Chögyam Trungpa Rinpoche

Let's look at how we block our sense perceptions. Habitually, we conceptualize so we hardly let an experience take place before we feel compelled to name it. We hold onto a series of clichés, influenced by expectations, and so develop set modes of relating to the world. We also have a tendency to cloud over and distort our perceptions because we have an omnipresent anxiety about our existence. We become preoccupied with self-preservation. Therefore, we have a dull, distorted view of the world. Our most basic obstacle is fear which makes us contract our sense perceptions. We get overwhelmed so we close down. When our anxiety subsides, our sense perceptions are no longer distorted by neurosis. We can be attentive without bias, judgment, or concept.

Experiential Work

To distinguish between our busy mind and still mind, we must do experiential work.

1. Get into discursive thought, even thoughts leading to emotions

2. Then drop them and directly connect to an object of sight

3. Go back and forth so you have the qualitative experience of both

The practice of opening to sense perceptions is to cultivate pure perception, to become sensate. Working with the senses brings us into nowness, sense of being, presence. We commit to the present moment and fully and completely experience our sense perceptions. We experience things as they are. It is an attentiveness without bias, not accepting or rejecting, not editing. It cultivates more relaxation and gentleness in relationship to our environment. We can just be and let ourself occur. We suspend our agenda and become receptive. We are more inquisitive to see things in their own nature, and experience at a deeper level. It cultivates a sense of appreciation.

Ultimately, we practice to intensify or intoxicate our sense perceptions. Our sense of self and our sense perceptions come together, concepts collapse and sense perceptions open. At that point, there is a dazzling luminosity. There is a sense that everything seems to emit light. It is the radiation of energy. At that point our heart opens. All of our sense perceptions are connected to the heart, so they dissolve into our heart. There is no barrier between ourself and our world. This practice can transform our relationship to the world.

We practice how to look, listen, smell, taste, and feel.

- By practicing how to *look*, we discover how to *see* with our whole being
- By practicing how to *listen*, we discover how to *hear* deeply with our body
- By practicing how to *smell and taste*, we discover how to *savor*
- By practicing how to *feel*, we discover how to be *sensual*

Five Steps of Experiential Work

Here are five steps for experiencing sense perceptions more fully. They work with the natural process of sense perceptions.

1. **Sense of being:** Establish a sense of being in the moment. Take in a deep breath and let it go. Let it cut through the cloud of distraction and preoccupation and put yourself on the spot.

2. **Sense of connecting:** Quickly engage one of your senses with an object. (Look at a tree, hear a car, touch your skin.) The abruptness cuts through thoughts and creates an open ground. Be inquisitive. Simply look at it as it is.

3. **Sense of merging:** Establish communication between yourself and the object. Linger and merge, draw it into yourself, join your being with it. A dialogue or play begins, a cosmic back and forth, without language.

4. **Draw in the energy:** Feel the energy of your object infuse your body. Feel the richness and power of embodying energy.

5. **Let the energy into your heart:** Rest in the bliss of feeling fulfilled.

Do this exercise with different sense perceptions in various environments. Use them as a quick break from work. Opening to your sense perceptions in this way is refreshing and invigorating. It's better than a cup of coffee!

Another exercise you can do to connect yourself with your senses is to take a walk, blindfolded, with a partner leading you. This is simple:

- Keep your feet on the ground and feel the space around you.
- Stay tuned into your senses.
- Discover how refreshing and invigorating it is to be in world of senses.

Each sense also has different mind:

Looking and Seeing—Vajra
The interest is in form, shape, and texture.

Smelling, Tasting, and Savoring—Ratna
The interest is in the objects of smell and taste: salty, sour, bitter, hot, sweet, and any variety of foods.

Touching and Feeling—Ratna
The interest is in kinesthetic awareness, an inner dance of sensation. We awaken our body through awareness of it: the weight, shape, tone (tension/relaxation), temperature, tingling and gravitate towards objects of touch: our body, cloth, feathers, textures.

Listening and Hearing—Padma
The interest is in all sounds: music, ambient sound, snippets of conversation, the absence of sound in silence.

Functional Touch—Karma
The interest is in making something happen, in performing activities that use our arms and legs hands, arms, feet, and legs.

The Interconnection of the Five Senses

Each sensory perception generally includes the others. When we see something, we may also hear, smell, and touch it. Subtle shifts in our awareness can take place. For instance, we can simultaneously *feel* an apple in our hand, bite into it and *hear* the crunch, and *taste* it.

A lot of levels develop. This takes place all of the time in whatever we do in our life.

In layering the energies and sense perceptions, we can simply look at an object. We move from outside to inside, getting deeper an object:

Buddha:
Experience the space and connect abruptly to an object

Vajra:
Look and then see the linear aspect, shape, form, design

Padma:
Hear and pick up on its texture, vibrations, radiation, communication

Ratna:
Smell and taste its quality, merge with it

Karma:
Touch it with an immense interest and make it functional

Three Levels of Perception

1. Perception as experience.

This is the experience of things as they are when we are not caught in the self-confirming ego.

2. Perception of appearance/emptiness.

This is the recognition that things are apparent yet not inherently there, a shifty and intangible quality. There is both a limitless variety of perceptions as well as the profundity of its emptiness. The vastness begins to be more familiar as a natural expression of wisdom. As Trungpa Rinpoche said, "We could mingle ourself with the mirage of sounds, colors, shapes, energies and emotions. It's a kind of celebration: there is joy, a dance taking place."

3. Perception of luminosity.

This is the awareness of the natural brilliance of our world. We have a sense of awe, respect, curiosity, and enjoyment. We feel both nourished and excited by the world's self-existing magic. It engenders a sense of sacredness.

• • •

Within the mahāmudrā, looking at the object of focus is an upāya [skill]: your focus is turned towards the object and you then allow the mind to rest settled into its own nature, relaxed and without any artifice. This is the mahāmudrā way of meditating. For example, if you were to meditate on sound as a focus, you rest one-pointedly on that focus, which functions as a focal support to keep the mind from wandering. While you are focusing on the sound, you should place the mind in the state of luminous emptiness, allowing it to settle into itself without any contrivance.

–Khenpo Tsültrim Gyamtso Rinpoche

Experiencing is believing. We can have a non-conceptual trust in our senses.

CHAPTER 13

Transmuting Your Confusion Into Your Brilliance

A problem arises when we tend to become too ambitions in terms of dealing with emotions, particularly those involved with the spiritual practice. We've been told to be kind, gentle, good people. Those are the conventional ideas of spirituality. When we begin to find the spiky quality of ourself, we see it as anti-spirituality and try to push it away. That is the biggest mistake of all in working with our basic psychological patterns...The idea is not to seduce ourself into trying to create a Utopian spirituality, but to try and look into the details of the peak emotions, the dramatic qualities of the emotions.

–Chögyam Trungpa Rinpoche

The Five Wisdoms are key to emotional intelligence. They show how our wisdom is at the very heart of our confused emotions. So, our primary inquiry here is the relationship between emotions and wisdom. This tantric view, joined with personal experience, creates a potent mix. When we

164

crack the nut of our fixated emotions, we are liberated into a non-self-referential perspective. This is the pith of any work we do with ourself.

The human condition is such that suffering is inevitable. Life is radically shifty and full of discontinuity, uncertainty, and impermanence. Life's choiceless conditions are the top four causes of suffering: birth, old age, sickness, and death. It's a package deal. Our emotions are an inevitable reaction to these life markers. Life's transitions are often when we get the most emotionally intensified. Yet emotions are fundamental in creating meaningful experiences. They underlie our ability to engage in social interaction, to comprehend meaning, and to choose appropriate behavioral responses for each situation in which we find ourselves. They run below the level of our behaviors and feel secret, very personal. No one knows our inner experience the way we do.

Working with emotions is one of the most challenging aspects of being human. If speed is the glue of habits, emotions are what fixate them. Then we believe them to be true. Strong emotions precipitate solidified opinions and concepts about people and situations. We become more exaggerated, like caricatures of ourself. When this happens, our vital energy becomes constricted. Neurosis is attracted to a small mind, not the big mind of awakenment. Though we need to realistically look at the painful aspects of our life, we could discover that the battle with emotional pain is unnecessary. We have a choice. We can suffer or use untoward circumstances as opportunities for transformation. We can see that what we experience as negative is just the raw and rugged quality of our energy. Our awareness makes our emotions workable. In short, suffering is optional.

Buddhist psychology distinguishes four kinds of suffering. The first is an all-pervading sense of discomfort and dissatisfaction. We have a kind of undulating nausea—as if breathing toxic air—with a sense of an unnameable threat. The second is the pain of alternation. It's so familiar: we get what we don't want, and we don't get what we do want. We are constantly buffeted about by this alternation. The third is that one painful thing is piled on another, and another: we lose our job, our partner leaves us, and we get depressed. The fourth is that we see our pain as a problem that we need to get rid of. Usually, we do not experience the pain, only our reactivity to it. We resist the pain because we feel it is going to overwhelm us. Then we only experience the resisting and at some point, the energy could explode. In the effort to avoid pain, we create more pain, more emotions.

Intensified Emotions

At the peak of an Intensified Reality, we experience an emotional knot. Without question, what gets us most in trouble is our intensified emotions. They are a vivid display of energy and are always in reaction to something: life transitions, childhood abuse or neglect, distorted views of reality, illness. Usually, we do not acknowledge or experience our emotions properly. We just want to release them: dump our passion on someone or kill someone. There may be times in our life when things are particularly intensified. We might feel like a pile of dry leaves into which someone threw a match. The conflagration gets hopelessly out of control.

We have wounds. We feel vulnerable. We have confused beliefs and repetitive storylines that constantly spin us into feeling bad: bad about ourself, others, and the world. We create defenses, armoring and coping strategies, to protect ourself. The more difficult our life circumstances have been, the deeper the wounds and the more defenses we have. In particular, childhood trauma can be unconscious but affect us long into adulthood as it is so hard to bring it to the light of day.

Our neurotic shutdown is how we say, "Stop the world. I want to get off!" The point at which it is most likely to happen is when our expectations of how things "should" be are insulted by reality. Reality breaks through our conceptual filter and we are shocked that it doesn't meet our expectation. We feel frustrated and react emotionally. We resist what's happening and withdraw into our shell. We can close down for an instant or for a lifetime.

Our reactions to painful situations become stored in our body. We are walking minefields carrying our wounds around like little time bombs. When someone or something presses our buttons, we literally explode. The chances are that we blame someone else for behaving in such a way (because they trigger us), but we forget that we are the ones with the open wound. In families, the synergy of the triggers and the defenses become deeply ingrained by constant daily repetition of the same patterns of behavior. We then pass along those same propensities into the next generation, and the next. We go for what is familiar.

Most often we feel bewildered by our emotions, particularly when we have conflicting ones. The love/hate equation of an intimate relationship is commonplace...and crazy making. "I love him, but I hate him when he does that. Why can't he be like I want him to be?" Emotional turmoil makes it nearly impossible to see any situation clearly, perpetuating our confusion. We feel vulnerable, get reactive, and are impatient for a resolution. We want to fix it so the pain goes away. It is often a question of what we can tolerate. What emotions do we find permissible? For instance, we might handle an aggressive situation but be totally dumbfounded by a passionate one. We also need to consider how much intensity can we withstand. "I love her but..." Could we possibly be addicted to the intensity? It's painful but it's comfortingly familiar.

We could be embarrassed by our emotions. We sense that our feelings are taboo or shameful, so we put a lid on them. When we judge ourself or react to someone else's judgment about us, we are more neurotic. We raise our defenses, project onto others, and create a world of confusion. So, shame is like a double whammy. We don't want to feel emotions, let alone express them, because we are ashamed. We do not want anyone near our emotions. We say, "I'm fine." FINE = Freaked out, Insecure, Neurotic, and Emotional. We might find it easier to wallow in our familiar neurosis than be liberated from it. But ignoring the pain and confusion is being blind to ego's manipulations that create our suffering.

When we see others being emotional, we realize that emotions are not personal, as we tend to believe, because everyone has them. Our particular mix is unique, but not the essential nature of emotions. What we think is so private is actually universal. The more personal we get, the more kinship we have with everyone. We find we do not have to lock our emotions in a box labeled "private." When there is a feeling of trust in being able to share, we break through and create a deep resonance with others.

Our personality has a lot to do with how we work with emotional intensity. Threatened by complexity, we demand clarity. Threatened with a lack of comfort, we get into poor-me territory. Threatened by loneliness, we get into seduction. Threatened by boredom, we want to do something, anything. Threatened by everything, we just want to ignore. Some people are naturally expressive. Think padma or ratna. Others tend to bottle things up. Think vajra or karma. In some situations, we might be more explosive, like vajra/karma in a business meeting, and in others more constrained, like with our intimate other. Or vice versa. In this way, we perpetuate a passive, innocent stance.

The Anatomy of Emotional Buildup

Emotions begin with the smallest flicker of a thought and then we attach meaning to it. Believing strongly in our thoughts, we identify heavily with our emotions. Our speeded up mental chitchat feeds and focuses the feelings, so we build a solid narrative to justify how we feel. Our emotion becomes big and we become small. It becomes the enemy and we become the victim. Then we "feel" the thought as a psychophysical experience. We develop a storyline which escalates and creates an emotional drama. Then we project our emotion on someone. "I'm angry at so and so," and justify it with "because she did such and such." Our storylines rekindle the emotions. We find ourself entrenched in the cycle of emotional intensity. Perhaps, later in the day, we will pass along that angry energy to someone else.

> Discursive thought might be compared to the blood circulation which constantly feeds the muscles of our system, the emotions. Thoughts link and sustain the emotions so that, as we go about our daily lives, we experience an ongoing flow of mental gossip punctuated by more colorful and intense bursts of emotion. The thoughts and emotions express our basic attitudes toward and ways of relating to the world and form an environment, fantasy realms in which we live.
>
> –Chögyam Trungpa Rinpoche

We identify with our emotional story lines strongly, so it is hard to relinquish them. They justify us, confirm us. "I am angry. I am jealous. I am morose. This is my truth!" We feel loyal to our version of reality. We hang on tight, as if by letting go of our emotions, we would dismantle our whole known world. If I am pining over a lost love, giving up that melancholy means that the whole drama of my affair is gone, which means that a part of me is gone as well. We then dump the emotions on ourself by bottling them up or dump them on someone else by acting them out.

When our emotions become too painful, our overwhelming desire is to get rid of them. We don't want to feel their intensity. We deal with this in different ways. Some of us suppress our anger or jealousy or passion by denying that we are feeling it. Others of us might get intensely angry, but are so caught up in our storyline that we are not even aware that we're feeling emotional. We just act them out by exploding or otherwise indulging our feelings. But this is just another way of not relating to the energy.

Our wisdom and our confusion are uniquely interwoven so by trying to get rid of "negativity" by trying to eradicate it or labeling it "bad," we are throwing away our wisdom. The best way to work with our heightened states of energy is to befriend them. As difficult as they are to work with, intensified emotions can be turned to our advantage.

Working With Emotions

Our emotions come to the fore to protect us from exposing our more vulnerable parts. The deeper the pain, the stronger our emotions. Stuffing this toxic material is unhealthy. The more we repress, the more it could lead to an explosion. Hoping our intensified emotions will somehow be neutralized will not work. There is overwhelming medical evidence that indicates that repressing thoughts and feelings translates into bodily disorders such as stress, indigestion, high blood pressure, and increase the likelihood of strokes, heart attacks, and cancer. Could this be the case of my mother who strongly held to Christian beliefs in not expressing negativity and became chronically depressed, had mental shock treatments, and died of cancer at the age of 57?

The gist is that we are not trying to get rid of emotions, but become conversant with our emotional landscape. They are intelligent, a form of communication. We need to be aware that we are having one. This counteracts what we usually do, either creating a big drama or shutting down. These are both ways of avoiding emotions. The importance of awareness is that emotions become "workable." We could pause and stay with the feeling. An emotion could be like a bell going off, a signal to catch our habitual response and try something new. Befriend them.

Catching ourself being ourself is the way to become familiar with how we repeatedly play our top-ten tunes that tell our story. Rather than getting caught up in the mental convolutions and storylines that create emotions, we could experience them directly, psychophysically, energetically. It might be the first time that we actually experience them. This makes it possible to experience the wisdom embedded in our confusion.

Habitually we focus on what triggers us, what we find threatening. "He really makes me angry when he does that," or "Why can't he just love me?" This is taking the wrong end of the stick. Rather than looking at the object of emotion, to blame or lust after, we could look at our mind that creates it. As much as we want to be loved and respected by others, we have more clarity when another is not the object of our anger or desire.

Generally, we want to get rid of our uncomfortable feelings either by justifying or squelching them. We just move on, avoiding our inner world and stick to our daily routines. My grandmother cleaned the house. Many become workaholics. So, it's important to get into the nerve, that unthinkable place deep inside our core fears, where powerful work can be done. We could dive deep and dare to swim in water in which we thought we would drown. When we finally hit bottom, we find limitless depths of softness and tenderness. We need to remember again and again that our sanity is primordial, and our emotional confusion is temporary.

Stages of Working With Emotions

In doing emotional work with people, I have discovered that there are primarily four approaches. Each has an efficacy. At best, they are practiced sequentially: first we stabilize. Second, we open our hearts. Third, we work with intensity. Fourth, we become impervious to emotional upheavals. We can see them as the cool, warm, hot, and impervious stages. Let's dive a little deeper into each stage.

Cool, Letting Go

This is the fundamental practice for finding release from our suffering.

The cool approach is commonly thought to be the primary Buddhist practice: to renounce, abstain, and turn away from the heat of neurosis. It's about cutting the seduction of emotions. It is a blunt and powerful approach. We become more aware of what is wholesome and unwholesome, avoiding the judgmental trap of good and bad. Wholesome gives us a sense of well-being and unwholesome feels psychophysically uncomfortable.

The cool approach is exemplified in mindfulness, practiced both in meditation and in everyday life. Time and time again, we acknowledge a thought, cut it, let go, and come back to the present. It's very black and white, and somewhat austere, but very powerful. Understanding the Five Psychophysical Aspects gives us the possibility of catching ourself before things become too hot and heavy in an Intensified Reality. We could see what triggered us, as in the first aspect, feel the energy in our body as in the second aspect, and so on. The result is that the ego's machinations become more transparent and we feel more simplicity, peace, and gentleness.

Warm, Letting Be

This is the essential practice of opening our heart.

As we begin to see through our story lines, we have less fixation on ourself and things that happen are not such a big deal. Our ability to let go gives space for our heart to open. Spaciousness allows more gentleness toward ourself so we begin to experience an inherent emptiness in ourself, others, and our world. Warmth embraces our neurosis, our wounds, and we allow them to just be.

Maitri, Loving Kindness

Before we go on to the hot approach, let's mention maitri. When energy becomes heightened, we need a very powerful tool—the tool of loving-kindness, or *maitri.* Maitri is an attitude of unconditional friendliness toward whatever arises. It is the key. It has no bias toward negative and positive, acceptance and rejection, good and bad. It allows us to melt and relax our constricted view and become more present, spacious, clear, and accommodating. There is a sense of workability.

Maitri is a catalyst for openness and openness a catalyst for maitri. It allows us to move into the parasympathetic nervous system. A smile is the "Yes!" of unconditional friendliness that welcomes experience without fear.

Maitri allows the energies to become wisdoms. When self-referencing, we inevitably go into the neurotic aspect of the energies. When we are open and warm, our wisdom shines brilliantly.

Here's the gist. Ego is the obstacle. Friendliness is the path. Wisdom is the fruition.

Maitri allows us to be who we are, accepting both our sanity and our confusion. It allows us to be in the present moment just as it is, without trying to cling to it or push it away. It stops our struggle and lets all of our colors shine. We breathe easily. Only when we love ourself are we lovable. Likewise, only when we love ourself, can we love others.

Aspects of Maitri

- Maitri has an element of *familiarity*. We know our habitual patterns like old friends so they don't throw us off so much.

- Maitri is *accommodating and accepting*. When we see the intensity of our closed energy, we no longer try to avoid what's happening. We allow it to be, and so expand our palette of acceptable energy states.

- Maitri *relaxes* us and allows us to be gentle and kind toward ourself. Our pain is still there, but instead of avoiding it, we care for it as we would care for an open wound.

- Working with maitri enables us to develop *bravery*, which means that we can touch our vulnerable, raw spots and still stay open.

- Maitri allows us to see that our life experiences are *workable*. When we encounter an unwanted circumstance, we don't contract and close, but open to the situation. We see it not as a crisis but as an opportunity.

- Most importantly, the quality of friendliness toward ourself is *unconditional*. We are friendly toward all aspects of our experience, especially the facets of ourself that we like the least. We can love ourself without reserve, with zero stipulations.

When we use maitri as a tool, we find that we could either laugh or cry. At the point when we laugh or cry, the struggle is over. There is a sense of breakthrough. We have broken through our sense of constricted self. We have touched our heart. We have found the key to the wisdom within us, which displays itself as colorful liberated qualities.

Tonglen

Tonglen is the primary practice to realize this. There are two aspects to the practice. First, we have a direct experience of suffering, the nitty-gritty of pain. Second, we have an unwavering belief and trust in the basic goodness of everyone. We hold the awake mind of unconditional spaciousness and infuse it with empathy and compassion toward the suffering. Both aspects are felt rather than conceptualized. We fully feel painful situations by breathing them into our heart and we breath out all that is good. It arouses our empathy in a psychophysical way. Because it works with the heart, it works with ourself as well as with another person or situation. We break down the barrier between self and other. Opening our heart creates a warm space where emotional intensity can relax.

Hot, Transmutation

This is discovering the brilliant wisdom within intense confusion.

Transmutation—which means to change or transform, not transcend or leave behind—is one of the hallmarks of working with the Five Wisdoms. We transmute neurotic energy by knowing it intimately. The cool and warm approaches lay the foundation: sitting meditation stabilizes us and tonglen opens our heart so we can meet the intensity. Having planted seeds of wakefulness in ourself, we have a sense of fearlessness and confidence. We use the powerful energy of confusion to awaken as the most skillful means.

Co-emergent wisdom, the inseparability of our confusion and wisdom, makes it possible to practice emotional transmutation. Co-emergent wisdom is there already, therefore we can do it, therefore it succeeds. We open to the energy of the moment and just stay with the emotion. Feeling the energy in our body, we get back to a more primal experience. From the tantric perspective, emotions are our good energy. They have intelligence, if we make friends with them. If we don't make friends with them, we are just in a battle. Rather than being caught in an undertow, battered by waves, and smashed onto the sand, we can go right into the wave. Our slogan becomes, "We can't stop the waves but we can learn to surf."

Emotions and energy are of the same nature, so emotions are best resolved energetically. Energy is both the medium and the means of transmutation. We intensify emotion to experience it vividly. When it is at a peak and our energy is negatively intensified, our insight and intelligence are close at hand. When we embrace the emotions that bind us, they are liberated. Energies that seem to entrap us become enriching and enlivening. Our emotional fixations transmute into our unique flavor of our brilliant sanity.

This is not about transcending our pain but going deeper into it, being with it. As Trungpa Rinpoche says, "The ground of manure is fertile soil," and "The problem with negative energy is that it does not enjoy itself. We could appreciate it as very real and alive." For me, no longer being in the good-versus-bad battle was a tremendous relief. We begin to see a shift. We no longer see our neurosis as something to push away and our sanity as something to hold onto. We see whatever arises as workable.

Our emotions can become more workable. Without having to suppress them or act them out, we could just acknowledge them. They cease to be a big deal. Our need to suppress them comes from thinking they are terrible, shameful, or that we simply will explode. Acting out is being carried away by them from a sense of panic. It's a kind of release but a false release. It generally reinforces them and they become even more powerful. A skillful way of working with emotions is to see them as just energy. Without the panic, we can deal with them fully and properly.

–Chögyam Trungpa Rinpoche

If we are in the emotion completely, it is no longer a threat because we have dissolved the separation between ourself and the intensity. We don't panic but invite the intensity, fully experience it, and become one with it. Our emotion is still alive and kicking, but we are not a slave to it. We are sympathetic toward it and give it space. When we give emotions space to live, they come into their own intelligence. When we begin to trust the experience of heightened energy, we can relax within that very intensity. The key here is that the more intensified our emotional energy, the more brilliant we will be! The traditional analogy used is the alchemical process of turning a non-precious metal into gold.

When we are in an intensified reality, the most powerful skill is the hot approach. Transmutation has to do with allowing the energy to build. No acting out! The key is not taking them personally, but experiencing them as energy. Experiencing emotions as energy makes transmutation possible. At its peak, we either pop or melt. This is not a trick and we can't fake it. We have to do it fully. It is a natural process and whatever is constricted will naturally release. It's like a sneeze or an orgasm: energy builds and then it releases. It is in keeping with our understanding of the natural process of the sympathetic and parasympathetic nervous systems. We could experience a quality of inner completeness with nothing hidden or excluded. We could allow our inner experience to be more clear, more whole. We could become less broken, less paranoid, less fearful and limited.

> If a person is able to relate fully and thoroughly with the emotions, then they cease to become an external problem. One is able to make very close contact with the emotions. Then the war between your emotions and yourself—you and your projections, you and the world outside—becomes transparent. This involves removing the dualistic barriers set up by concepts.
>
> —Chögyam Trungpa Rinpoche

Transmuting could be gentle or more intense. The main point is to bring the emotions to our heart, where body and mind come together with a palpable feeling of warmth. We feel comforted and nourished by the openness of our own heart so the tension in our body unwinds. When we feel our heart, we may feel sad. Don't let this surprise you because underneath most intensified emotion is sadness. Sadness is the bittersweet quality of our genuine being. It feels very real, so we are attracted to it. When sad joy permeates our being, we may also feel empty but full. Since the heart and eyes are connected, we might experience tears of sad joy. This is the ground of authentic existence and we may find ourself more in touch with the world.

We are given opportunities all of the time to wake up or go to sleep. We could cling to a toned-down, conventional, less challenging cozy existence. Or we could open to the raw, colorful, brilliant aspects of life. Working with energy in this way is not about pacifying it or making it all OK. Working with energy is about fully feeling the energy. It makes this practice both delightful and challenging. Transmutation is the magic of Tantra. However, we can become intoxicated with the energy and feed on it. This makes this method more dangerous and it can get very messy. But when we have done it once, it's much easier to do it again and is extremely empowering. It takes only one match to light up a dark room.

We could begin to understand the benefit of being stuck in unfavorable circumstances. "What a wonderful opportunity to open further," we could say. Our stuck point is our work point, no more and no less. In this process, the differences between our neurosis and our sanity becomes more slippery. This was vividly portrayed in a dream I had in which I was being blown by a very strong, forceful wind along city streets. I was stunned when I realized I was flying. Flying! The feeling was dark, ominous. Then, as if in instant replay, I was doing the exact same thing and the feeling was light, inspiring. I realized then that it is possible to have the exact same experience with either state of mind.

Tantric Viewpoints

The tantric viewpoints are the basis for transmutation and emotional wisdom. Below are some of those viewpoints.

- There's a bedrock of energy that is primal and self-existing in which intense light and intense darkness co-exist.

- Co-emergent wisdom, the simultaneity and inseparability of confusion and sanity, is seeing wisdom in the darkness of confusion.

- Energy is neutral and has its own intelligence. Our reaction to it is what is confused or sane.

- Emotions are a vivid display of our energetic style which intensifies when life pushes our buttons.

- Emotions are energetic, so emotional fixation can only be resolved energetically. We employ the powerful energy of confusion to transmute them. When we give intensified energy free rein, it releases naturally and intelligence arises from it.

- The point at which our energy is negatively intensified is the most opportune time to work with it because our energy is most vivid. Our very fixation is an opportunity to see our wisdom.

- The intelligent way to work with painful emotions is to fully relate with their energy. If we do this, and don't put up resistance, the emotions don't overwhelm us and our battle with them becomes unnecessary.

- Our sanity is inherent and our confusion is impermanent. We can align with sanity without discarding our confusion. We can discover that any state of mind is workable.

- An attitude of unconditional friendliness, maitri, toward whatever arises is the catalyst to turn all that is confusing into brilliant intelligence.

- The problem with our confused energy is that we do not enjoy it. We could appreciate it as very real and alive, as fuel for the fire of wisdom.

- When our energy is stuck over a period of time, we experience an imbalance in our psychophysical being, leading to mental and/or physical illness.

- We can recycle energy into wisdom. We can build up and regenerate energy instead of expending it. The more we recycle our energy, the more we have. It's ecological and more sustainable.

- When we manifest our wisdom, we align ourself with the totality of the Five Wisdoms and ride the energy of the moment. We experience our connection to everyone and everything in an energetic matrix, the mandala.

- The Five Wisdoms posture practice is the exemplary way to work with our emotions as it gives us firsthand experience of our energy.

- When we have a sense of how to work with energetic reality, we can creatively apply our understanding anywhere, anytime, no matter what we are doing.

Impervious

This is the fruition of working with emotions.

This is the highest level of working with emotions. Traditionally it is called self-liberation. Imperviousness is based on an unwavering confidence that the essential nature of everything is pure and empty. Therefore, everything is self-arisen and self-liberated by its own nature. Emotions never leave the ground of emptiness, like a snowflake falling on a hot coal. Confusion is consumed in space.

This is not so much a practice as having the realization of sacredness. There is no method, no reference point, no watcher, no trace, and nothing to hang onto. There is only the spontaneous occurrence, of which we are part. We don't need to do anything. We ride the energy of the moment. Spontaneously everything comes into its wisdom. This is only possible when we are completely aligned with the view that we are intrinsically, brilliantly sane and the world is fundamentally, basically good. Then neurosis has no hold on us. This viewpoint depends on having cultivated confidence, gentleness, and maitri by practicing the cool, warm, and hot approaches. We become fearless and without doubt. We can rest in the essence of bliss, luminosity, and non-thought experience.

There is a pitfall to this approach, which is also true of the cool approach. If we haven't done the good, deep work of the hot approach, with all its nitty-gritty mess, we could bypass the good manure of who we are. We have avoided facing the parts of ourself that we like the least. This is spiritual by-passing.

Four Stages With a Metaphor

Here, in summary, are the four stages of working with our emotions:

1. **Cool:** cutting disperses the clouds
2. **Warm:** melting sees that the clouds are not so solid
3. **Hot:** transmuting sees the sky and clouds as inseparable
4. **Impervious:** self-liberating, it recognizes that there is only sun

When we recognizing the inseparability of neurosis and sanity, essential change comes about. We go beyond aligning with sanity (the sun) as opposed to confusion (the clouds). We embrace all aspects of who we are. When our sun and our clouds come together, we are a rainbow. Our wisdom embraces both our sanity and confusion. Let's go for the rainbow!

Emotional Wisdom: Brilliant Sanity

When emotions are genuine, they have unconditional qualities. They arise from a spacious mind without the fixation of ego. We can experience their flavors, textures, and temperatures, yet not be seduced by them. They ring true and feel wholesome. We feel the living aspect of emotions rather than the frustrated aspect. There is no self-referencing so there are no territory or boundaries. There is nothing to fight for, promote, or defend. We don't indulge our emotions so we don't feel their constriction.

We learn to welcome our emotions as a vivid display of energy. We drink life straight up, undiluted. We wear emotions like ornaments. Our actions are accomplished spontaneously without the obscuration of solidified emotions. When we embody the Five Wisdoms we are authentically, powerfully present. We have confidence, self-respect, and dignity. There is also a deep sense of relaxation. We can just be who we are, true to ourself. What a relief! We do not have to put on a persona or mask. We do not have to play a role so someone will like us or hire us or give us a grant. We feel synchronized, integrated, balanced. Most likely, our sense of humor will come out. Our presence radiates.

The Five Wisdoms: The Simultaneity of Confusion and Sanity

The transformative power of working with the Five Wisdoms is that we don't reject any part of ourself, but rather see the wisdom within all that we are. We have the liberty to be who we are unconditionally. The basic premise is that sanity and neurosis are not separate, rather, they are different qualities of one indivisible, essential nature. Each energy is neutral and teeters on a razor's edge of going toward wisdom or falling into confusion. Everything we think, feel, say, or do could have a neurotic twist or a wisdom twist. Here is a snapshot of the inseparable nature of the confusion and sanity in each of the five:

Buddha: Spaced out inertia is the all-accommodating space of totality.

Vajra: Anger is ego's insistence on being right, embedded in which is a clear, precise intellect.

Ratna: Neediness is inseparable from the deep satisfaction, and composure of equanimity.

Padma: Obsessive passion and manipulation to get what is most pleasurable are based on a keen discriminating sensibility and intuition.

Karma: Competitive speed and being in control are capacities to accomplish actions effortlessly.

Contemplate the Transmutation of Each Energy

When we are open, the Five Wisdoms become five qualities of intrinsic sanity.

- **Buddha energy is all about space:** space feels constricted when neurotic; all accommodating space in its wisdom
- **Vajra energy is all about perception:** convinced of a biased insight when neurotic; a mirror-like wisdom, seeing things as they are, in its wisdom
- **Ratna energy is all about substantiality:** feeling unworthy and needy when neurotic; a sense of equanimity and fulfillment in its wisdom
- **Padma energy is all about passionate connection:** insecure and manipulating when neurotic; having keen discriminating insight in its wisdom
- **Karma energy is all about action:** speedy and controlling when neurotic; all accomplishing action in its wisdom

Going Forward

On this journey of emotional investigation, we can't necessarily do it on our own. It could seem impossible to do any kind of practice when we are in an intensified state. Because of this, it is important to relate with someone else, so we neither bottle up nor act out in impulsive ways. If we don't have enough maitri in ourself, we need to seek it in a friend, a meditation instructor, or a therapist. It is best to work with someone who understands energetic work. Working in a group with the Five Wisdoms posture practice and emotions gives us firsthand experience of our energy and a radically accepting community.

CHAPTER 14

Quintessential Being: Your Wisdom Anatomy and Sexuality

Fundamentally, Tantra is based on a process of trust in ourself that has developed within us, which is like a physical body. Tantra involves respect for our body, respect for our environment. Body in this sense is not the physical body alone; it is also the psychological realization of the basic ground of sanity that has developed within us...The practitioner has been able to relate with himself or herself to the extent that his or her basic being is no longer regarded as a nuisance...We have finally been able to relate with the basic form, the basic norm, basic body. And that body is what is called Tantra, which means "continuity," "thread."

–Chögyam Trungpa Rinpoche

We live in a culture that is very disembodied. Many of us primarily live in our heads. Most of us no longer work on the farm, grow our own food, or build our own homes. We live in a technology world where we work at computers, and surf the internet on our phones. We live in a world of information and ideas where we sit in offices and go to meetings. The lack of physical interaction with our world causes a tremendous energetic imbalance for us. We hold stress and tension in our bodies and block our good energy. We get ill.

To counteract this, we seek out various healing modalities, a large percentage of which work with the body: massage therapies of all sorts, yoga, the gym, acupuncture, bioenergetics, and so forth. This effort to reclaim our bodies is wonderful but perhaps we can go further. What would it take to train ourself to live in balance with our energies all of the time?

What Is Body?

Primarily we understand our body to be a physical organism, a biological model. Our body's systems—skeletal, muscular, organ, endocrine, gland, nervous, circulatory—are incredibly intelligent and are at work for us all of the time. We experience all of our sense perceptions through our body. Our body's movements take us into action. Our body, emotions, and thoughts are always working together: we have a thought that turns into an emotion and an emotion that is felt in the body. So, when we pay attention to our body, we find that it is constantly speaking to us about our state of being. Are we hungry? Are we angry?

This thing we call our body is a continual reference point for us. We identify with it and are attached to it. We hold onto our body literally for dear life. We are our body; being without it is death. Whether we happen to like it or not, we still experience it and talk about it as "ours," something we regard as our personal property. The more we pay attention to our body—to feed, to cloth, to beautify, to heal—the more we are convinced it is ours. It gives us the most certainty that we exist. It is not so much *who* we are, which is a psychological orientation, but *what* we are, which is physical.

However, this conventional view makes our body too heavy, too solid, too just there. It is hard to imagine it being anything else but "real." If we stop here with our understanding of body, we miss the dynamism of embodied energy.

> ...body is a sense of a working base that continues all through Tantric practice. Thus, Tantric practice becomes a question of how to take care of our body, our basic psychological solidity, our solid basic being...Body is the practitioner's fundamental sanity.
>
> —Chögyam Trungpa Rinpoche

We can dissolve the illusion of a separation between mind and body. They are intimately connected, pervading and mirroring each other. There is no identifiable boundary between body and mind: we are psychophysical. Body directly influences mind and mind influences body. The body is the essential basis for enlightenment. We discover this when we first start to meditate.

Negative psychological patterns are held in our body and the body keeps the score. As well, we can activate our body's capacity to heal. When our bodily systems are out of balance or blocked, we experience negativity; when harmonious and fluid, we have a sense of well-being. Also true is that when we are in our heads, we don't integrate our senses, let alone our sensuality and sexuality. So, our body becomes frozen. The good news is that our body can heal our mind and our mind can heal our body.

The deepest understanding of body is that it has as much to do with energy as matter. Shamanistic Bon, Tibet's indigenous religion, Tantric Buddhism, and Native American traditions are imbued with this awareness. Western science now has an understanding of energetic body, as in neuroscience. Contemporary healing modalities see that there is more to our body than the conventional biological version. Take, for example, the Frequency Specific Microcurrents devices which send electric currents to the body's systems for healing.

Embodiment

All spiritual traditions are about how to let go of conceptual mind. Practices move us from constricted states to expanded states of consciousness that include the body. Embodied practices emphasize personal transformation through the direct experience of nonverbal wisdom. Somatic, visceral awareness is the primary vehicle in Tantric Buddhism. The body is seen as a repository of wisdom, an indestructible living force, sensitive and intelligent.

Tantric practices are based on trust in our body as the basic ground of sanity, full of potential. They give us access to the vast amount of energy stored in our body, much of which is unconscious. Our body shows us the way, opening us to different bodily experiences. We experience a sense of goodness in our basic being, then a genuine pride and joy. From a Tantric point of view, our natural state is blissful. We can train ourself to go there. Bliss on demand!

When in a state of bliss, we open to our surroundings and awaken our sense pleasures. The psychophysical becomes psycho-sensual. Opening to everything, and appreciating things as they are, creates a continuity of awareness. We are perpetually present, attuned to the energy of our body and senses. This creates a tremendous potency in our being.

We care for our physical body so that our wisdom body is accessible. We come to respect it, treat it as sacred, and honor it as a vehicle for transformation. There are many tantric practices and rituals to this end. It is the foundation needed to access and reinvigorate the subtle energetic body. Our body is the temple of enlightenment.

All tantric practices work with our body so it is not so much about hearing teachings and doing formal practice but receiving *transmissions* to direct embodied experience. When we bring awareness to our body, we open to the unconscious where we encounter our awakened state. The unconscious becomes conscious. When attuned in a fully embodied way, our concepts drop away. Embodiment anchors us in the present moment. This is extremely liberating. The mind chatters away and creates dramas only to the extent that we are not embodied.

The paradox here is that the more we are present, the more we are absent in the sense of not maintaining a solidified sense of self. We discover that there is nothing solid to our body. It is not the solid entity that we commonly experience. We discover deeper and deeper levels of our own non-existence. The more profound the emptiness, the more powerful the energy that arises. This becomes a perspective for our entire life and is tremendously helpful at death. In fact, the process of dying is considered an opportune time to become enlightened. Our human body is precious precisely because it is impermanent. Just let go of that cumbersome body and go!

Great wisdom resides in the body, precluding all concepts.

–Hevajra Tantra

Wisdom Anatomy

In tantric understanding our inner anatomy is an elaborate system working with the subtle energetic body. There are many sources to these very profound teachings, both public and restricted to the initiated. They require careful guidance because working with the inner yoga can be very intense as we meet our energy more directly. Therefore, instructions on the specifics of tantric practices are best transmitted from an authentic teacher to a committed student. I have done such practices over the last forty years. Here, my interest is in extracting the essence of these practices and presenting an understanding of them in simple terms that is suitable for anyone. They are also the basis of the Five Wisdoms postures.

Wisdom already exists in us. We are born with wisdom anatomy. We can't see it and it cannot be detected by physical measurement so it has to be pointed out to us. It's innate yet not made of flesh, blood, atoms, or particles. This anatomy has three components: channels (Sanskrit: nadis), energy or wind (Sanskrit: pranas), and seeds of energy (Sanskrit: bindus). The nadis/channels are a vast network of meridians or pathways that run throughout our body. Pranas/winds, or breath energy, flows along the paths, having various functions and directions. Bindus, minute spheres of energy as powerful as uranium, are a type of consciousness which ride the flow of energy. The energy centers (Sanskrit: chakras) accumulate specific qualities of energy in accordance with where they are located in the body.

Imagery is often used to describe this system. The nadis are like a railroad track. Prana is the train that rides on tracks. Bindu is the passenger, a conscious, awake quality that is the true, natural state of mind.

When we are born, our subtle energy is in balance and energy circulates properly. A healthy baby is like a baby Buddha. No wonder everyone loves them! In the course of life, particularly when we are ill and hope and fear proliferates, our subtle body is disturbed and our energy becomes distorted. Then energies circulate too fast, or are blocked, or go in the wrong direction. Excessive thinking dries up the bindus and they start to diminish. We could get depressed, easily scared, have anxiety, and a lower libido. Energetic practices allow the circulation of energy, re-tune our body, and revive the bindus.

Nadi, prana, and bindu each have two aspects: pure and impure. Impure nadis give rise to samsara's confusion and obscurations. When purified, they fully manifest as wisdom nadis. Pure bindus are free from all mental elaborations. Nadi, prana, and bindu are the basis of purification, inseparable from the essence of the true nature of mind, self-aware wisdom. They take us to complete enlightenment.

> By putting one's awareness in the body you find that the further down you go the more primordial, unconditioned and unmanifest is the energy you encounter. The chakras begin at the perineum, which is the most primordial level of awareness, and as you go upwards, they are more connected with expression. At the navel there is a sense of the earth, stability and equanimity; at the heart is a feeling of warmth and compassion; the throat is about communication, expression and connection; and the head is less a conceptual centre than a place where the energy reaches a crescendo. So the different chakras have very different feels.
>
> –Reginald Ray

The central channel is the key to understanding how we can come into our wisdom. It is at the very center of our torso. We visualize it as thin as a straw to create a sense of precision, yet as we deepen our practice it becomes as vast as a cathedral. It is quintessentially still. When subtle mind enters the unconditional space of the central channel, all confusion and emotions dissolve. It removes the veils to primordial luminosity. The deeper meaning of the central channel is that enlightened potential is already present within us as unconditional space and unconditional awareness. I think of it as the ultimate vacuum cleaner or cosmic garbage disposal!

The fruition of inner yoga practices is that we click into the basic luminosity of the primordial ground by visualizing light. Light is inseparable from energy so it is the conduit. The primary practice for achieving this is chandali (Sanskrit) or tummo (Tibetan). The progression of the practice goes like this: with awareness, we move the prana and bindu along the nadis, raising heat from the lower chakras and bringing down cool light from the top of the head. When the lust of the lower chakra encounters the coolness of the crown chakra, it turns into bliss. That energy will naturally go to the heart and purify the emotions.

Chandali is ultimately about emptiness, non-duality, being in the now. It is an ordinary and extraordinary experience. This has been personally helpful in so many ways: practicing non-conceptually, having the visceral experience of bliss and joy, experiencing inner and outer luminosity, and deepening an understating of the Five Wisdoms postures.

Tantric Sexual Practices

A principal imagery in tantric practices is that of yab-yum, a female and male deity in sexual union. As well, female and male genitals are powerful symbols in themselves. This image symbolizes the fundamental nature of reality: the primordial union of emptiness and manifestation. The yum, the feminine aspect, is the expression of emptiness. The yab, the masculine aspect, is phenomenal appearance. Deities are visualized, or sensualized, as empty but with a form. This translates into all phenomena as seen as empty but with form: appearance/emptiness. Deities are an expression of wisdom and compassion. Yab-yum practices engender these views in the practitioner.

Most significantly, it is through the use of the polarities of feminine and masculine sexual energy that tantric practice transforms ordinary passion into liberated spiritual energy. It purifies the body and accelerates the removal of emotional and mental obscurations. Through practice, we unite the innate feminine and masculine energies within our body. The deepest realization is that our essence is bi-gender and that awakenment does not belong to either sex.

Three traditional practices may be given by a tantric guru. The first is doing a practice that includes a yab-yum visualization, reciting a liturgy, saying a mantra, performing mudras (hand gestures), and working with breathing.

Secondly, chaṇḍali practice works with the nadis, pranas, and bindus, moving and holding energy in specific ways. This generates heat and, absorbed in embodiment, one becomes totally free from concept. It brings the practitioner into a full embodiment of these energies in a visceral way. By this means, one enters a state of bliss. Here are some excerpts from a song by Milarepa, a yogic adept:

> My body is rainbow-like in the sky of
>   appearance emptiness
> Not turning that into a mental fixation craving is
>   consumed
> Speech is sound and emptiness—like an echo in
>   an empty dale
> With neither good nor bad about it, to indulge
>   or refuse are consumed
> Mind is luminous emptiness—like the light of
>   the sun and the moon
> Without the slightest bias in it, the idea of a self
>   is consumed
>
> . . .
>
> Seeing reality's face, there's no mistake here
> The prana is drawn to the center and hits the
>   spot
> The white [male] and the red [female] elixirs
>   meet face to face
> Bliss luminosity non-thought experience just is
>
> . . .

Appearance and emptiness blend into one, what
  bliss!
Emptiness no longer intellect's realm, what
  relief!
Confusion consumed in space, what a wonderful
  sight!

The most advanced practice, karmamudra, is that of sacred
sexual union with a qualified and appropriate consort. Some
Tibetan Buddhist teachers see karmamudra practice as necessary to attain enlightenment in this lifetime. At times and
places the men and women doing this practice have lived and
practiced together and have achieved realization. Though the
male deity is generally thought of as the dominant figure with
the female deity as consort, historically women have trained
men in the practice.

Karmamudra is talked about as the quick path to transform
ordinary passion into liberated spiritual energy. A distinctive
feature of this practice is not releasing into orgasm but contain-
ing and spreading the energy through one's body. Uniting with
another in nondual bliss to infuse one's body with vital sexual
energy is profoundly transformative both spiritually and physically. This experience of open abandonment and intensity is
completely fulfilling. However, the practitioner can become addicted to bliss and miss the point that the ultimate realization is
emptiness.

At the deepest level, lust for another is to dissolve the sense
of other. Ultimately, the sexual act of uniting with another is a
symbol for making love to the world. It is a state of connectedness with all phenomena: interbeing. One can resonate with all
we experience and ride the energetic wave of all that happens.
Engaging in constant intercourse with the phenomenal world is
an experience of endless great bliss that results from that mating.
Space is one's ultimate consort.

"Nonthought" is an experience of being completely present in nowness. It is available to everyone, but the vajrayāna tradition provides powerful and skillful methods which accelerate inner development in direct and tangible ways. Ordinary methods of meditation practice may only slowly or intermittently grant the benefits of nonthought in the practitioner's experience. Cultivating great bliss is a powerful tool which greatly hastens the removal of emotional and conceptual obscurations in one's practice. When one is able to clear away these obscurations, wisdom and compassion arise spontaneously.

–Chögyam Trungpa Rinpoche

Sexuality is a total experience of joy that comes from being completely in the realm of nonthought. It is why people are so obsessed with it. It also could be rare in our life. There could be fear around it. So, sexuality is a controversial issue. Unfortunately, it mostly gets distorted into self-serving instead of self-transcending. Because of this, the practice requires considerable purification of one's emotions, particularly the habitual grasping and fixation we have toward an object of desire. Gaining stability through mindfulness and awareness is an absolute prerequisite to do yab-yum practice.

The passionate quality of human experience can only be liberated through desire itself; a "mingling of passion and absence of passion"…[it is] difficult to honor passion without being overwhelmed by self-centered desire for gratification. Experiencing intense passion without succumbing to gratification is at the heart of practice and separates sexuality in Buddhist Tantra from ordinary sexuality.

–Judith Simmer Brown

Then There Is Tantric Tango!

Tango is an interesting model to examine the essence of an intimate exchange of energy. Any dance or activity that is about connection is extremely powerful and tremendously fulfilling. Making love, contact improvisation (a dance form), horseback riding, padma energy exploration, and tango all have this in common. Much to the surprise of one of my tango partners, I once blurted out, "Dancing with you is like riding a horse!" The synergistic experience of movement, grounded in energetic exchange, is a delightful sensation. Tango aficionados say it's better than sex!

The essence of tango is an embodied symbiotic experience of the masculine and feminine energies. It is joining with another at a very subtle level, from which flow a myriad of movement possibilities. We begin with the leader leading with clarity and purpose, and the follower responding with softening and surrender. The role of follower has to be as strong as the role of the leader. In deep resonance with each other, the response of the follower can then influence the leader's next lead. This reciprocal relationship, with both people riding the energy of the moment, is the epitome of nondual union and, we could say, the epitome of good collaboration. We come to a tangible sense of what it means to lead with clarity and purpose as well as follow with grace and ease. At an elemental level, leaders are clear, pure water and moving air, and followers are dancing fire and grounding earth.

The Five Wisdoms inform tango by giving us five key principles for becoming sensitive to when and how to lead and follow. A tango dance always begins with the partners in a quiet presence (buddha), where they open to connecting with each other (padma). From there, the leader initiates the movement (vajra/karma), and the follower responds (padma). The dance then becomes the expression of the joining put into action (padma/karma). If we start right off with karma action we miss the essence, of tango. Ratna enters the picture later, with embellishments, sometimes led and at other times spontaneously coming from either partner. We can then use these same principles to make collaborative partnerships more effective. This is tango teamwork.

> I think the reason dance has held such an ageless magic for the world is that it has been the symbol of the performance of living. Many times I hear the phrase "the dance of life."...The instrument through which the dance speaks is also the instrument through which life is lived: the human body. It is the instrument by which all the primaries of experience are made manifest. It holds in its memory all matters of life and death and love.

> –Martha Graham
> Preeminent choreographer
> and dancer of the 20th century

> Trust only movement. Life happens at the level of events, not of words. Trust movement.

> –Alfred Adler

In programs with Khenpo Tsültrim Gyamtso Rinpoche, we manifested embodiment as enjoyment. We danced and sang. We heard the teachings and expressed them in song, dance, poetry, and theater pieces. We memorized songs; we *knew them by heart*. There was a pervasive experience of joyous engagement with each other. We become part of that experience and it became part of us.

We lived fully!

We got outrageous!

We celebrated!

PART IV

A Bigger World Awaits You

CHAPTER 15

The Inevitable and the Essential Journey

In our own lives, we feel a sense of confusion—it seems to be confusion—but that confusion brings out something that is worth exploring. The questions that we ask in the midst of our confusion are potent questions, questions that we really have. We ask: "Who am I? What am I? What is this? What is life?" and so forth. Then we explore further and ask: "In fact, who on earth asked that question? Who is that person who asked the question 'Who am I?' Who is the person who asked, 'What is?' or even 'What is what is?'" We go on and on with this questioning further and further inward. In some way, this is non-theistic spirituality in its fullest sense.

–Chögyam Trungpa Rinpoche

We are all journeyers through life. For some of us, this is more conscious than for others. Once born, inevitably there are going to be life situations and occurrences that are going to be challenging. Each stage of life presents us with new challenges: growing up in a family, going to school, becoming socialized, working, getting married, parenting, etc. When has parenting seemed beyond the beyond in our ability to deal with our children in a sane way? How many children have felt the same about their parents? How many have been crippled by their education rather than enlightened by it? How many have had their lives crumble upon losing an intimate partner or a favored job? Or both at once? So, our life could be disappointing. We might have reached a certain level of despair, desolation, or hopelessness. We could have arrived at a sense of empty-heartedness.

Perhaps we have a good life. Things seem to rock along. There are minor irritations but, all in all, we manage. We see no need to dig deeper. Then one day everything falls apart. We find ourself in the middle of one of life's major dramas. A life crisis comes as a surprise, but it is inevitable. We can either become a victim and be in a constant struggle, or we can be proactive, be a warrior. We will either be beaten down by these challenges, or, with luck, have them be transformative opportunities.

So, it seems there is an inevitable journey to our life for which it seems essential to prepare. How do we meet the major challenges of our life, such as illness, loneliness, or loss of heart? We see that having good intention can guide our way and we can move along the path with confidence. Establishing a way of working with ourself with a disciplined practice gives us the inspiration to be alive.

> Genuine inspiration is not particularly dramatic. It's very ordinary. It comes from settling down in your environment and accepting situations as natural. Out of that you begin to realize that you can dance with them. So inspiration comes from acceptance rather than from having a sudden flash of a good gimmick coming up in your mind...Inspiration has two parts: openness and clear vision.
>
> —Chögyam Trungpa Rinpoche

In these times, when both our internal bewilderment and the external forces of calamity and destruction rage on, we owe it to ourself to chart a course to align ourself with our inherent sanity. When aware of this journey, we have the opportunity to look at where we have been, where we are now, and where we would like to be. This larger perspective is in itself empowering. For me this journey has come to be essential.

The notion of journey brings up some interesting para- doxes. For one, we actually do not know where we are going until we get there, and even "there" seems to be rather illusive. In a dance theater piece, I told a little story of trying to get somewhere and could not seem to get on the right bus. Finally, I got on a bus and asked the bus driver where he was going. He said you never know until you get there. The philosopher Mar- tin Buber is in accord. He said, "All journeys have secret desti- nations of which the traveler is unaware." Most poignantly, the only way the journey unfolds is to be in the moment. Each unique moment opens to the next one and the next. Everything is known in its own time.

Personal Change: Motivation and Resistance

The journey from where we find ourself to actualizing our highest potential and living our deepest values has been ex- plored since the birth of the human species. It is in the nature of being human to ask the questions that make this journey a possibility. We are perpetually intrigued by who we are, what this life is about, or simply how to get through the day with more ease. Perhaps we have a yearning for a deep spirituality. Some time ago, a message came to me through a dream. The message was clear that we have to change our dreams, our sto- ries, our life. In the dream, I am very absorbed in trying to de- cide which way I want my life to go.

At the same time, we resist moving into a new way of being, making a change. Whether it is keeping to a new type of diet, establishing a daily meditation practice, or keeping a New Year's resolution, we too often resist personal change. We think starting tomorrow is good enough. I call this the mañana yāna. Mañana is Spanish for tomorrow; yāna is path: the tomorrow path.

Why is our resistance so strong? It is because we are, at every moment, in a delicate balance between our confusion and our sanity. Our propensity to create our own suffering and chaos is in equal proportion to our potential to recognize our sanity. We don't realize this. We habitual deny the very best of who we are and entrap ourself in our confusion. This is why it takes a good deal of effort to make changes in our life. It is only when we clearly see what is most wholesome that we can really make a commitment. We might find that if we neglect our meditation, we botch things up at work.

Our ability to take on the journey has everything to do with both our motivation and capability. Climbing Everest is potentially possible for everyone but few have either the inclination or the means. However, what is true of the journey of working with our minds and bodies is that we slowly acclimatize ourself to higher and higher levels of understanding and experience. Once we taste the freedom of being liberated from our struggle, we thirst for more refined ways to bring this about. Each day we find that it is not "just another day" but another day with real purpose. This is what takes us along the path. For those of us who aspire to reach the top of the mountain, we find that there are more than one way up. As a Buddhist saying goes, "If we are facing in the right direction, all we have to do is keep on walking."

The Price of Wisdom

The metaphor of journey has long held meaning for me. As a dancer, I choreographed hundreds of dances and dance-theater pieces. At one point I realized that most of my later pieces were about a journey. So, meeting Trungpa Rinpoche, a teacher who could take me on an inner journey, was very compelling. I remember distinctly feeling that it was not that I understood the teachings, but that I trusted them.

We can talk about the external journey: what we did when and where, and the fantastic adventures we had. It is helpful to understanding the external forces that have been at play in our life, the causes and conditions that have come together to create our life's circumstances. However, ultimately the very personal inner journey is more meaningful. Obviously, the vicissitudes of our outer journey inform the inner journey and vice versa. When embraced fully, the highlights of our inspirations and the valleys of our despair provide a certain authentic symbolism for our life.

The essence of the contemplative approach to living is that the inner journey unfolds by being aware of our internal process twenty-four hours a day. It brings immediacy in relating to life's experiences. Things become very personal. The empowering effect of discovering something, rather than being told something, is what creates an inner strength. Training people through experiential learning is of paramount importance. As a Five Wisdoms Training participant said, "I and the other participants *had a voice,* and that is perhaps the most essential ingredient to embodied learning. We *created* the training, both on an individual and group level." Accepting with a deep knowing that we are always in process, that there is no end product, and that our life is marked with impermanence, is the shaky but exciting ground upon which we stand. A willingness to hang out in that space gives us the inner strength to live life fully.

The bad news is that we are falling. The good news is that there is no ground.

–Chögyam Trungpa Rinpoche

The journey has no name. The destination is unknown. We don't know where we are going. What is it like to open to the unknown, or at least that which cannot be understood at the present time? The answer and the reward are in daring to undertake the journey. The sense of movement from one stage of our life to another, moving through the seasons of our life, is what gives us the very vitality of our existence. If we look around at those who are not moving, we see the alternative: living in a cocoon.

Though we do not know where we are going, there is a sense that by living fully in our current situation, the present moment, whether wonderful or horrific, that life will give way to the next phase. Allowing painful deaths to give rise to joyful births, embracing the embryo of an idea that could come to fruition perhaps in an unexpected way, are all part of our daring to step along the path, to let our journey unfold.

Though we journey into the unknown, at any given time we can choose our course of action. As in the game Dungeons & Dragons, which my son Julian played into adulthood, making the right choices in adverse circumstances is extremely empowering. As a grown man, my son is a skillful strategist in his business.

Undertaking our life's journey is like giving birth to ourself. Most of us think that once we are born, that's it. But to be reborn again and again creates a fresh atmosphere in our life. At the same time, we are dying. Once born, we are instantaneously candidates for death. Death does not just happen once. There are small and big deaths all along the way.

In the book *The Way to Shambhala*, Edwin Birnbaum writes of an ancient Tibetan text in which a father is explaining to his son how to travel to the kingdom of Shambhala, an ancient enlightened society that is both part real and part mythical. It begins with known places in India that we can visit today. Then the route goes north into Nepal. The father then describes mountains and finally, we come to a valley, an enchanted land where jewels hang from trees and diamonds sparkle in the rivers. This journey is a metaphor for how the external journey of our life can become an inner journey of awakening.

Inspired by this account and living in Nepal at the time, I took a solo trek along the route described in the book on the Everest trail to Tengboche, a Tibetan Buddhist monastery. As it was just before the monsoon season, the trail was mostly deserted. In the morning I would hike; in the afternoon it would rain and I practiced meditation and wrote poems as a way of chronicling the trek. For me, this was a blend of an outer and inner journey. Ultimately, it was a journey toward inner realization. From this complete merging with my surroundings, I created a dance theater piece called "The Mountain." From reading the book, to doing the trek, to creating and performing the dance theater piece, an outer and inner journey unfolded.

In the spring of 1998, my father, then aged 82, my son Julian, my daughter Karuna, and I took a three-generational trip to Turkey. The trip became both a chance to see some of the places where my father and I grew up as missionary children, and also as a time to deepen our connections with each other. My father and I both had manuscripts of our books along; mine was of my first book, and his became the book *The Things We Cannot Say, A Cultural Encounter East vs West*. His book is about early Christian missionaries venturing into the Ottoman Empire, each group having a set of unconscious assumptions about themselves and the natural order of things. Dad and I read each other's manuscript and had some very heart-to-heart discussions. This trip transformed our relationship, creating a much deeper love and respect for each other.

Julian wrote his own book, a documentation of the trip entitled, *Turkish Delight...And Other Tales from Over There*. It begins simply. "We went to Turkey. We had to. It was in our blood." His book is filled with exciting and humorous anecdotes, like one where we were stopped by the police as we were looking for a hotel in a new town. As the police approached, "Mom" addressed them in fluent Turkish. They ended up escorting us to the hotel! My children had a wonderful time. It was a very bonding experience which is felt to this day. It was a rich time for this intergenerational family connection, truly a trip worth taking.

The inner journey can be every bit as dramatic as an outer journey, and, if met bravely, it can be vastly more life transforming. For example, there can be a journey with our constricting emotions. Denying them gets us nowhere. It just pushes them into the subconscious where they grow like monsters. Bringing our emotions into the light of day, however, can get quite messy. Creative expression can be useful in that process. We balance between open, creative self-exploration and discipline. As Merce Cunningham, preeminent modern dance choreographer, once said, "Too much discipline dulls the mind; too much creativity makes the body flabby," or mind mushy, I would add. Our outpourings take us into the process of transmuting our fixated emotions into wisdom. I took a year after my mother died to create a dance for her called "Elegy." It was an intense journey of letting her go, coming to understand death, and the mourning process.

On the journey, we are told to trust our experience. We could ask, "What if our experience is utter confusion? What can we trust?" The point here is to trust the process, the journey. Staying open in the midst of chaos, keeping our wits about us, takes the fearlessness of a warrior in battle. In this same vein, every breakdown, rather than being a crisis, can be an opportunity, a breakthrough, to a new way of seeing and being in the world. Allowing a part of ourself to die makes room for the birth of the new. There is no need to be sorry for the pain we suffer. The pain is what allows the journey to happen. Why do many people live the most fully when facing a major illness? Why is life so vibrant when we are in a major crisis?

At some point we all have to face our fear. That we have fear is the very reason, in fact, to undertake the journey. We must go beyond our fear. All of our neurosis, our confusion, our suffering arises from fear. Our reaction is to manipulate the world to keep our fear at bay. This creates an endless perpetuation of neurosis as we bury ourself under layer after layer of armoring and coping strategies. We can begin to recognize and work with our core fears, the paralyzing states of mind that hold us back. As we unravel our protective armoring, things will get worse (more confusing) before they get better. However, we find that when we relax, our fear dissolves in a flash. We will then taste the intoxicating drink of fearlessness.

When we hold a black-and-white view toward our experience, we are convinced that sometimes things are good and sometimes bad. As we move along our path, we see that good things can be disguised as bad things and bad things disguised as good things. In fact, we see that what was difficult was probably the best thing that happened to us. The distinction between good and bad begins to melt away. Things just happen. Whatever happens, happens. We can respect the flow or pattern of our life and have more understanding of who we are. My slogan for this is, "If one wonderful thing doesn't happen, another wonderful thing will"

My husband and I deciding to separate catapulted me into the most challenging journey I ever had. The turmoil of emotions, the intensity of fears, the solidity of my neurotic limitations was beyond anything I had experienced. Yet, I stayed open to my experience. The process took years. It was the most life transformative period of my life. During that time, John and I worked together as practitioners to bring out the sanity of our decision. Not feeling comfortable with the traditional notion of divorce, we found other ways to talk about it. I wrote a short practice called "The Sadhana [practice] of Dissolving a Relationship." John offered the Mahayāna understanding called "Freedom from the Four Extremes." This is a teaching connection: not together, not separate, not both, not neither. Five years later we did a ritual with our two children, Karuna and Julian. We called it "Appreciating the Dissolving and Aspirations for the Evolving." Not having attachment to each other, which leads to expectations of each other, we are now able to see each other more clearly.

In Ursula La Guin's "The Earthsea Cycle," the protagonist Ged is a young wizard in training. His misfortune is that he unleashes an evil spirit. The story unfolds as this evil spirit pursues him far and wide through a mythical world. In the far reaches of this world, he finally confronts the demon, only to find that it his shadow self. We all run away from the parts of ourself that we dislike the most, and project it out as if it is something real and external to us. Facing our inner demons and fears takes the bravery of a wizard-warrior like Ged. Ultimately the demon is an illusion, and therefore there is nothing to fear.

At times, we are able to completely let go of our resistance. I had a dream in which I was in a big open space and suddenly took off into the air and, to my amazement, kept going higher and higher. I was flying. I was flapping my arms but it did not feel like I was exerting much effort. The feeling was, "This is easy; anyone can do it. You just have to let go of any idea that is holding you back." On the one hand I was elated I could fly; on the other hand, it felt very ordinary.

The Lonely Journey

For many, one of the most challenging aspects of this journey is that we have to do it alone. Why? First of all, it is accepting what is. We are alone. Though during our life, we have both the joy and struggle of relating to others, in essence we are alone. We come into the world alone, and we leave it alone. Accepting loneliness as our path has profound implications.

Some people find being alone is easy and being around people lonely, perhaps because it is more difficult for them to connect. Others, who are more relationally oriented, find that being alone is a struggle. Still others feel the most fulfilled when being around animals, creating art, or walking in nature. For some, however rich their external world, there is always a deep loneliness, a hole at the center of their being.

Too often, particularly when we don't feel good about ourself, we cling to others to save ourself from ourself. No wonder our relationships often don't go well! When we feel OK about who we are, we are like trees standing tall in the forest together yet with space around us. When we are constantly leaning toward another for support, we give away our strength. We begin to feel weak. At best, our relationships to others and our world come from a deeply rooted depth and richness. Of all the talk about love in relationships, loving oneself, enjoying oneself, being with oneself is the most transformative kind of love. The good news is it is where we can affect the most change. Further, it is the only way to make loving others possible. It is the place to start.

Whether we are lonely or not has to do with our capacity to connect with an inner world of aliveness. Whatever our style, cultivating quality time alone enhances our ability to understand ourself and relate to the riches of the world. In doing so we could discover that there is a journey from a painful loneliness to a fulfilling aloneness. There is a sense that in being alone we are incubating life.

Heart Failure

The most crippling experiences of our journey are the times when we have a loss of heart. We lose the sense of the preciousness and vitality of life. We would rather not be involved. We have no interest in anything. The sense of moving forward on our journey comes to a standstill. Life stagnates. We become the living dead. We say we are depressed. This is certainly true for me. When not in touch with the wisdom within, I feel lonely and depressed. This is precisely the time that the potential for transformation is most ripe. Yet, for some this can be the black hole in which people live out the rest of their lives.

We can experience depression as a chronic situation in our life, or merely as a flash in the moment. Though we can obviously use therapy to work with the situation, what is interesting to look at within the context of artful living is to see our depression as the rich manure of our being. We can take heart that we are experiencing something so intensely that we are consumed by it. We have arrived somewhere. But where are we? We are here, slumped into a rotten feeling. Good. Fully acknowledging where we are and being inquisitive about it are the very tools we need to carry on. We can take a look around and see that, in fact, it is as good of a place to be as anywhere else. Having a sense of equanimity to whatever arises allows us to be inquisitive about absolutely everything that occurs. There is no need to be reactive. Good and bad goes out the window. It, whatever "it" is in the moment, just is. No Big Deal.

At times, we fall. A favorite saying is, "On the spiritual journey, we always fall forward." Every fall is an opportunity to bounce back up. There is also room for mistakes. As Trungpa Rinpoche put it, we have to be willing to be a fool and not so self-protective.

Going to the Heart

Our cultural surroundings affect who we are and how we manifest. We do not live in isolation. We need to find those places in the world that bring out our best, that literally bring us to life. Living in or traveling to the places that nourish us, makes it possible for us to engage fully. My mother-in-law went to southern France every year to paint. For her, this was the place that inspired her. We can, without much effort, learn to create an environment that makes us flourish, even if it is one corner of a room in a studio apartment.

At the age of two I went to live in Turkey with my missionary parents and I have lived many places. I find that I have always gone to the heart of things. As a classical ballet dancer, I lived in London. As a modern dancer I lived in New York City. As a dancer exploring the creative edge, I was in San Francisco in the 1970s. When I was in the process of integrating Buddhism into my dancing and teaching, I went to the Naropa Institute (now University) in Boulder, Colorado. When Buddhism became a primary focus in my life, I lived at Karmê Chöling, a Shambhala retreat center. My choice for a retirement community is Enso Village which has core values that align with mine.

Braving the Journey

Traveling alone can have its dangers. Perhaps we fear being alone, or that we are unworthy or frustrated in our inability to clear our mind of hassles. Perhaps we are so stuck that it seems impossible to move into a situation with better prospects. At times we may need guides along the way. A good friend, a therapist or a coach, a meditation instructor, or a spiritual teacher can provide a trustworthy place for us to work with the obstacles that have overcome us.

Again, my thoughts turn toward Etty Hillesum, the Dutch Jewish woman whose diaries during the World War II German occupation in the Netherlands became the book, *An Interrupted Life.* Walking along the barbed wire fence of Auchswitch by moonlight, her thoughts turn to the beauty of the world. Though she worries about such things as her poor feet that might not make the enforced prisoners' march, she is ultimately undaunted. The horror of her outer circumstances made her inner journey all the more profound. I am awed by the inner resources that made her journey so compelling.

Trungpa Rinpoche made a dramatic escape from Tibet at the age of sixteen. As an abbot of a major monastery in eastern Tibet, he took responsibility for leading around 150 people over the Himalayas in the winter while being chased by the Chinese. At one point, not knowing what to do, he found a secluded valley and meditated for a month. After coming to the West, he also went through a dark, difficult period. He was trying to understand how to teach people in the West. A retreat in Bhutan turned things around. He decided to break from tradition, give up his monk's robes, and forge a new way of teaching.

We will find that meditating on a regular basis provides the most support in working with our state of mind. Taking time for more informal reflection can also serve us well. As more familiar worldly attachments loosen, we have more allegiance to the inner journey. Though I grew up abroad and traveling for work and pleasure has long been a way of life, I often find that the sights, sounds, and tastes of foreign countries are not as compelling as what reveals itself in the inner journey. Seeking further external entertainment ultimately does not seem to be the point. Being in solitary retreat in a cabin in the woods on a yearly basis are the times I often feel my life is the richest.

A haiku I wrote:

In the confines of my cabin,
most notably I experience
freedom

No Place to Go

An authentic journey moves us from one place to another going both higher and deeper. Higher in that we actually feel lighter. Deeper in that we feel more grounded, on the earth. The process of working with ourself is marked by a sense of shedding what is not needed rather than taking on something from the outside. The path unfolds in equal proportion to our willingness to shed layers of our protective armor. As we shed, there is a tangible sense of lightening up. Less encumbered by our solidified views and habits, we walk with a lighter step. We also feel our feet on the ground. As human beings, upright mammals, we have both an affinity to the celestial realms and a connection in an immediate way to the good earth, our primal mother.

Ultimately there is no place to go. Just being is magical. Sitting, observing a blade of grass, or just being simple, simply being, is not only OK, but completely fulfilling. This is our day, our life. What more could we want?

This quality of just being, resting in space, was made very vivid in a dream I had in which my house was made of light. It was an ordinary house, but it was made of light and it floated in the air, like a celestial palace. I heard a voice say, "You don't have to become it; you are it. You don't have to do anything; just be. You don't have to go anywhere; you are there."

This short story is about the experience of just being, with nowhere to go:

I am the boy who lives by himself. I don't do anything in particular, I just live: that's the way I am…The sort of things that interest me are stones and rivers and trees and clouds. Since long ago I have had no parents or brothers and sisters, so I just live alone. Sometimes I want to do like the grown-ups, but then I realize there's no point in that. I have my own world to live in and I'm known as "the boy who lives by himself." When I was born, no one gave me a name. Perhaps my parents did give me a name, but somehow it never entered my mind. So, I remain nameless…I suggested to him [a friend] that he should be nameless like me. At first, he didn't like the idea. He said, "If I didn't have a name, how would I know who I am?" I found it difficult to explain to him in words, so I just said "Well, why don't you give it a try and see what it's like?" So he did… Now he was able to see what his nameless self was really like and he became like a tiger who has broken his chain…Today is the first day of my journey, so here I am, playing in the road. I've only traveled 50 yards or so, but it would take the grown-ups ten years to learn what I've learned in this one day.

–Chögyam Trungpa Rinpoche

Cultivating a sense of inner journey provides us with an inexhaustible source of fulfillment for life on a very uncertain planet. We could say it is essential.

CHAPTER 16

The Dharmic Journey

This path entails uncovering three basic human qualities. They are natural intelligence, natural warmth, and natural openness. Everyone, everywhere, all over the globe, has these qualities and can call on them to help themselves and others.

—Pema Chödrön

It is such a mistake to assume that practicing dharma will help us calm down and lead an untroubled life; nothing could be further from the truth. Dharma is not a therapy. Quite the opposite, in fact; dharma is tailored specifically to turn your life upside down—it's what you sign up for. So when your life goes pear-shaped, why do you complain? If you practice and your life fails to capsize, it is a sign that what you are doing is not working. This is what distinguishes the dharma from New Age methods involving auras, relationships, communication, well-being, the Inner Child, being one with the universe, and tree hugging. From the point of view of dharma, such interests are the toys of samsaric beings—toys that quickly bore us senseless.

—Dzongsar Khyentse Rinpoche

In this chapter we are moving on in our journey to look at some of the basic tenants of Buddhism which are the ground for our study of the Five Wisdoms.

Educating ourself in the Buddhist teachings, or dharma, is a threefold process of learning, contemplating, and embodying. Learning involves studying the dharma. Contemplating means that our study, practice, and everyday experiences begin to mix together and inform each other. Embodying means that there is no separation between what we have learned and practiced: we live the dharma.

We can hear the same dharma hundreds of times, but each time it is different. Why? Simply because we have different levels of understanding as we move along the path. For example, we begin to understand that acquiring is not emphasized as much as shedding. The measure of accomplishment in practice is the shedding of our ego and the arising of wisdom and compassion. There is also another magical combination: having a teacher or teachers, the teachings, and a community of practitioners. All three confirm and encourage our experience as a practitioner.

Buddhist teachings show us what is real and true only to the extent that we have internalized them. We find truth experientially. The fundamental longing we have for an awakened mind compels us to search for it outside of ourself. We listen to teachers and read the dharma. However, it is of primary importance to always come back to the simple truth that an awakened mind exists within us. We tend to forget and obscure our brilliance, so we need the continual discipline of meditation to bring us back. That is why we practice.

When we refer to a spiritual journey, we are not talking about ambition and struggle but rather aspiration and effort. Aspiration is the sense that we are inspired into nowness, this very moment. Effort is that discipline is necessary. So, there is the inspiration and then there is the exertion needed to realize it.

Everything that comes up in our life is put on the path and, in essence, becomes practice. Nothing is rejected or treated as bad. Everything is workable. The journey is transforming confusion into wisdom. Because of this, we need to start where we are, our confusion and suffering. However, we can use our confusion to wake us up. It is our good energy. To reject the experiences that shape us is to deny a part of ourself. Let's not put it in the trash. Let's conserve our energy and recycle it. We can go into our distress rather than try to get out of it. We stay with it rather than deny it. We have to look at the nitty gritty of our lives, those aspects of ourself that have us spinning around day after day. Rather than getting caught in some grand view, let's look at where we find ourself.

On the spiritual path we have no way of knowing where we are going until we get there. We have no known destination. It's more like an adventure. We get on a train from which we can't disembark; we ride on and on and on. We go the entire distance because if we quit, a sense of being unfinished begins to haunt us. Yet there is no sense of mistake. On the spiritual path, we always fall forward. At some point we are introduced to the realization of ordinary mind, seeing the nakedness of reality as it is. It is very ordinary, just ordinary experience.

> The everyday practice is simply to develop a complete acceptance and openness to all situations and emotions and to all people, experiencing everything totally without mental reservations and blockages, so that one never withdraws or centralizes onto oneself.
>
> —Chögyam Trungpa Rinpoche

It makes no difference how long darkness has been in our life. The light of wisdom can dissolve our distress in an instant. We can drop the ways we distrust and diminish ourself: hesitation, lack of confidence, doubt, and self-absorption. We could develop much greater trust in ourself to jump into our life in a fuller way. We could embrace a quality of inner completeness, allowing our experience to be more whole and less broken, paranoid, fearful, and limited.

The Four Noble Truths

The Four Noble Truths are a nutshell version of Buddhism. They are the overriding understanding of everything. suffering exists; suffering has a cause; cessation of suffering is possible; there is a path to relieving suffering. Everyone wants to be relieved from suffering so the place to begin is first to acknowledge we are suffering. Second, we can look at how and why this suffering occurs. Third, we see the possibility of being liberated from suffering and experience cessation. This is the motivation for our practice. Fourth, we learn how to do that on a genuine path of practice and study.

1. The truth of suffering

Suffering is real. Life always involves suffering. Even when things seem good, we always feel an undercurrent of anxiety and uncertainty inside. So, we need to acknowledge our suffering in a very immediate and visceral way. Then we can feel the immense suffering in the world.

Five kinds of suffering (adapted from the traditional three kinds of suffering)

1. **Basic anxiety:** an all-pervasive discomfort, a sense of undulating nausea
2. **The pain of alternation:** whatever it is, it will change
3. **Inherent pain:** the situations of birth, old age, sickness, and death

4. **The perfect storm:** painful situations piled on top of each other

5. **The pain of pain:** the pain in trying to avoid pain

2. The truth of the cause or origin of suffering

The cause or origin of suffering is 1) craving, our never-ending desires, and 2) fundamental ignorance, our mistaken belief that we are a separate, independent, have a solid "I." The painful and futile struggle to fulfill our desires and maintain a sense of solid self, perpetuates samsara, conditioned and cyclic existence.

3. The truth of cessation

The good news is that our obscurations are temporary. When we relax, pain has no hold on us and we experience intrinsic health. We see that it is possible to observe the clouds without getting sucked into them. The absence of struggle leads us to the discovery of cessation. We drop the effort to secure and solidify ourself and discover wakefulness, nowness. An awakened mind is always available to us. There is newness in every moment.

4. The truth of the path

The journey from confusion to wakefulness is possible. The study of dharma and the practice of meditation is what works. We can live authentically and develop wisdom.

…recognizing our suffering is the starting place and inspiration of the spiritual path. [the] second noble truth was the cause of suffering. In the West, Buddhists call this "ego." It's a small word that encompasses pretty much everything that's wrong with the world. Because according to the Buddha, all suffering, large and small, starts with our false belief in a solid, separate, and continuous "I," whose survival we devote our lives to. It feels like we're hopelessly caught in this bad dream of "me and them" we've created, but we can wake up from it. This is the third noble truth, the cessation of suffering. We do this by recognizing our ignorance, the falseness of our belief in this "I." Finally, the Buddha told us that there is a concrete way we can get there, which basically consists of discipline, effort, meditation, and wisdom. This is the fourth noble truth, the truth of the path.

–Melvin Mcleod

The Three Marks of Conditioned Existence

Another nutshell view of Buddhist truths are the three marks of conditioned existence, samsara. They are simple truths about our existence that cannot be denied. We could experience these three marks very simply and straightforwardly.

1. Impermanence

Nothing lasts forever: things come together and fall apart, decay. There is also psychological impermanence: thoughts and emotions arise, dwell, and dissolve. We cannot hold on to what we have either in ourself or in the phenomenal world. Arising and dissolving marks our life. Denying this dynamic puts us on autopilot. The realization of impermanence makes a pivotal difference in our experience. Tuning into the dance of life and death makes us more alive.

2. Egolessness

Ego is our attempt to shield us from impermanence. Egolessness points to the truth that everything is subject to change, so there is no solid self. There is nothing to hold onto in terms of a permanent state of mind or body.

3. Suffering

Impermanence and egolessness boycott our continual effort to maintain the way we want things to be. So, we suffer. We experience frustration, anger, depression and all sorts of extreme states of mind in our effort to deny the truth of suffering.

The realization of these three make a crucial difference between a routinized, uninspired life, and a life worth living. Everything in our existence arises and dissolves. We can tune into an ongoing life-death dance. Each gesture could arise fully, alive and fresh...and then be gone. When we ignore these truths, we go on a kind of autopilot.

Karma

Buddhist teachings on karma are very helpful in unraveling the conundrum of human existence. In a nutshell, karma is an understanding of cause and effect: our thoughts, feelings, and actions and their resultant effects. It's very logical: past karma effects present karma, and present karma effects future karma. It is a perpetuation of conditioned existence. We do something upright and create good karma. It feels wholesome. We do something dishonorable and create bad karma. It feels unwholesome. Most have experienced the felt sense of when we are aligned with ourself and our world and when we are fighting it. So, karma is about choice, not fate, as is popularly thought.

Karma is about what we are born with and what we are born into. Our personal karma is an essential consciousness that is our pattern integrity, our unique combination of energies. So, it is not Jane, but Jane-ness, an is-ness that is Jane. Collective karma is what we are born into, life situations that arise co-dependently through complex causes and conditions. Our families, peers, ethnic groups, society, and culture affect us. They mold us to what is desired and acceptable. In particular, there is intergenerational family karma which profoundly affects our world views, emotional reactivity, and self-worth. We also might find that we are in the middle of a war, a disaster, or famine. Bad things can happen to good people.

Our personal karma and our life situations are constantly informing each other. The question comes up, "Whose movie am I in?" Or, "How did I get in this mess?" We are at a loss as to know who is running the show. We might have a sense of trajectory about our life, but it never seems to go that way. As we exit the womb, there should be a sign: "Caution: hazardous road ahead." So, how do we navigate our own propensities in the context of external situations? What do we think? What do we feel? What do we say or do? What roles do we play? Do we become a victim? A warrior? A heroine? A decent human being? We have propensities and we have possibilities, which can lead us to feeling victimized, or can lead to an awakening. We can begin to see that life will give us the experiences we need to make it meaningful.

It is hard to catch ourself being ourself because it all happens so fast. We are not aware of the moment-to-moment formation of ego. In the midst of a situation, we tend to decide what to do based on impulsive reactions rather than our innate wisdom. We dig ourself deeper into our hole. If we are aware of our habitual patterns, we have a choice; if we are not, we are slaves to them. When we become aware, we can catch ourself and dismantle this momentum. It is our ignorance that does not see how we create ourself.

We are not stuck with our karma, the causes and conditions that brought about where we find ourself. It is just the cards we have been dealt to play this game of life. How we play our hand is up to us. Paying attention to how we are with different situations and circumstances, we see how the context can either inspire or depress us, enliven or crush us. Our life situations create either confusion or sanity. For example, one person might love the challenge of having a new computer system at work; for another that same situation might be debilitating. So, one person could get the promotion and the other person could get fired. Some life situations ripen our karma, and, like a ripe fruit that is punctured, it gets very messy. The juice splatters all over the place.

Three members of my dance company and I co-created an improvisational dance play in three acts called "Breakgame." Its message was that life is a game, an illusion, and that we can wake up from it and see our foibles. Act I was a ritualized card game in which metaphorically our karma was dealt to us. One of us would get the Ace of Spades which we had designated as the winning card. In Act II, we played out our neuroses, expressing emotions and tensions in our interactions. We would have sudden gaps of realization that it is a game. Not knowing who had the winning card provided a certain electricity in our interactions as the piece progressed. In Act III, the winner revealed themself, and danced having transcended the game. In the epilogue, this person watched as the whole cycle seemed to start again. This is our life. From moment to moment, we never quite know how to play our cards, or when realization will dawn.

Having found ourself here, it is our job to navigate our karma. The good news is that awareness is more powerful than karma and allows us to work through it. Quite simply, if we pay attention to what we think, feel, say, and do, and are able to act in ways that are in line with our understanding of cause and result, we have taken the first step of being on the path. We see that we can do anything with a neurotic twist or a wisdom twist. The most important thing is awareness. It is always on the mark.

> We are here because of our past karmic situation, but what we are going to do is up to us...The emphasis on practice is because it is the only time in your life you can steer your karmic situation.
>
> –Chögyam Trungpa Rinpoche

The big picture here is that the perpetuation of karma is true both in this present life as well as throughout lifetimes. Rebirth is a profound tenet of Buddhism but hard to understand. It makes sense if we understand that there is a consciousness, an energetic integrity or energy pattern, that goes from one life to another. But it's not a specific person. Grandpa isn't reborn as grandpa, but his energy goes on. Our body is a good example of pattern integrity. The cells in our bodies are dying and being replaced throughout our lives, but there is still a sense of "I." We can say, "I am a persistent pattern." We have pattern integrity. So, at death our personal pattern integrity or consciousness goes on but not the personal self. Then this more abstract consciousness manifests in a new specificity.

Aversion, Renunciation, and Inspiration

Being on a genuine path and becoming a dharmic person, we realize our tastes change.

Aversion

Most of us have a fundamental dissatisfaction with our life. There is a sense of complaint, grudge, and blame. There is a lack of joy at being alive. When we discover this in ourself, we begin to feel a distaste for samsara, both our own egoic agendas as well as the spinning world of confusion around us. We have more discernment of what is wholesome and what is unwholesome. This leads to renunciation, which is a pivotal point.

Renunciation

Renunciation is basically saying no to what is not wholesome. Externally, it is simplifying our life and not getting distracted by entertainment. Internally, it is not catering to our hopes and fears and creating emotional dramas. There is a sense of surrender. Our approach to life could become more simple and direct. This kind of renunciation may seem unattractive at first but we could begin to appreciate it because it allows us to come to a deeper sense of ourself. We could develop a yearning toward wakefulness. Sitting meditation could become more and more attractive. It could be the very ticket that allows us to experience a sense of ease, our sweet spot.

> Renunciation in this instance is not just throwing things away but, having thrown everything away (or given everything up), we begin to feel the living quality of peace. This peace is not feeble peace, feeble openness, but it has a strong character, an invincible quality, an unshakable quality, because it admits no gaps of hypocrisy. It is complete peace in all directions, so that not even a speck of a dark corner exists for doubt and hypocrisy. Complete openness is complete victory because we do not fear; we do not try to defend ourself at all.

> —Chögyam Trungpa Rinpoche

Inspiration

Eventually, we arrive at inspiration—a fundamental desire to be decent, upright, and good. We take responsibility for ourself. We are inspired by the energetic, living quality of openness.

Discipline, Meditation, and Insight

Discipline (shila), meditation (samadhi), and insight (prajna) are three prongs essential to following the dharmic path.

Discipline

To develop genuine mental discipline, we cultivate an attitude of simplicity, eliminating unnecessary complications. Discipline develops intuition, which in turn produces insight. It's like rubbing flint and steel together, to get a spark of intellect.

Meditation

Meditation is our actual practice. It is an attitude of bare attention, a capacity to just be in a very direct, simple, precise, dynamic stillness. It is a way of making friends with ourself. Traditionally, it is called the practice of dwelling in peace. We rest in a cradle of loving kindness. It also helps us develops intuition, which is seeing things clearly without questions or doubt.

Insight

Once we are more tamed, we experience more space. Insight arises out of that. Insight is seeing directly and concretely how the mind functions moment to moment, like learning its geography. It is unbiased knowledge of our world and our mind. It also provides inspiration for intellectual study.

> ...to develop a genuine mental discipline, it is first necessary to see how we continually burden ourself with extraneous activities and preoccupations. In Buddhist countries, shila might involve following a particular rule of life as a monk or a nun, or adopting the precepts appropriate to a Buddhist layperson. In the Western secular context, shila might just involve cultivating an attitude of simplicity toward one's life in general.
>
> –Chögyam Trungpa Rinpoche

Meditation, Our Fundamental Discipline

Meditation is the keystone that allows us to progress on the dharmic journey. It infuses a sense of discipline throughout our life. Every moment, we become aware of when we are awake/open and when we have gone to sleep/closed. We don't just have a session of meditation and then flop. We become a reasonable person and pay attention to every detail of our life: our clothing, grooming, environment, eating, and sleeping.

With meditation, we develop a natural and dignified way to do everything. Then there is no such thing as same old same old. The things we do every day—brushing our teeth, combing our hair, cooking dinner—have a seeming repetitiveness. But with meditation, a kind of intimacy could take place with our daily habits. We call this art in everyday living.

There is a threefold process involved. Initially, we just do it: fake it until you make it. Then, there starts to be an inner feeling in what we are doing. Finally, we realize we are sacred being living in a sacred world. This is an awakened world, but only people who are awake see it that way.

Nowness and Aloneness

Nowness is the essence of meditation. Our practice is not aimed at achieving a higher state, but simply being without any object or ambition, being here right now. When things are simple and direct, we can be mindful of one thing at a time. That one-pointedness, that bare attention, is the basic point. We can rest our mind in nowness. Each breath is a unique expression of now and fully felt. To experience nowness, we need to be alone. A necessary part of being a practitioner is coming to terms with being alone where we can touch the core of our being.

> Usually we regard loneliness as an enemy. Heartache is not something we choose to invite in. It's restless and pregnant and hot with the desire to escape and find something or someone to keep us company. When we can rest in the middle, we begin to have a nonthreatening relationship with loneliness, a relaxing and cooling loneliness that completely turns our usual fearful patterns upside down.
>
> —Pema Chödrön

Another aspect of nowness is relaxation. It allows us to be in the moment. We unplug, stop, and just be. As Karuna Rockwell, our family equestrian, says, "Getting a horse to relax is primarily about letting them know you are listening, which lets them know you are aware, which gives them the feeling of safety they get in a herd."

Especially if you meditate intensively over a long period of time, you might feel very sad at times, for no particular reason. The process of breathing out, dissolving, and being mindful while you maintain a good seat brings a feeling of sadness and aloneness. You feel vulnerable and raw. The more you sit, the more you experience this kind of sadness. Externally you maintain your posture, but inside you begin to dissolve and become like gelatin. You feel jellified and droopy all over. That is a good sign—fantastic, actually. You might become the best jellyfish, the very best. We have that kind of droopiness and those jellyfish-like possibilities of being gentle and soft, raw, without skin, without even bone or marrow.

–Chögyam Trungpa Rinpoche

Aloneness and sadness are the heart openers. Sometimes it could be unbearably painful. To experience aloneness, we need to create ways to withdraw from the normal routine of our life. We could take the space created by our practice as our protection. We could also practice being silent. Periodically maintaining silence is not taking away our liberty to speak, but appreciating the freedom of silence.

Meditation practice takes place on a personal level. Great intimacy is involved. It has nothing to do with achieving perfection, achieving some absolute state or other. It is purely getting into what we are, really examining our actual psychological process without being ashamed of it. It is just friendship with ourself.

–Chögyam Trungpa Rinpoche

Nowness is a more vast way of being, a constant sense of having a miraculous birth. Our normal mind cannot engage depth because it is too self-involved. Nowness can be scary, like taking our hands off of the steering wheel. We realize that when we really open up to our world it is not about us. When we realize this, our personal self can step out of the way and we can go for the ride.

> Nowness is the sense that we are attuned to what is happening. The past is fiction and the future is a dream, and we are just living on the edge of a razor blade. It is extraordinarily sharp, extraordinarily tentative and quivering. We try to establish ground but the ground is not solid enough, because it is too sharp. We are quivering between that and this.
>
> —Chögyam Trungpa Rinpoche

Emptiness, Shunyata

The more we taste the very ephemeral, fleeting quality of all we experience, the more we see things as they are. We can begin to see the stillness, the spaciousness, within the activity itself. The final experience of emptiness or openness is a state of basic existence, in which there is no distortion of any kind whatsoever. Basic existence is not influenced by primitive emotions or primitive beliefs. Everything is seen clearly, precisely, right on the point. In some way, at some level, everyone knows this. My father often quoted a Turkish saying, "Buda gecer," meaning, "This too will pass."

> Understanding shunyata means that we begin to realize that there is no ground to get, that we are ultimately free, nonaggressive, open. We realize that we are actually nonexistent ourself. Then we can give. We have lots to gain and nothing to lose at that point.
>
> —Chögyam Trungpa Rinpoche

Wisdom

Profound wisdom does not change, but each time we revisit a teaching, we have changed, so we go deeper. Understanding is a process, and the product of understanding is self-existent. Wisdom is like buried treasure. The digging process takes effort.

Wisdom has no beginning or end. It is not an it. It is in the moment and outside of the moment, both precise and expansive. We are already liberated, but haven't noticed. Stop, look, listen, feel, smell, taste.

Spiritual Journey

The journey's end is also its beginning. It is committing to an ongoing process. We could become determined in our pursuit, not looking for pleasure but for truth. The dharma is so real that we feel something is finally happening. At the same time, it is groundless. Ultimately the spiritual experience is an indefinable, ineffable experience.

> However, the path itself must eventually be abandoned, just as you abandon a boat when you reach the other shore. You must disembark once you have arrived. At the point of total realization, you must abandon Buddhism. The spiritual path is a temporary solution, a placebo to be used until emptiness is understood.

–Dzongsar Khyentse Rinpoche

CHAPTER 17

Discovering
the Tantric World

It is necessary to understand and relate with the five buddha principles (Five Wisdoms)…so that we can begin to
understand what Tantra is all about. If Tantra is a mystical
experience, how can we relate it to our ordinary everyday
life at home? There could be a big gap between tantric experience and day-to-day life…Working with the buddha
families we discover that we already have certain qualities.
According to the tantric perspective, we cannot ignore
them and we cannot reject them and try to be something
else…They are the only potential we have, and when we
begin to work with them, we see that we can use them as
stepping stones…They provide a bridge between tantric
experience and everyday life.

–Chögyam Trungpa Rinpoche

In order to approach Tantric Buddhism, we need to have an
understanding of some fundamental Buddhist perspectives.

The Three-Yāna Journey

Buddhism is commonly understood as one thing, but actually there are many schools. Trungpa Rinpoche presented his teachings in a three-yāna (vehicle or path) approach. The yānas unfold the teachings and corollary practices to meticulously fine-tune our consciousness. The path has a distinct sense of journey. Each vehicle has a particular focus and imparts a particular flavor of wisdom. However, like peeling layers of an onion, we go to a deeper understanding in each subsequent level. This comprehensive journey provides a powerful way to discover our essential nature and innate brilliance.

Buddhism is a non-theistic spiritual path based on experience and realization, not divine authority. This makes it especially suited to those who consider themselves spiritual but not religious, the fastest-growing demographic in the U.S. The word spiritual refers to a belief that there's more to life than what appears on the surface. Buddhism is also considered the world's most developed science of mind, making it very accessible to the non-religiously oriented.

The emphasis is on direct experience not mediated through concept. We are not even bound by the goal of liberation. This makes the journey very real—sometimes irritatingly real. We do not get trapped in a spirituality that is aggrandizing our ego, nor by-pass the mundane aspects of life to attain a transcendent state. We are willing to get into the nitty-gritty of life. We also do not depend on anything outside of ourself, as in theistic traditions, to save ourself from ourself. It is all within us, we only have to discover it. A process of stripping brings us to our genuine being.

All Buddhist teachings come from personal experience so there are often seeming contradictions or discrepancies. But why not? We each have our way of perceiving and interacting with the world. We each have our language, our way of communicating, and each language offers a slightly different perspective. Making the teachings immediate to our life is the journey.

Hīnayāna

The first vehicle is the Hīnayāna where we are introduced to sitting meditation. This gives us the opportunity to face ourself very intimately. We begin to catch ourself being a nuisance to ourself, seeing the suffering and confusion we create for ourself and others. Because of this, Hīnayāna emphasizes discarding, renouncing, or turning away from the heat of neurosis and attachments. We practice letting go the agitation in our body, our erratic breathing patterns, and the wildness of our mind. We become "tamed." In some ways this yāna paints a very black and white, good versus bad, picture. However, being able to discriminate what is wholesome from unwholesome is essential to provide some sense of settling and peace within ourself. We begin to enjoy making things simple. Trungpa Rinpoche once said, "Never forget the Hīnayāna."

Mahāyāna

The Mahāyāna brings us into bigger view. Having cleaned up our act, so to speak, our neurosis becomes more transparent. We make friends with ourself by finally accepting and acknowledging ourself. Being less identified with a sense of self and pushing our own agenda, we see that the purpose of our life is much bigger than just our own welfare. This is a big leap. Our situation opens up tremendously. We become more sensitive to others and our surroundings and discover the warmth of a compassionate heart. At the same time, we begin to see the transitoriness and non-substantiality of everything. Having discovered these things within ourself, we want to share them with others. We take the big step of vowing to put others first. We bring the warmth of compassion to every situation we encounter.

At this point we are awakening to what is traditionally called buddha nature, an awake state of being. We can experience it, rest in it, and live from there. It frees us from the sense of constriction we have about ourself. When we limit our potential, our abilities, we live in a world governed by a small mind and conventionality. In discovering our awake state, we open to a sense of the big mind. Once we have confidence in our own wisdom and goodness, compassion for others arises naturally. This confidence allows us to be both gentle and fearless. We could have the eyes of wisdom and the smile of compassion. We find that we feel happier.

Every difficulty is due to a lack of wisdom and compassion. Wisdom can cut through to realizing what is true. Then we need the medicine of compassion. Too much kindness is idiot compassion, like when our trying to help goes too far. Sometimes we need harsh compassion to wake us up.

In the Mahāyāna, we discover three qualities within us:

1. a sense of spaciousness, timeless and open

2. luminous and clear awareness

3. spontaneously arising compassion

When these three are brought together, we gain an enormous sense of confidence. Most of us don't experience this, but finding those qualities in ourself is empowering. We find they are always developing within us, as if we are pregnant with our true self. In the context of the Five Wisdoms, our essential nature is the magical ingredient that turns raw energy into wisdom.

Transition to Tantra

There is a continuous process through the yānas, and the more we appreciate the previous yānas, the more we are able to understand Tantra. From the first awakening of our desire to work with ourself to the point of discovering our wisdom nature, there is a continuity in our personal process of ripening and freeing. We have listened to the teachings and have done our meditation practice. We have worked on cutting through the perpetual agendas of ego and conventional dualistic logic. We have worked on letting go of our reference points. Our meditation practice has created a softness, gentleness, and open heart. We are less swayed by the storms of emotional upheavals and life circumstances. Within us, there is a growing devotion to the path of awakening and to an authentic teacher. We appreciate their profound wisdom, teaching style, and skillful means.

The primary view is that Buddhism is a path of personal realization and compassion toward others. Most traditions think of this as full enlightenment. The process of being marinated in emptiness and infused with warmth are essential to being able to take on the energy of this last yāna. Tantra holds the primary view of Buddhism and provides further skillful means to bring it about. The previous yānas process us, make us workable, so we are ripened. However, they are only steps along the way. With Tantra we have more tools to work with our slippery ego! We take a fresh look and begin to see very naturally. This is known as ordinary mind, just seeing things as they are. We develop a sense of complete command. Having a keen understanding of how our mind and body operate, we are ready for a more powerful set of teachings.

The Hīnayāna and Mahāyāna are the vehicles of *cause* bringing us slowly toward realization. Vajrayāna, or Tantra, is the vehicle of *result* as it takes the realization of our awakened mind as the path. A dedicated practitioner does not by-pass earlier yānas, but also does not need a complete achievement of them before going on. Having the whole map at our disposal provides inspiration, and we aspire to go further. We come to appreciate the need for a solid foundation to have a golden roof.

Years ago, during a meeting with the dance faculty at Naropa Institute (now University), I had an exchange with Trungpa Rinpoche's regent Osel Tendzin. I commented that I felt I had danced myself into stillness. After the chaos and turmoil of a professional dance life, I had found the gift of the Hīnayāna: simplicity. Great! He looked at me and said, "Why not stillness into dancing?" I took this as an invitation to enter the Vajrayāna. I find it to be a metaphor for the journey. Yes, we need simplicity, and yes, we need to dance!

Tantric Buddhism

If the previous yānas are the rivers that flow to the ocean, Tantra is the immovable, indestructible ocean. We are already enlightened. We just have to realize it. And it *is* realizable. We began with some kind of bewilderment and ignorance. Now we have a transcendental, universal bewilderment in the best sense, an awe at the magnificence of our world. Initially, we were bound by our neurosis, and then we were liberated from it. Now we are bound by a deep commitment to a path of liberation.

Tantra is about direct *transmission,* a direct introduction to the mind of ultimate realization. Formal transmission stops our mind. There is a sudden intoxication of nowness. It is a direct *experience* of that realization in the moment. Words give us inferential understanding. This is direct experience. It is an invitation to a more vast way of being that cannot be shaken. There is a fundamental trustworthiness.

Tantra is essentially teachings for being fully in the world. So, instead of renouncing the world, we return to it, with a difference. We awaken to the world we live in, a reality ever deepening and expanding. Having been trained and processed, we have wise eyes and take a fresh look. Because our perception has changed, the world begins to be a different place: alive, colorful, brilliant, and intelligent. It is powerful, magical, and outrageous. It is full of all-pervasive, all-encompassing wisdom energy. We realize how things are, the truth of the truth with no room for falsity. We get fully involved in our everyday life with a new perspective. There is a sense of delight and fearlessness. We are more open, clear, and compassionate. We are more cheerful and there is more room for a sense of humor, play, and joy. My father, a Quaker, and I had many conversations on spirituality. I feel a particular resonance with this quote:

> I cannot believe that God does not possess one of the blessings of his creation: the gift of laughter. I must know that from time to time, God's laughter echoes among the stars.
>
> —William L. Nute Jr., my father

The basic point is that we have come beyond a dualistic perception of existence. Here too there is a sense of progression. When we stabilize our mind and rest one-pointedly, we begin to see the self-nature of mind, its extraordinary ordinariness. When we see that mind has no basis, we experience simplicity. When we are free from the fixations of this and that, and transcend our habitual patterns, we experience one taste, the equality of all. Freed from the conventions that separate meditating from not meditating, we discover the state of non-meditation, or constant meditation. There is a sense of complete absorption in being here now and relating with what is here.

> In the tantric notion of indestructibility, there is no ground, no basic premise, and no particular philosophy except one's own experience, which is extremely powerful and dynamic. It is a question of being rather than figuring out what to be or how to be...the speciality of vajrayāna is the

enormous appreciation of relative truth, which brings us skillful means as well. The problem with our lives is not so much that we don't understand enough Buddhist philosophy, but that we don't know how to live as Buddhists, as the followers of the dharma.

—Chögyam Trungpa Rinpoche

Tantra is an esoteric tradition that has been held as rare and supreme. So tantric teachings are said to be secret, both in the sense that they cannot be understood by the uninitiated, as well as not being proclaimed publicly. The secrecy protects both the teachings and us. We might think we understand them but they can be co-opted by ego. We could simplify their profundity, come away with a distorted view, and most likely reject them. Traditionally, Tantra had been practiced by yogins and yoginis, men and women, living outside of the boundaries of conventional society to circumvent the need to conform. Now, more of these teachings have moved from the esoteric into the public domain. As the Dalai Lama said, the time for secrecy is over. This is good news! Deep answers are needed now more than ever.

Mahāmudrā

The hallmark of Tantra and the primary context of Five Wisdoms are the teachings of Mahāmudrā and Maha Ati (AKA dzogchen). They emphasize embodiment and the immediacy of experience, bringing us into a fuller kind of existence. They have the power of grounding wisdom energy within us as well as embracing everyday reality.

Mahāmudrā is a synonym for such-ness, here-ness. It is not simply awareness, but an enlightened state of being. We simply rest in the very ordinary mind of nowness. This leads to a true understanding that there is no goal, only this moment. We feel the totality, the unceasing wisdom play of the phenomenal world. It is inviting us to participate. We experience our world as apparent yet empty. It becomes less solid and more illusory, like a dream. We enjoy our sense perceptions and mingle ourself with the sights and sounds and tastes of our world. There is a tangible atmosphere, a quality or texture to our experience that is both ordinary and magical.

One of the ways that Mahāmudrā is practiced is by celebrating. My experience of the program environment created by Khenpo Rinpoche for fourteen years at Karmê Chöling retreat center was magical. The day begins at seven in the morning with exercises interspersed with singing, dancing, and playing, and progresses to presentations of song and dance in the evening. There was a sense of moveable feast throughout the day and into the night. It was a magical environment where wisdom and freedom were brought together. Creating this magical situation was Khenpo Rinpoche's gift to us.

> Mahāmudrā, which is the basic nature of mind, is beyond words...As a result of the posture that you have developed through meditative discipline and the awareness techniques you have been using, such as following the breath, you begin to notice that there are moments of gap, moments of fresh outlook, moments of letting go, and moments of a natural sense of existence. There are moments of natural relaxation. This is the practice of Mahāmudrā, which cuts through any habitual tendencies, any thought processes that could create problems...One's whole practice should be based on the relationship between you and nowness.
>
> –Chögyam Trungpa Rinpoche

Not maintaining the view of Mahāmudrā is a momentary error or mistake. We forget, we freeze. Wisdom becomes hidden. Though we have forgotten, we have not strayed far because the error is also included. Ha ha! Gotcha! It acts as a source of awareness, a reminder. Our mistake is reversed and we wake up in the moment. From the perspective of the Five Wisdoms, it is perpetually aligning ourself with the wisdom aspect of the energies.

At times, I have had penetrating experiences of Mahāmudrā mind. A favorite practice is to do grocery shopping in this state of mind. Everything around me becomes penetratingly delightful. On a solitary retreat, I would sit for hours on a high rock overlooking a vast valley encircled by mountains. Timelessness and spacelessness were both magical and ordinary. My heart kept opening and opening as tears ran down my face.

Maha Ati

Mahāmudrā works with the texture of our world, the nitty gritty of our experience. It is a way to navigate the path; with Ati we have already arrived and we rest there. We see there is no need to strive as the journey no longer needs to be made. We might think that we need never have made the journey at all. Yet it was necessary to acclimatize ourself to the final shock of a big mind. It is the end of the journey because there is an absence of journey. The sense of journeylessness, neither journey nor journier, brings out pure brilliance. Its simplicity is disarming.

The view of Ati is necessary because we have to let go of the very mind that got us here. It is a further dissolving into larger space, the greatest opening of our mind. Mind becomes nothing, so encompasses everything. Awareness is non-awareness. Awareness of something binds us. So non-awareness is the best kind of awareness. With Ati, a big mind just got bigger. It is like outer space—unconditionally vast and completely fathomless. The radiance is unceasing. The attitude of Ati provides a new dimension of shock. It is like the sky is falling and there is no escape.

We have come a perfect 360 degrees, back to square one. We have used up, or run out of, any form of defending ourself and we no longer have the hassle of maintaining ourself. All relative reference points and notions of good and bad, simplicity and confusion, don't apply. We find there is freedom beyond conventional norms. Just being becomes an expression of bliss. Disarming ourself completely and thoroughly heightens the possibility of bliss. Great bliss is invincible and victorious, a fundamental relaxation and ultimate nakedness. There is a sense of great purity. We see all phenomenon are equal in their true nature, apparent yet empty.

With Mahāmudrā we are in a colorful world, enjoying the Five Wisdoms. There is space but always a texture to the space. With Ati, there is just luminous space. In Mahāmudrā, our neurosis and wisdom are inseparable. We burn our neurosis in the wisdom bonfire. In Ati, neurosis is self-liberated on the spot, like a snowflake hitting a hot coal. It dissolves instantly because space is invincible, primordially pure from the beginning. In Mahāmudrā, whatever happens has inherent wisdom. In Ati, nothing happens. We are awake all of the time. Being awake reaches its full measure as great brilliance and luminosity. We are not the king or queen of the universe; we are the universe.

The Indestructible Vehicle

Tantra is called the diamond vehicle, because it is indestructible like a diamond. It is the truth of the truth and once realized, it will never be diminished. It's like reaching the highest, most glorious peak. Our state of being is transformed into the highest unwavering awareness, empowering beyond compare. Tantric realization is maintained by a commitment to remain in the view and not wander, so there is a sense that our mind is always protected. We are not swayed by the petty whims of our neurosis. It is impossible to forget or stray from the view because any slip or mistake is included. The occurrences of the day are perfectly pure, apparent but empty.

Traditionally, there are warnings about entering the Vajrayāna as there is an inherent danger in working with energetic reality. There are stories in the tradition that make this approach look ruthless to the point of uncompassionate. We could either be scared or attracted by such a world. Because the path of Tantra is experiential, our life becomes very real and very direct. We do not know what we will discover, so we could have misgivings or fear. It is often called the quick path as its methods are so powerful. Tantra is also very demanding. This is not a Sunday-go-to-church kind of spirituality. Ultimately, it is not about feeling good or being nice, but waking up. We could be open and intrigued, but at the same time, Tantra is not for the faint of heart.

> ...ego can only handle a low voltage of the electricity of reality...If you suddenly plug into a power plant that is radiating Vajrayāna energy, exposing you to the naked reality of the world, ego's wiring will melt...The Vajrayāna path is like putting a chemical compound on a lead plate. It begins to eat you up and also begins to make some patterns. Wherever you're not eaten up, it begins to create some kind of work of art [the best of who you are]. And what's reproduced from that plate is called Tantra...
>
> —Chögyam Trungpa Rinpoche

There was an amusing moment when we were all sitting around in a faculty meeting at Naropa Institute. The publicity department had proposed putting the word "contemplative" into our by-line and we were discussing the ramifications. Some thought it would make us look wishy-washy. Someone said it would make us sound like zombies. Then Peter Orlovsky, longtime companion to Allen Ginsberg, said, "Why don't we say, 'hot contemplative.'" Tantric Buddhism is definitely hot contemplative!

Perhaps we had hoped an awakened mind would create some stability. Yes and no. As we say, "You can't stop the waves but you can learn to surf them." The fact that we find ourself on shaky ground is actually good news. It is acknowledging the inseparability of our existence and non-existence. Like a sand castle, now it is here and then, with the next big wave, it is gone. This leaves us with a certain sense of bewilderment. And why not? Rather than perpetually acting from ego's perspective to manipulate the world to our advantage, we find ourself at a loss. We are more confused and more sane at the same time. We could feel a sense of freedom and excitement, a willingness to experience life directly. This is the gateway to transformation and liberation. Something real is happening. This indefinable, ineffable experience rings true. It penetrates us to the core. The fundamental truth is that the basic sanity of enlightenment is irritatingly possible. The problem is that we don't prefer sanity.

Enlightenment is ego's ultimate disappointment.

–Chögyam Trungpa Rinpoche

Enlightenment is permanent because we have not produced it. We have merely discovered it.

–Chögyam Trungpa Rinpoche

Enlightenment is like witnessing the brilliant sun for the first time in the morning. It is like seeing the beautiful flowers that grow in the wood, the frolicking deer, a bird flying proudly, or fish swimming. Life is not all that grim. In the morning you brush your teeth, you can see how shiny they are. Reality has its own gallantry, spark, and arrogance. You can study life while you are alive. You can study how you can achieve the brilliance of life.

—Chögyam Trungpa Rinpoche

We have been indoctrinated that if we don't use the conceptual mind, we can't function. But here is the great switcheroo, we actually function much better! Vastness becomes the backdrop to all our actions. We develop an efficient radar system that intuitively synchronizes with the coincidence of the moment. By encountering our world more directly, we function more accurately. We are awake rather than learned or clever. The conceptual mind clouds things by always having a bias, an allegiance to something. It is very plodding, always going through linear logic, black and white, right and wrong, for and against. It cannot engage with the depth because it is too self-involved. It does not see the big picture, so actions could be flawed. The gist is that we need to give up ego's power to realize a greater power. It gives us more sense of freedom to deal with things properly.

> When we begin to look beyond duality, we see that it is not just empty and nonexistent. We begin to realize that beyond egohood, there is still tremendous aliveness, vitality, strength, and energy. This aliveness and energy is luminous and bright, and it contains tremendous wisdom.
>
> —Chögyam Trungpa Rinpoche

In embracing Tantra, we acknowledge everyone's potential to be a fully realized human being. We trust in our body, trust in our senses, and trust in our energy. There is the sense that things are already elucidated. Our only job is to see them and not be afraid of seeing such nakedness. We feel we have been confirmed in who we are, what we are. Not knowing who we are, we have been holding our breath. Now, there is a sense of wholesomeness in ourself and in our world.

Enlightenment is intimacy with all things.

–Dogen Zenji (1200–1253)

At this point the world is our teacher. As tantrikas, we re-possess the world and see it in an enlightened way. We are continually open to the feedback that comes from the phenomenal world. Duality is not a problem, it just is. We created samsaric reality by our neurotic projections. Now we identify with our basic sanity and discover the pervasive communication between the world and ourself.

Mind and its projections are innocent. They are very ordinary, very natural, and very simple. Red is not evil, and white is not divine; blue is not evil, and green is not divine. Sky is sky; rock is rock; earth is earth; mountains are mountains. I am what I am, and you are what you are. There are no obstacles to experiencing our world properly, and nothing is regarded as problematic.

–Chögyam Trungpa Rinpoche

We discover that nothing is permanent but impermanence; nothing is continuous but discontinuity; everything is apparent yet not inherently existing. Since the relative world comes together through causes and conditions, it is not permanent. Commonly, we define our existence through our experience, but our experience arises out of a false sense of reality. We take things to be real, have a physical existence, and do not take to heart "Here today; gone tomorrow." Birth, old age, illness, and death all point to the truth of impermanence. Life is like a dream, apparent yet having no intrinsic reality. This allows us a lighter way to be involved with life.

Being unencumbered by our habitual ways of being, we can engage freely and dynamically with energy. Seeing and experiencing reality directly and spontaneously, we are more present in our being and more genuine in our actions. This experience has been called "beginner's mind." Suzuki Roshi, a Zen Buddhist teacher, once said, "In the beginner's mind there are many possibilities, but in the expert's there are few." Suzuki Roshi has also called this the mind of readiness which is cultivated as a way of being. The mind is always open, flexible, and inquisitive.

Wisdom is pure awareness or knowingness that sees the way things are. It sees the truth, or higher truth. A *sense* of wisdom is expressible in words, but the *experience* is inexpressible. As our capacity for awareness increases, the depth of our wisdom increases. We increasingly move away from our rational mind to one of pure awareness. Simply put, aligning with ultimate wisdom is like having a deep reservoir of unshakeable strength. Rather than being buffeted by the ups and downs of daily occurrence, we can rest in the ultimate view of emptiness. Rather than being made uneasy by the clouds, we can align with the vast open sky.

This state of mind allows us to distance ourself from the entanglements of outer circumstances which make our life unstable. If we have the ability to rest in equanimity, we relax. Trungpa Rinpoche had some great ways of driving this home: NBD means "no big deal" and CCL means "couldn't care less." We do care, but at some level nothing is that important. The particulars of our existence come and go. There is a sense of workability. Whatever arises we meet directly with the view of the inseparability of confusion and wisdom. Therefore, there is no reason to regard anything as a problem.

We have developed our ability to work with a lot of power and so gained strength. We have nothing to fear, so we have no reason to regard things as threatening. We have a bird's-eye view, a big perspective. We have an increased capacity for compassion, wisdom, and discipline. We can relate to greater pain and sadness because we are not bound by our conceptual mind. We can be anywhere and become anything, but we are always connected with what is needed. Profound wisdom does not change, but each time we re-visit a teaching, we have changed, so we go deeper. Wisdom has no beginning or end. It is in the moment and outside the moment, both precise and expansive.

The metaphor of the seasons is an apt one in terms of looking at this journey. We are born in the middle of winter, frozen, but we see that winter has an end. We begin to feel spring, some kind of thawing, softness. We cultivate our field, spread manure, and sow seeds. The journey continues and we have summer where there is an opening, a flowering. In the fall, we celebrate our good harvest. We go through this journey again and again. We feel further ripened with each cycle. Our existence begins to change.

CHAPTER 18

A Radical Perspective
on Wisdom

There is a vast store of energy which is not centered, which is not ego's energy at all. It is this energy which is the centerless dance of phenomena, the universe interpenetrating and making love to itself...And this energy is always ongoing, whether or not it is seen through the confused filter of ego. It cannot be destroyed or interrupted at all. It is like the ever-burning sun. It consumes everything to the point where it allows no room for doubt or manipulation.

–Chögyam Trungpa Rinpoche

In this chapter we are going to look at expanded states of consciousness—where our conditioned mind has less of a hold on us—and the relationship between Tantra and quantum physics in seeing that all is energy.

When the word wisdom comes to mind, we tend to think of a wise person, a profound book, or an ancient lineage of teachings. We might understand what wisdom has come to mean in a particular culture. In Japan and China, truth is expressed as heart-mind. Quakers speak of wisdom as "the inner light" and "the light in the world." The hallmark of Buddhist

252

traditions is the teachings on emptiness, shunyata, the realization of which brings inner peace. Tantric Buddhism has a radical perspective, shedding quite a different light on our understanding of wisdom.

Energetic reality is the touchstone, the heartbeat, of Tantra. It is an understanding of primordial dynamic energy that is the basis of our existence, vast and ungraspable. This immense unoriginated powerful energy is all-pervasive, unconditional, unbiased, and indestructible. It is without seeming cause. In this primordial sense of space and time, we can energetically experience a positive life force as a transpersonal knowing or intuitive understanding. It allows us to see the energetic reality of the Five Wisdoms Energies.

Tantra sees the world as a living web of profound interconnectedness. This view of interconnection is seen in aboriginal cultures, some religions, contemplative traditions, and by emerging scientific paradigms. It is an experiential, inclusive spirituality. It sensitizes us to the rhythms of nature as well as lending clarity to all human interactions. As such it serves as the basis for action that is both compassionate and effective. This view is as ancient as primordial time and as new as quantum physics.

The primal energy of cosmic space, constantly in flux, is immeasurable and ongoing whether we are aware of it or not, like it or not, or learn to ride it or not. There's nothing we can grasp. The continuity of birth and death takes place every moment, every instant. Impermanence is the continuity. It is impartial, not something we can manipulate. It is indifferent to our ups and downs. We can't make deals with energetic space because it couldn't care less. We are not front-and-center in terms of the cosmic world. Space is an obstacle to our ego, it stops us in our tracks. Trungpa Rinpoche said space is "powerfully uncompassionate." It's analogous to our perception of death. It is both threatening and uncompromising. However, it also liberating. We can't get stuck in space!

We come to a realization of this ultimate reality through awakening to it, not through reasoning mind. Contemplating the infinite is hard to do. It is our fear that makes us narrow our perceptions and habitually tend to our everyday world. We keep ourself busy to avoid the vastness of space. However, we first open to it in glimpses when we begin to appreciate the empty gap of non-thought. We could find ourself absolutely nowhere, suspended in some kind of space. Such experiences could occur throughout our life. Once we experience the empty space, nothing can shake our knowing it. It becomes a powerful self-existing truth. We then see the world as ephemeral, both existent and nonexistent. It brings a sense of peace, free of the reference points of subjective and objective reality and the fixation that causes our suffering.

Space, the Final Frontier

Buddhists have a lot to say about space. Where other people go blank, we start talking. As my then twenty-year-old son said, "Only a Buddhist talks about space for hours on end."

Conventionally, we think of space as empty, open, nothingness, unobstructed, the great beyond where nothing is happening. It is what is between objects, and a table or person is a solid entity. We assume objects are real.

When we look out, it all seems pretty real. Moreover, we think of ourself as solid, me, and space is all that is not me. So, we are constantly creating a boundary protecting ourself against space. It becomes the walls of our fortress. If we are solid, then space is a threat, it's our undoing, our death.

The boundary is also the walls of our prison. We imprison ourself by the very creation of a boundary: stuck, frozen, solid, heavy, numb. We are captured inside our world, separate from the world out there. We try to relate to our world through gloves, but it doesn't work or satisfy. Because of this, we are constantly in a struggle with space, trying to maintain our ground but at the same time, not suffocating or strangling ourself. We are constantly asking ourself how open, or how protected we need to be in a given situation. Those little flickers of mind shut us down—"Oh, I'm not going to say hello to that person." "No way, I can't go along with this, it's against my principles." And that's what we're doing all of the time, close off, withdraw, don't get near. We sense a threat and become fearful, losing touch with a free-flowing sense of ourself.

Quantum Physics and Tantra

It is exciting to see that the forefront of scientific discoveries and Tantric Buddhism have a deep resonance with each other. For instance, catching up with the Buddha, science declares that everything is energy! Whether it's understanding the cosmos through quantum physics or understanding our inner energy through the polyvagal system, there is much that can be said about the relationship between the observable world and the spiritual realm.

First, a disclosure: I am neither a scientist nor an academic. I teach Tantric Buddhism in a very experiential way. My deep-dive has been into Buddhism, not science. Yet, the reason I feel I have some sense of quantum physics in a valid way, particularly the work of David Bohm, and dare to bring it up here, is I understand Tantra. Tantric practitioners have a first-person approach, experiencing reality through contemplative practices. They do not need proof. Scientists have a third-person approach, looking at objective reality. They like proof.

Both Tantra and quantum physics understand that the space of totality is imbued with self-perpetuating energy constantly in flux. Space and energy can be seen as synonymous! Space is full, not empty. It is solid, in that it is full of relative things. Space is not static but full of change and transformation.

From the tantric point of view, energetic space has three basic qualities: vastness, accommodation, and acceptance. It lets things happen to their fullest extent because it is not conditioned. It does not depend on dualistic concepts and the relative world. Space is where all of the action is. It has tremendous power and is invincible.

Although we mostly think of the world in terms of material existence, its basic vitality or vibrant aspect is energy. Energy pervades every aspect of the phenomenal world. It is the quality, texture, ambiance, or feeling tone of the animate and the inanimate, the visible and the invisible. It manifests in the places and situations all around us like landscapes, seasons, colors, the elements, and environments. It is in the soft rolling hills and jagged peaks, winter and summer, a cozy living room and an airport. The energy of the phenomenal world is everywhere!

At times we see chaos and confusion and become entrenched in it. At other times we awaken to the beauty and order of reality. What happens is sometimes predictable and sometimes surprising. When we are in tune with the energies, we experience our connection to everyone and everything in an energetic matrix. This is the mandala.

The mandala of unconditioned being is primordial intelligence, a transcendent knowingness. It has no limitations. How do we experience it? We *feel* it—a non-referential, unbiased, transpersonal knowing or intuitive understanding of the totality and interconnectedness of everything. We meet the world directly with the myriad of combinations of our wisdom energies.

Understanding the world in this way may seem foreign. It's true. Quantum physics shows us that nothing is as it seems, or as we have known it to be. It sees that the world is made of energy constantly in flux, that energy is the basis of everything, and that our world has much more to do with dynamic play than matter, substance. This points to the natural instability and constant change that is in fact the nature of the world.

The day science begins to study non-physical phenomena, it will make more progress in one decade than in all the previous centuries of its existence.

–Nikola Tesla

Ready for a deep dive with David Bohm? He went way beyond the understandings of quantum physics to fully embracing the relationship between science and spirituality. He's the man! His deep friendship with Jiddu Krishnamurti, a spiritual teacher and philosopher from India, was helpful. This friendship confirmed, in an experiential way, what Bohm was discovering through physics.

His theory has what he calls the Implicate Order and the Explicate Order. The Implicate Order is an ultra-holistic cosmic view. The underlying theme of his theory is the "unbroken wholeness of the totality of existence as an undivided flowing movement without borders." He believed that the bizarre behavior of subatomic particles might be the result of unobserved sub-quantum forces and particles, a hidden-ness which may be reflective of a deeper dimension of reality. He maintained that space and time might actually be derived from an even deeper level of objective reality. The layers of the Implicate Order can go deeper and deeper to the ultimately unknown. It is this unknown and indescribable totality that Bohm calls the holomovement. He explains that the holomovement is the "fundamental ground of all matter."

In the Implicate Order, everything is connected and "everything is enfolded into everything," as Bohm states it. This enfoldment takes place in the movement of the electromagnetic field and also in that of other fields (electronic, protonic, etc.). Electromagnetic energy (such as light or heat) does not always behave like a continuous wave. Therefore, light has a dual character. Under certain circumstances, it may display wavelike aspects, movement; and in other circumstances, it may have the characteristics of particles, solidity. This dynamic energy has the potential to become manifest reality because the sub-atomic particles function as both waves and particles, energy and form, depending on circumstance. When unobserved, they act like waves, energetic flow. When observed, energy consolidates into physical entities.

In this dimension of reality, any subatomic particles that have once interacted can instantaneously "respond to each other's motions thousands of years later when they are light-years apart," Bohm says. This particle interconnectedness is intrinsic because they are connected in the Implicate Order. Such movement of light waves is present everywhere and, in principle, includes the entire universe of space and time. So, in theory, any individual element could reveal information about every other element in the universe. These fields obey quantum-mechanical laws, implying the properties of discontinuity and non-locality. This means that few things can be predicted; there are only the probabilities of any particular outcome.

The Explicate Order is where things are unfolded rather than enfolded. It is secondary, derivative. It flows out of the law of the Implicate Order. Within the Explicate Order, there is a "totality of forms that have an approximate kind of recurrence (changing), stability, and separability." According to Bohm, it is these forms that make up our manifest world.

Everything that is and will be in this cosmos is enfolded within the Implicate Order. There is a cosmic movement to the process of enfoldment and unfoldment, in endless feedback cycles that create an infinite variety of manifest forms and mentality. The universe is endlessly recreating itself. The implicate is the source of all that becomes the explicate. Bohm believed that a fundamental Cosmic Intelligence is the Player in this process engaged in endless experimentation and creativity. This Player, the Cosmic Intelligence, is in constant movement accruing an infinity of experienced being!

Have I lost you? Don't expect to grasp this all at once. But let's go on.

Let's look at some parallels between Bohm's understandings and Tantric Buddhism. Both see that a web of energy, the fundamental ground of all matter, is un-originated and indestructible. It makes up all existence and contains all of the information of the past, present, and future. Both see that everything is connected in a constant dance, what scientists call quantum entanglement and Tantra calls the mandala. Quantum entanglement means that particles are energetically entangled and will remain affected by one another regardless of physical distance. In Tantra, the mandala is the timeless interconnectedness of everything.

Both speak of the natural instability and constant change in our existence as the nature of the world. Another parallel is that scientists understand that sub-atomic particles can manifest as energy and form, and Buddhists understand dimensions of reality, the subtle energetic and the manifest. Energy materializes and thus creates the manifest consensus reality.

Auspicious Coincidence and Riding Energy

Conventionally, we think that we need to manipulate the world to get what we want. As a result, we often become confused when trying to decide how to act. In fact, we don't have to exert energy, we only need to join with self-existing energy. The world presents us with occasions when energy comes together in time and space and creates a confluence of circumstances to which we can respond directly, being in tune with what is going on. Like kayaking or skiing, when we surrender to the natural flow of movement, we don't think about what to do next, we just do it. When we connect with energy, synchronicity happens as a matter of course.

When we open to the matrix of energies, we ride the coincidence of the moment. All is clear and precise and we act in response to the situation. There is no goal other than responding to the moment. When we know how to ride the energies, our actions are a spontaneous and appropriate response to whatever situation we are in. We feel the confluence of energies and align with it. Tantra calls this auspicious coincidence. Auspicious coincidence is within the manifest reality of the Explicate Order but is beyond the linear understanding of cause and effect, as it arises from the Implicate order. It is beyond karma. What happens happens.

Our ego is constantly trying to deny this reality. We are generally unable to experience the energetic dimension because we are so busy creating a protective shell for ourself. We put great effort into grounding ourself in what we take to be real in a palpable way. It is hard for us to accept that this fleeting, transient, impermanent situation is actually the reality of our existence. However, this is exactly what the Buddha realized over 2500 years ago. Science is finally catching up with the Buddha!

Edgar Mitchell, who was part of the Apollo 14 lunar team, experienced an astonishing change of consciousness, a spiritual awakening. He came to see that the cosmos has a deeper aspect to it, a purpose and intelligent design. He saw this through an inner knowing beyond the rational intellect. He then devoted himself to the study of the human mind so that he might help raise awareness of the divinity within us. He founded The Institute of Noetic Sciences (IONS). Noetics is the study of consciousness. The institute focuses on scientific investigation of a wide range of phenomena and issues involving human awareness. In 1978, Dr. Willis Harman, the president of IONS, said,

> ...the noetic sciences are...the esoteric core of all the world's religions, East and West, ancient and modern...A noetic science—a science of consciousness and the world

of inner experience—is the most promising contemporary framework within which to carry on that fundamental moral inquiry which stable human societies have always had to place at the center of their concerns.

Crazy Wisdom

In Tantric Buddhism, crazy wisdom is another radical perspective on wisdom. It is embodied in teachers who have the highest realization and who break the boundaries of conventional norms. Such teachers meet the world at a cosmic level, which can seem crazy in conventional thinking. It is the absence of dualistic thinking, the ultimate thinking outside the box, a penetrating intelligence which knows no limits. Trungpa Rinpoche was a crazy wisdom teacher.

> Those who danced were thought to be insane by those who could not hear the music.
>
> –Source unknown

Crazy wisdom holders experience sacredness at a primal level. They communicate an extraordinarily ordinary presence by just being, and yet at times can act in outrageous ways. At times, Trungpa Rinpoche was so powerfully direct that it was truly terrifying to be around him. His words could be transmitted not by linear, logical thinking but by creating incidents and environments or atmospheres. In this way, everything becomes a teaching. They accept the social norms of society but continually color it with insight and craziness at the same time. Such realized beings are not shackled by self-serving ego and so transcend the fear of birth and death.

The reality of the world could be called self-secret. Something spiritual or mystical in this sense means something that strikes the truth. True spirituality is an absence of frivolity, an absence of belief in good and bad in the religious sense, an absence of religiosity. It is that which is contained in the living situation, which speaks truth, which reminds you of the natural situation of things as they are.

–Chögyam Trungpa Rinpoche

Crazy wisdom has a sense of being eternally awake. There is a simultaneity of immense vision, control, and relaxation. This awake mind feels young, innocent, and free; a childlike quality that is fresh, inquisitive, and sparkling. It is not caught up in hope and fear. There is no room for doctrine. It has no concern for good and bad, whether this or that exists, or the threat of death. It is indestructible as it is without cowardice and paranoia. Within a sense of emptiness there is a sense of potentiality. It is empty but also fertile and tangible.

I am particularly struck by a crazy-wisdom holder's attitude toward death. His Holiness Karmapa was lying on his deathbed when visited by a senior student who was sobbing. His Holiness said to the student, "This is nothing." The phrase *there's no such thing as dying to be done* means that we become one with everything. What is emphasized is that if we have not been able to achieve this understanding in our lifetime, death is an opportune time to do it. In letting go of our body, that which grounds us to this material dimension, we are liberated. Khenpo Tsültrim Gyamtso, when one of his students told him she had cancer said, "How wonderful! What a great opportunity!"

Crazy wisdom is crazy gone wise, rather than wisdom gone crazy. It is an embodied power that can make straightforward decisions to care for whatever needs to be cared for. It tunes into cosmic energy and then executes whatever needs to be done. It has to do with radiating, communicating, and acting. It's an energy that continually regenerates rather than depletes itself. Because it cuts through conventional norms, it actually relates more properly with the world. It brings a certain practicality to life in that there is the ability to operate without ego. It's absolutely wise, doesn't allow compromise, and so is somewhat heavy-handed. It thrives on dangerous energy.

> Wisdom does not permit compromise. If you compromise between black and white, you come out with a grey color—not quite white and not quite black. It is a sad medium rather than a happy medium—disappointing. You feel sorry that you've let it be compromised. You feel totally wretched that you have compromised. That is why crazy wisdom does not know any compromise.
>
> —Chögyam Trungpa Rinpoche

The Five Wisdoms Energies

Primordial energy cannot be appropriated by anyone, yet it has characteristics. The cosmic web of self-existing primordial energy is the dancing ground of the Five Wisdoms Energies. We discover that energy breaks out into different reflections that we experience as different characteristics, textures, qualities, and tones: a violent storm, a capricious teenager, or an aging grandmother. The way these patterns of energy manifest are somewhat predictable so we can categorize them into five different energetic styles or families. They also merge and layer, become dominant and recessive, strong and gentle, and there are countless permutations.

In human beings, the energy is psychophysical. We experience a particular quality of emotion and we also feel it in our body. Energy permeates all of our relationships as well as our philosophical beliefs. The energy of the phenomenal world also rubs up against us, creating a dynamic tension. So, our personal energy is constantly in the flow of the self-existing energy of the totality.

The Five Wisdoms are our starting point to experience embodied wisdom. They allow us to go beyond a conceptual understanding of wisdom into the direct experience of energetic reality. We develop an unbiased, transpersonal knowing or intuitive understanding that points to a multi-level experience, both embodied and ethereal. This *is* tantric wisdom. Then we begin to realize the value of wisdom. It is priceless.

CHAPTER 19

Your World Just Got Bigger

We can begin to have extraordinary panoramic vision with no limitations. We drop our reference point, so we can go anywhere. When we choose to go with a particular energy, a particular direction, our choice is not based on a sense of agenda. We have directionless direction. It is an entirely new approach to time and space. We can approach time because it is timeless, we can approach space because it is spaceless. There is a direction because there are no directions at the same time. This opens up tremendous possibilities of another way of looking at the whole thing. Without reference points we can't keep track of anything. Wanting to keep track would be like wanting to attend our own funeral.

–Chögyam Trungpa Rinpoche

Expanded states of consciousness can revolutionize your understanding of the self and create a deeper connection with who you are…interconnectedness with life impacts your relationship with the world.

–Dan Siegel

In this chapter we are going to look at the mandala principle. It sees the cohesiveness of all existence, the fabric of the universe, a dynamic synergistic system of infinitely interconnected energy and interlocking relationships. It's essence is that of a continual dynamic of arising, dwelling, and dissolving. It is constantly in flux.

We discover that the microcosm of our life, and the macrocosm of the universe are inextricably interconnected. We could experience a tremendous expansion of our inner life, pushing through boundaries of the self into the inseparability of inner and outer vastness. We come to a deep knowing that everything and everyone is connected to everything and everyone else. It is a penetrating insight into *interbeing*—a word coined by Thich Nhat Hanh. As he said, "You cannot just be by yourself alone. You have to inter-be with every other thing."

> We do not need to invent a ground of connectedness, but only to realize it. We are all one, but we do not live in that knowledge. Human beings need to become more aware of the interrelatedness of their existence.
>
> –Charlene Spretnak

Everything is many layered and interwoven, existing interdependently: if that exists, this exists; if this exists, that exists. We are affected by all that goes on around us at many different levels. Every action we make sets in motion interdependent causes and conditions beyond comprehension. Just think, that we were born and live in this world is due to inconceivable circumstances.

We realize we do not live in a vacuum, but are deeply connected to all that exists. We see that wholeness is our natural state and unrelated separateness is an illusion. When we work with reality properly, a rapport takes place between us and the external world. It creates a network or system of circulating relationships. Ignoring the relationship between ourself and the outside world creates problems. As we are becoming more and more aware, the separate self now threatens the survival of our species.

> It really boils down to this: that all life is interrelated. We are all caught in an inescapable network of mutuality, tied into a single garment of destiny. Whatever affects one directly, affects all indirectly. We are made to live together because of the interrelated structure of reality.
>
> –Dr. Martin Luther King Jr.

All that is conditioned comes from this unconditioned space, as we see in the Implicate Order and Explicate Order. The continual dynamic of arising and dissolving gives rise to endless expressions, the energetic dance of all phenomenon. Everything is spontaneously present in ever-changing patterns: circulating, interconnecting, and interweaving. Energy is cohesive, self-organizing, and has energetic integrity.

Like a mirror, the mandala reflects everything equally. It does not accept or reject; it encompasses everything. Any one aspect of the mandala can evoke anything else in the limitless expanse of space and energy. We could experience connections between the smallest experience and the vastest experience, from the most ordinary to the most sublime.

The mandala perspective offers us the opportunity for a lifelong, very rich and very deep, understanding. When steeped in the mandala perspective, our responses are appropriate because we are connected. We could be anywhere and become anything, but we are always connected with whatever is needed.

The Mandala of Phenomenon

Let's look at mandala from the perspective of how the elements come together to manifest our world. The forces of nature are elemental energy in the raw. Earth is solid, firm, and trustworthy: a good foundation and nourishing ground. Water is fluid, changeable, it can be forceful and flowing or still and reflective. Fire is playful and intense, quixotic and passionate, and impossible to grasp. Air might manifest as a light refreshing breeze, or as a harsh hurricane. The elements that create the manifest world are the same as those which constitute our body. We are born, come into being with the elements; we die as the elements dissolve.

Mother Nature has a constant momentum. There is a time to create summer and autumn and winter and spring. There is a time for snowfall, and a time for rain or a hailstorm. We know that the tides are connected to the moon, the seasons are connected to the earth moving around the sun, and the weather is connected to an infinite number of variables. Astrology understands that the positioning of the planets and stars at our birth dictates the energetic aspect of who we are. All processes are exquisitely natural.

Sometimes the forces of our world are destructive, like a tsunami or a perfect storm that wreaks havoc. Sometimes those forces are benevolent and create an inviting environment in which we can relax, come to a sense of peace, and enjoy ourself. Some places, perhaps sacred to many people, give us inspiration. We call them our retreat or power spots. This is also true of people. It does not take much for a leader in power to create mass destruction. As well, leaders who are aligned with benevolence can create tremendous good.

Ultimately, deep ecological awareness is spiritual or religious awareness. When the concept of the human spirit is
understood as the mode of consciousness in which the individual feels a sense of belonging, of connectedness, to the
cosmos as a whole, it becomes clear that ecological awareness is spiritual in its deepest sense.

—Fritjof Capra

A mandala can also be in time, showing the progress of a
day or a course of action. Buddha energy has a sense of accommodation or basic space. Vajra is connected with dawn, when
light is first reflected on the world. It is a symbol of awakening,
a sharpness of experience. Ratna is connected with midday,
when we begin to need refreshment, nourishment. Padma is
when it is time to socialize, to make a date with our lover.
Karma is when all is accomplished and our day is complete.

Orderly Chaos

Trungpa Rinpoche termed the mandala principle "orderly
chaos." The confused or chaotic mandala is samsara, the world
of constriction, small mind, tunnel vision. It's the way we most
commonly experience the world. We go around and around
with our favorite top tunes and believe our story line. Maintaining ego is oriented toward security and so creates territory
and boundary, which creates a dualistic world of this (self) as
opposed to that (other). We are fixated on what we hold dear.
This is familiar and safe, *that* is unknown and a threat.

However, the samsaric mandala and the wisdom mandala
are interdependent, equal, and reciprocal. Confusion is the dynamic aliveness, and awareness sees that the confusion has a predictable order. Confusion and sanity commingle. There is
nothing to get rid of and nothing to gain. All is included. The

Five Wisdoms perspective points to the indivisibility between samsara, the cycle of birth, suffering, and death in our conditioned existence, and nirvana, a transcendent state in which there is no self and no suffering. We tend to see them as polarities: the confusion and pain of our samsaric existence, which we want to get rid of, and the spaciousness of awakened mind, which we long for. What we begin to see is that wisdom lies within confusion and it becomes clear that the wisdom mandala is born out of the confused mandala.

> We fail to regard samsara as something very powerful, very energetic. We tend to dismiss it as belonging to an area of mistake, not realizing that the mistake has been made seriously and meaningfully.
>
> –Chögyam Trungpa Rinpoche

When we begin to have a felt sense, as opposed to a conceptual idea, that the energy of the universe does not belong to anybody, we awaken to the mandala of freedom, a big mind. We transcend ego's game of duality, which deliberately obscures the vast vision of the mandala. We open to the magical aspects of our world. There is a sense of wholesomeness and vividness to everything. We feel nourished, healthy, and strong. We feel more alive. It can be heartbreakingly beautiful and feels like we could stay there forever.

Since the wisdom mandala is born out of the confused mandala, we only experience it when we enter the confused mandala. When we stay with the confusion, a primordial intelligence or transcendent knowingness arises. It is pervasive, extraordinarily awake, lively, and powerful. This is the mandala of freedom, of a big mind, of an inborn intelligence. It is without origin. It is a greater atmosphere, a whole sphere expressing the vivid reality of life. The main point is that we can't dictate what happens, not because we give up trying, but because phenomenon is self-existing. The resistance to seeing the totality is fear. When we let go of our struggle and pain, the energy of the mandala flows. The mandala slogan is "What happens happens."

> There is chaos of all kinds developing all the time: psychological dis-order, social dis-order, metaphysical dis-order, constantly happening. If you are trying to stop those situations, you are looking for external means of liberating yourself. But if we are able to look into the basic situation, then chaos is the inspiration, confusion is the inspiration…we could relate with the whole process with the basic understanding that confusion is a stepping stone. Confusion means wisdom from that point of view.
>
> –Chögyam Trungpa Rinpoche

We are not trying to stop chaotic situations, but accept them and get into them, daring to experience the vital force of confusion. Confusion is the starting point because it invites further questioning, which reveals clarity. We wake up in the midst of the confusion. Turning away from the confusion is spiritual bypassing. It's a question of whether we're willing to accept the claustrophobia as brilliant or not. The possibility of awakening is ever-present. If we really understood the link between the mandala of confusion and the mandala of awakened awareness—not just conceptually but viscerally—we'd be pretty enlightened!

Nowness

Nowness is the sense that we are attuned to what is happening. The past is fiction and the future is a dream, and we are just living on the edge of a razor blade. It is extraordinarily sharp, extraordinarily tentative and quivering. We try to establish ground but the ground is not solid enough, because it is too sharp. We are quivering between that and this...This razor-blade quality is something more than psychological irritation. Life as a whole becomes penetratingly sharp—unavoidable and at the same time cutting. We could say that is the living description of the truth that life contains pain. According to Buddhism, life or existence is defined according to the truth of suffering, which is the razor blade.

—Chögyam Trungpa Rinpoche

Finding ourself living on the razor blade is actually good news. We begin to see that confusion acts as a continual sense of awareness is our path. We could become very alert, completely attentive, and willing to meet each situation. We are not trying to make things more harmonious, homey, and peaceful. Life becomes unavoidable and penetrating. It creates tremendous room for fearlessly working with the actual situation rather than trying to get rid of it.

One of the keys to experiencing the mandala is being in the present moment. In the moment we either say "Yes!" and wake up or "No!" and go back into duality. Being in the now has no past, present, or future, but is timeless. The past is fiction and the future is a dream. We are totally in tune to what is happening on the spot. The world opens in that moment. We make a shift from seeing through a self-identified lens to seeing the dynamic energy of the big picture. We transform our view by opening to a larger awareness. We see that each experience is layered, interdependent, interlinked. This depersonalization of awareness is very liberating. We become involved in forces and dynamics bigger and more independent than ourself.

The buddha energy wins the day! Holding the buddha energy of all-encompassing space, we have an unbiased, transpersonal knowing or intuitive understanding which enables us to see the mandala. It is an experience of feeling completely adequate with no need for conventional logic. It is a firsthand experience of things as they are. It is an awareness without purpose or goal, impartial rather than latching onto one point of view. We are open to all directions, all possibilities. The attitude is, "I am flexible. I can roll with the punches, sail with the wind, ride the waves, kayak down the river." It takes being fearless, confident, and trusting. What's wrong with this picture? Nothing. We change our attitude and relax as it is. Ultimately there is one wisdom: awake.

As we have seen, habitually we have a watcher, a commentator, making sure we keep track of everything so we stay within our comfort zone. Our slogan is, "I have to survive," or "Make this work for me." Without our familiar reference points, we feel we would die. In fact, we do die. We shed our identity, our ego. We dissolve our defensive armoring and step out of our constricted ego sphere. We stop manipulating life's situations to our advantage. We allow whatever is happening to be as it is. We go for the ride, rather than steer the ride.

There is a sense of vagueness: directionless, timeless, and spaceless. But that vagueness is very lively and opens us to tremendous possibilities. The ultimate experience is seeing the energies as facets of one whole. There is more spontaneity and freedom to move and play. We become instinctively attuned rather than relying on concept. There is no longer a watcher because we are included. It is being in the zone. It is extraordinarily awake ground.

Instinct here is an experience in which you feel that you are completely adequate, that you do not need the aid of conventional logic, or any proof of anything. It is a sense of a firsthand account, firsthand experience, actually experiencing. At that moment you do not watch yourself experiencing, you simply just do experience. It is very straightforward.

–Chögyam Trungpa Rinpoche

Being in the moment and seeing the big picture is a more skillful way of finding our direction than convoluted logic. When seen precisely, every situation offers guidance and what to do becomes clear. Habitually, we want to secure our future right now. We imagine all sorts of situations and so make plans. We get into a great deal of paranoia and panic. But if we see the present situation as it is, it could be quite simple.

When we no longer need to control and manipulate the world to our advantage, we have emerged from our constricted ego-sphere. We drop the storyline, relax, and allow the energy to be as it is. We ride the energy of the moment, bringing whatever quality of energy is needed to the situation. We respond in tune with what is happening. Our actions are spontaneous and appropriate. We could be light and full of humor.

We could choose to deny the opportunity that is presenting itself to us or, more effectively, ride the wave of coincidence. When we surrender to the natural flow of energy, the auspicious coincidence, we don't have to think about what to do next. We bring wisdom activity, motivated by compassion, into play. Allowing ourself to fit into the big picture—without manipulating or scheming—is a powerful experience. This is how we learn to ride the energies of the mandala.

In any given situation, we are in a mandala. There is a mandala of our home and family members. When we go into a restaurant or any other place, we experience the mandala of the people and environment. We see the general patterns, either pleasant or unpleasant. For me, when I choose where to sit in a home, a meeting, or a restaurant, I am very conscious of the energy dynamics and find my seat accordingly. Having this kind of relationship to our world is extremely empowering. The mandala perspective wakes us up.

Still vivid in my memory is the time when I was going through an unfamiliar airport and came into an enormous open hall where people were coming and going in all directions. I suddenly stopped. Time seemed to stand still and my awareness became vast. The people moving through the space were energetic beings in a cosmic dance. It was dream-like: vivid but illusory. There was a sense of connecting with everyone and everything in the moment. Another time, jet lagged in the Amsterdam airport, I was lying on a bench for a while. I heard announcements for departing flights to all corners of the world: Jakarta, Mozambique, San Francisco, etc. I felt myself shift from my self-identified lens of tracking the time until my flight, to a larger awareness of global connectedness. I was part of a bigger picture. I found that depersonalization of awareness very liberating. It was actually soothing, comforting.

We can discover for ourself the richness of living in a multicolored world. This living web of interconnectedness sensitizes us to the natural rhythms and energy of society, politics, organizations, events, and so forth. Thus, it is the basis for action that is both compassionate and effective. It lends clarity and focus, as well as joy, to working for a better world.

Co-Emergent Wisdom

Co-emergent wisdom is the magic potion that turns all that is confusing into all that is awakened, as we saw in transmuting. The power of working with this perspective is there is no need to shed or reject anything. Rather than letting go, we let be. Letting be means we find our wisdom within our neurosis.

We can appreciate the full spectrum of who we are and what is, rather than being dumbed down to ego's sphere. This profound teaching is the most powerful transformative aspect of the Five Wisdoms. It makes it possible to see the mandala of orderly chaos.

Our realization of co-emergent wisdom is when we simultaneous *experience* confusion and clarity. As we saw with orderly chaos, they are inseparable and interdependent, not polarized as we commonly think. When we enter the confusion, our clarity is also right there, and intelligence is born out of the confusion. For example, when someone is angry, they are also clear. It's just that they get overly pushy about their clarity.

We usually don't take confusion seriously, seeing it as a mistake rather than being inquisitive about it. So, our very confusion is our wake-up call. Whatever horrible thing happens is actually a precious opportunity because it is in that kind of intense experience that our sanity is most available. This is brilliant sanity. We are not just sensible but creative and visionary. It gives us the feeling of being completely adequate. We don't have to overthink everything. We can just experience. So! It turns out that chaos is our inspiration; chaos is good news.

Co-emergent wisdom opens us to the dynamic play of the mandala. We meet our world nakedly without trying to protect ourself. It's like being on a first date. Where will this lead? We don't know what is going to happen. There are so many positive or negative, creative or destructive, painful or pleasurable possibilities. We could feel more shaky and tentative because we can't establish ground. We might jump to solidifying the relationship because we can't stand the uncertainty. We could feel insecure, full of both hope and fear. Trungpa Rinpoche put it succinctly, "The bad news is that we are falling; the good news is that there is no ground."

Our problem is that we are constantly trying to maintain some situation, trapping us in a dualistic world. Usually, we think we should get rid of the troublesome world and create a perfect utopian world. I was working with an IT person who was constantly making mistakes. It was so frustrating. Then I realized that, as an elderly person, he may have some cognitive issues. Whether this was true or not, the thought opened me to seeing the situation for what it was. Co-emergent wisdom makes us impartial so our world becomes more workable. We develop a more sympathetic attitude toward it.

An interesting perspective in understanding the mandala is that everyone is guilty and no one is to blame. Everyone is guilty means that everyone has played a part in a given situation. No one is to blame means that all occurrences are part of a dynamic synergy. Blaming is like quicksand. It takes us deeper and deeper into a solidified sense of us and them, dualism created by a self-protecting ego. Rather, we can feel the freedom of dancing with energy, as I pointed out in the example above.

We are constantly given chances to either cling to comfort in the darkness or open to brightness and light. The darkness could feel more comfortable because it is familiar. The light could feel delightful, but also challenging. Co-emergent wisdom is daring to expose ourself. It can happen spontaneously, in a flash, bringing with it a sense of great joy. At the same time, a sense of commitment is needed to plant the seeds of wakefulness deep inside us. Then, through continual allegiance to sanity, it can happen more and more. We can take the light road in any situation. As I like to say "The secret to a happy life is not to take life so personally." This means our self-protecting ego becomes irrelevant.

Settled into ourself with a sense of stillness, we can just be. When just being, we open. It may not be everyone's experience, but here are some possibilities. We could arrive at a sense of empty-hearted awareness. We could feel lonely. Yet, from my experience, the feeling of being alone and the feeling of totality go together. It can actually feel very romantic because when we opening is inviting the magic of the world With an awakened consciousness, we can have a deep internal awareness of the whole. We could feel a sense of belonging, of connectedness, to the cosmos as a whole.

> A drop in the ocean partakes of the greatness of its parent although it is unconscious of it; but it dries up as soon as it enters upon an existence independent of the ocean... Consciousness is a deep internal awareness of the whole.

> —Mahatma Gandhi

CHAPTER 20

The Dimensions
of Reality

The body, appearance emptiness, like a watermoon
Move and move and rest within movement emptiness
Speech is sound and emptiness like an echo
Speak and speak and rest right within sound emptiness
Mind is luminosity emptiness inexpressible
Think and think and rest right within the inexpressible

–Khenpo Tsültrim Gyamtso Rinpoche

We commonly understand there to be two levels of reality: our everyday consensus reality, and, for those
spiritually inclined, a transcendent reality. We understand these as a sense of secular and sacred. These two levels of
reality are also common to Tantric Buddhism, though we are
going to go beyond these descriptions in this chapter.

Two Truths: Relative and Absolute Realities

There is a progression to our understanding. As we saw in
Chapter 7, we create our version of reality—a dualistic world
of *this* and *that*, *me* and *them*—with our neurotic projections. We

see ourself and everything out there to be truly existent. Through our meditation practice, we begin to see that both ourself and phenomenon are not quite so solid, and that they seem more transparent. The fire is hot and could burn us but ultimately it has no inherent existence. We intuit this rather than conceptually understand it.

Then we get a glimpse of ultimate wisdom which is all-knowing and not of the relative world. It is open, vast, undifferentiated, unconditional, and profoundly good. It brings a sense of peace, free of the vice-grip of our neurotic patterns. We experience this as being wakeful and clear. Ultimate wisdom sees that everything is transitory, impermanent, and illusory. It's easy to say, but hard to realize, being as fixated as we are on the apparent solidity and convincing reality of all we experience. However, we could also get seduced by transcendent reality. We could long for an experience that is larger than ourself, thinking it is the only place to be, and get caught in the trap of spiritual materialism.

Finally, we see that our everyday world and ultimate wisdom co-exist. We see the inseparability of relative appearance and absolute emptiness. We relate to our ordinary lives in a direct way, yet are sustained by the inspiration and protection of the absolute. We can trust in both. We can deal with whatever situation that arises because it is fundamentally empty. The realization of appearance/emptiness is the understanding of absolute truth. Gaining certainty in this allows us to be both fully in the world as well as relate to a spiritual dimension. Absolute truth is like the keel of a boat giving stability; relative truth is like the rudder that steers and the sails that work with the wind.

We may have had experiences of the relative and ultimate but had not known what to call them. I experience them particularly when traveling. Waking up in a new place is disorienting. I could be awake and my mind could be completely open yet not know where I am. This usually feels very refreshing to me, but could be scary for others. My mind habitually searches for some reference points. I wonder where I am, what time it is, what I am supposed to do today. I start to get my bearings. "I am in Amsterdam. I have come here to teach. It must be Thursday. I need to call so and so to make sure..." Establishing outer reference points confirms that I exist. Generally, we feel more safe and comfortable in the relative world of things to do and people to see and places to go. Losing reference points also has some comical effects, as when, on returning home, I have forgotten how to use the phone or find myself putting a cucumber into the utensil's drawer instead of the refrigerator. (This happened!)

In summary, we could say that first we are ensconced in relative reality, then we discover the ultimate, and then see their inseparability. We see emptiness is full and fullness is empty, a Buddhist conundrum that turns our mind inside out.

Three Truths and the Three Modes

Relative and absolute realities are common to all Buddhist traditions. The specialty of the tantric tradition is the subtle, energetic dimension. The world most immediate to us is solid, concrete, and tangible. The energetic plane is the subtle energy in constant dynamic play that radiates and speaks to us. For instance, there is an energetic difference between a table made of metal and a table made of wood. They speak to us in different ways. The mental plane is hidden and has no inherent existence but is experienced by us as thoughts, mental models, and fantasy. So, the energetic dimension is actually a bridge between apparent reality and non-inherent reality.

Commonly, we know that we have a body made of flesh and blood, an inner energetic emotional world, and a mind full of thoughts, daydreams, and so forth. We could talk about them as three modes: physical, energetic/emotional, and mental. They are our body, speech, and mind; our outer, inner, and secret aspects; the gross, subtle, and inexpressible. They are interdependent and inseparable. Body has a quality of solidity, speech has a quality of expressiveness, and intelligence has a quality of clarity.

Our entire existence has to do with our body, our speech, and our mind. Awareness of our physical actions, communication patterns, and style of thinking empowers us to deal with reality properly. When we are at our best, they are synchronized and we are more integrated. What we think, feel, say, and do are synchronized. Body is appearance/emptiness, speech is sound/emptiness, and mind is clarity/emptiness. The true nature of our body, speech, and mind is open, spacious, and relaxed.

These three spheres exist in people, places, and situations. With practice we can begin to see that they co-exist in the present moment. Our first impression of anyone or anything is their outer form, their physical presence. When we stay with the direct perception of the basic quality of solidity, we pick up a vibration and intuit an inner landscape, how they/it energetically speaks to us. The energetic vibrations could be subtle or extraordinarily powerful. For instance, if an angry person walks into the room and starts shouting, we feel the energy of anger. Through experiencing their body and speech modes we have an understanding of their mental mode, their mental contents.

Let's dive deeper into each mode.

The Outer Mode

In the outer mode, manifest reality is tangible—tables, trees, people—so we take them to be real. We know our body and all phenomenon are made of the five elements. Our sense faculties act as a bridge to connect us to the world. So, there is always an intermingling of our body and outside phenomenon. We experience this mode as dualism: perceiver and object, a solidified self and not self. This is the world we know and take for granted. We work with this reality on a day-to-day basis in our life.

The Inner Mode

The inner mode is the communication or radiance of physical form, a dynamic play of subtle and not-so-subtle energy. It's our emotional landscape and expressive characteristics. We experience the ambience, feeling tone, qualities, and textures of our world. Our energy radiates who we are and in turn the world speaks to us. It adds emotional vividness to a perceptual world. We pick up the vibe and grok—words from the 1960s that mean intuitively knowing what's going on.

This dimension is about the communication between our outer and inner worlds. This is the dimension of sense consciousnesses, the energetic fields between our sense faculties and the objects of perception. As psychophysical beings living in a multidimensional world, there is a reciprocal relationship between us and our world. So, we experience the outer dimension through our sense perceptions as well as our six sense, intuition.

There is a natural illusory, dreamlike quality to this inner world. We can't pin it down like we can the outer world. It is more fleeting, more ephemeral. It is important because it links body and mind, the material and the ethereal. Because energy is fluid, it is in this dimension that we are able to transmute all that we experience as constricted energy into expansive energy.

This energetic dimension is the domain of the Five Wisdoms Energies. As such they are a bridge between manifest reality and the ephemeral realm. Through practice, we realize the truth that things are apparent but empty, existing and not-existing, being here and yet being questionable. This gives us a profound understanding of things as they are.

The Secret Mode

Who knows our mind better than we do? The mental mode is hidden or secret because it is only known to ourself. On the one hand, it is psychological. On the other hand, it has the potential to be vast and boundless with no essential, inherent existence. It is a primeval, intuitive intelligence or knowing that is transpersonal. Everything we experience is like a dream, movie, or cyberspace: fleeting, impermanent, and illusory. Since no one can really know our thoughts and emotions in the way we do, it creates a sense of loneliness—we experience our world alone. Because of this, there is a fundamental tenderness to existence. This creates a level of wakefulness.

Ego, our stronghold of personal identity, fiercely sabotages our accessing this dimension because it is a death sentence to ego. The feeling of nonexistence is very threatening. "It's all fun and games 'til someone loses an I." However, the good news is that at a tantric level, there is a positive experience of nonexistence because we are tuned into the magical possibilities of life. We see that the three dimensions are actually what promote creation, joy, and ultimate aliveness. It's a world of benevolent compassion and wakefulness free of ordinary, arising of experience, emotions, thought patterns, habits, challenges, and interrelations.

Paying attention to the three modes, we become more open and aware. We find that we have no problem dealing with the vicissitudes of our life. We can relate with whatever arises quite simply.

Quality and Action

We can go further in exploring these dimensions. Quality is the unifying principle that brings the three dimensions together to see the whole texture. We are able to identify which five energies are present.

Action arises as an expression of the manifested form, the energy of speech, the intelligence of mind, and the texture of quality.

The Energies In Action

The Five Wisdoms can only be fully realized when we understand these three dimensions to wisdom. They connect us to the dynamic play of energies in both our body and the phenomenal world. Because the energetic mode is their domain, they play an important part in the interplay between absolute and relative reality. When we embrace the ever-dynamic flow of this mode, we experience a basic sense of lightness, pleasure, and playfulness. There is juice and vitality to our existence. Gaining certainty in this transforms the basic fabric of our existence.

Perhaps we cannot imagine what it would be like to drop our conceptual fabrications and operate from a deeper source. But working with the five energies, we come to see that thoughts are not very deep; the body works at a much deeper level. We could say that thoughts are sparks; the body is a burning fire, the light of which radiates wisdom. When we rely on the natural energetic process, there is a sense of both looseness and wakefulness, a sense of heaviness and lightness, of being utterly dull and being extraordinarily colorful.

The Three Kayas

In traditional Tantric Buddhism, the three planes of enlightened existence are known as the three kayas. The transformation of the three modes into the three kayas is the basis of the tantric path and the transformative power of the Five Wisdoms. They point to the interplay of space, energy, and form in ordinary life as well as in the awakened mind.

The dharmakaya is the ultimate level. This basic ground—vast, boundless, and undifferentiated space—is the profundity of our existence. It is the emptiness of the mental mode, a state of mind that is open, free, and spacious. We have always had this openness. When the Buddha realized this, he claimed he was the enlightened one.

The sambhogakaya is the subtle energetic dimension, the psychophysical realm of communication and expression with qualities and characteristics. It is the body of stimulation, enjoyment, and intelligence as well as of joy and bliss. It is many colored like a prism or rainbow. Everything vividly speaks for itself so experience is very direct, definite, and clear. It is the play of the phenomenal world, which we experience through the Five Wisdoms Energies.

The nirmanakaya is body manifestation on the physical plane. Enlightened beings appear in a physical body as someone whom we can see, talk to, and for whom we can cook lunch. Buddhas can actually manifest in any physical form—not simply as spiritual teachers—in response to what beings need. Their skillful means, compassion, and resourcefulness are expressions of wisdom.

To put it simply the dharmakaya is about absolute space; the sambhogakaya is about radiance; the nirmanakaya is about manifest form. In reverse order, there is what we experience directly and think of as "reality," a more subtle level that we intuit, and the non-dual aspect that we "know" but is inexpressible. With practice, we can move from external forms, to inner experience, to emptiness.

The svabhavikakaya is the unity and inseparability of all three. Total wakefulness, or enlightenment, is realizing the presence of the three kayas in the moment: boundless space, wisdom energy, and manifest appearance. Yet, as we know, some religions disregard or distrust the life of the body, and many secular cultures ignore spiritual development.

The three bodies of wisdom can also be seen as a creation story because energy is the movement from possibility to actuality. From the boundless space of the dharmakaya energy arises, first as sound and then as light, to become the five energies of the sambhogakaya which then manifest in material form in the nirmanakaya. Creation goes from the highest, most-liberated consciousness to the lowest, most-limited physical manifestation. This is not as far-fetched of an idea as it might seem. It is not a sense of creation like the Big Bang. It is the sense that creation happens in every moment: there is space; there is expressive energy; there is form.

CHAPTER 21

Embracing Your Feminine and Masculine Energies

Exploring the masculine and feminine dimensions of the Five Vital Wisdoms gives us deeper experience of them and with that comes a potential for deeper healing and liberation, because the polarity and union go all the way to the deepest levels of Tantric meditation where bliss-openness wakes us up to the nondual nature of our being and reality.

–Sydney Leijenhorst

N eed we say that of all the many ways we could talk about characteristics of energy that the feminine and masculine are distinctive and obvious to everyone? Clearly, the feminine and masculine are universal principles that come into play in all spheres of life and at every level of human experience from societies, cultures, and politics to everyday activity and momentary perception. They have cosmic proportions and yet are very immediate in our life. What is the first question we ask when a child is born? They appear as primary orientations in several esoteric traditions: the Taoist Yin and Yang, the Hindu Shakti and Shiva, the Tibetan Buddhist Dakini and Daka, or Yogini and Yogin.

Feminine and masculine energies can either create tremendous turmoil or tremendous harmony. Feminine energy is spacious, accommodating, nurturing, warm, receptive, emotional, process-oriented, intuitive, and spontaneous. It is associated with energetic heat and intensity. When indulged it can become self-serving, fickle, provocative, and sharp. Masculine energy is focused, direct, clear, logical, action-oriented, goal-directed, reason-based, reliable, and problem-solving. It is associated with steady power, strength, solidity, resiliency, and groundedness. When self-serving it is dominating, authoritarian, and controlling.

Unfortunately, most of us find ourself full of confusion and emotional distress with these seemingly oppositional energies: never the twain shall meet! Yet each energy has its wisdom and a deeper understanding of them can bring new insight at a personal, interpersonal, and a societal level.

The Tantric View

Buddhist Tantra has a rather radical view: to have a union and balance of feminine and masculine energies within ourself. So, it's not about gender. Feminine intuition and masculine skillful means can intertwine naturally. Both women and men can learn to come into a healthy, integral relationship with them because they exist innately within us. Discovering how we can embody and express both, we can heal our inner fragmentation. We awaken to the full spectrum of who we are.

At a cosmic level, the union and balance of the feminine and masculine is expressed as EVAM. E, the feminine principle, is unconditioned vast space, unchanging and powerful. VAM, the masculine principle, is manifestation, action. Brought together E and VAM join spaciousness and energy, vastness and potency. This union is cosmic reality.

Tantra not only places great emphasis on the body, but in particular focuses on the feminine as an embodiment of wisdom. The feminine principle symbolizes a fundamental reality: the ineffable world which we cannot grasp. It has no substantial existence. It is unconditional, unnameable, unoriginated, and unceasing. As primordial intelligence, it is an atmosphere of openness and all-pervasive accommodation. It is transcendental knowledge, full of precision and brightness. It is ultimately resourceful and full of potentiality.

An epithet for the Buddha, the awakened one, is Bhagavan. Bhaga is the Sanskrit word for vagina. A Buddha dwells in the bhaga, the wisdom space of the feminine, and so looks at the world through the eyes of the primordial feminine. As such, he is engaged in constant intercourse with the phenomenal world and experiences endless great bliss that results from that mating.

This space of vast emptiness accommodates everything. It is the primordial mother, the mother principle, the womb of reality giving birth to all things. It is essential vitality, fertile and creative so it has a mercurial, vibrating quality. Women are a physical manifestation of this as progenitors of life. They embody space in their reproductive organs, their vaginas representing space full of the potentiality of thousands of eggs. Feminine manifestation is embracing, nurturing, generating, soft, and gentle.

In phenomenal experience, whether pleasure or pain, birth or death, sanity or insanity, good or bad, it is necessary to have a basic ground. This basic ground is known in Buddhist literature as the mother principle...the mother-consort of all the Buddhas...As a principle of cosmic structure,

the all-accommodating basic ground is neither male nor female. One might call it hermaphroditic, but due to its quality of fertility or potentiality, it is regarded as feminine.

–Chögyam Trungpa Rinpoche

The sacred feminine is mysterious. It is hard to pinpoint
and eludes definition. It is attuned to nature and sensuality,
engenders sacred sexuality, and invokes poetry. Though we
cannot necessarily understand it, we also cannot ignore it.
Trungpa Rinpoche has described it as humming in the background, an underworld that is self-secret, and that our everyday reality cannot see it. The surface world goes on
nonchalantly ignoring this extraordinarily powerful undercurrent. We can most readily access it through practices of embodied meditation.

Every woman of true royalty, owns a secret land more real
to her, than this pale outer world.

–Robert Browning

This unfettered space of mind is where the mind awakens.
It allows insight, thought arising from non-thought and dissolving back into non-thought. It is a big mind, a best mind, a
vast mind. We all have the basic accommodation and fertility
of the feminine aspect. Connecting with space liberates us in an
instant. It allows us to step back, watch what is going on, and
then gives us the confidence from where we can make decisions and execute actions.

In this cosmic picture, masculine energy comes from the
empty space as an urge to manifest. The expressive power and
play of emptiness is the beginning of all perceived reality. We
form steps out of the world of the formless. It is all that we
know in our tangible reality, both animate and inanimate—the

seasons, the weather, the elements…everything. Masculine energy is fearless and sharp, ready to act, ready to manipulating the world to accomplish what it wants.

It may seem that the feminine comes first, but actually feminine and masculine energies arise simultaneously. They are always and forever in union and constantly giving birth to reality. This primordial unity of our reality is a profound understanding. Our downfall is forgetting this. Masculine energy has the potential for tremendous heights of accomplishment. However, when we disregard that manifestation arises from the feminine, we are perpetually caught in an excessively masculine world. When overly involved with action, we create endless confusion and suffering. In union with the primordial mother, the masculine softens. Without that embrace, the world becomes locked into an aggressive frozen duality. So, this basic cosmic structure is necessary to our sanity. The immaculate space is uncorrupted by dualistic confusions so it safeguards against ego's impulses.

The natural chemistry between men and women is a powerful expression of the fundamental dynamic between feminine and masculine energies. Tantra uses this natural dynamic of sexual attraction. Sexual desire is an aspect of yearning for completeness.

> …wholeness is to discover, through desire, the interrelatedness of masculine and feminine qualities on all levels of experience. The sharp edginess of women reaches for the blunt pragmatism of men; men yearn for the emotional intensity of women. Sexual yearning is, at its heart, no different from spiritual yearning. Appreciating contrast and complementarity is central to the tantric practitioner's life, as is tracing the dance between men and women in ordinary discourse. And sexual passion is a central expression of this dynamic, which goes to the heart of the body and mind.

–Judith Simmer Brown

Dakinis

This discussion would not be complete without the mention of dakinis. In Tantric Buddhism dakinis represent the manifestation of energy in a female form. In this sense every woman is a dakini. They can be your mother, your aunt, your sister, or your lover, young, old, ugly, beautiful, and both playful and aggressive. As worldly dakinis, they own their femininity.

Wisdom dakinis are the essence of wisdom. They break conventional norms and transcend the conditioned existence of samsara driven by ego. They embrace life in which all experience is seen as sacred. They are linked with the symbolism of space embodying the inseparability of emptiness and wisdom. Uddiyāna is the legendary dwelling place of wisdom dakinis, a land of exceptionally beautiful and independent women. They are not symbolic, but flesh and blood women practitioners of Tantra.

In Tantric Buddhism, arousing passion is central to its practices. Dakinis activate the powerful and transformative energy of the passionate feminine. They can play a great part in an individual's attainment of enlightenment, removing physical and spiritual hindrances and awakening spiritual qualities. Practices focus on the inner channels, winds, and energy centers. They are done either on one's own or by engaging with another in sexual union to generate great bliss. Dakinis can act as messengers or guides. Therefore, a Tantric Buddhist practitioner takes refuge in them.

> The heat and intensity of women's energy can trip intense emotional triggers, which can create enormous chaos. This chaos can be beneficial when intractable situations present themselves...when stubborn logics and habitual styles are employed, penetrating insight can liberate the ponderous environment into chaos, even when it manifests as intense emotionality...The sensitivity of women's intuition can see

injustice, emotional subtlety, interpersonal dynamics, and hidden meanings. When there are imbalances and obstacles in specific environments, the sharp and penetrating qualities of women can identify them and adjust them. This emotionality can also be very warm, generating compassion and care for others…her power is very definite, penetrating, and even threatening in its directness…[their] fierceness is not emotional but a sharp energy of wakefulness.

–Judith Simmer Brown

There are three ways to access dakini wisdom. You can invoke them in traditional tantric practices which includes descriptive prose, elaborate iconographic visualization, hand gestures, and mantra. She is usually depicted as dancing in the sky as she is dynamic energy in space. Secondly, there is a practice working with the subtle energy of your channels and chakras to arouse embodied bliss. The third practice is sexual union. Dakinis sing and dance and overflow with happiness and pleasure generating expansive bliss. When in meditative absorption with them, you experience their bliss. She is your consort and companion and there is reciprocity of helping each other on the path.

The idea of an enlightened, sacred feminine energy that was also naked, dancing, and fierce was something I had never experienced, and it touched me deeply. I couldn't put into words the effect it had on me, but it was something significant and new…an image of spiritual enlightenment of female divinity that is active, dancing, fierce, free, and wild… beyond the grasp of the conceptional mind…spiritual and erotic, ecstatic and wise, playful and profound, fierce and peaceful…By activating the dakini power within us, we have an inner resource that should never be underestimated.

–Lama Tsultrim Allione

By invoking a wisdom dakini, a practitioner can develop a sensitivity to the energy of enlightened awareness. The dakini can enter their stream of consciousness and awaken them. As dynamic energy, the dakini represents the path of transformation. Specifically, this is the alchemical transmutation of the energy of intensified, confused emotions into the energy of enlightened awareness. Sometimes the energy needs to be forceful, so a dakini has a wrathful manifestation. This is the profound method of the Anuttara Tantras of the Kagyu Tibetan Buddhist lineage.

> Dakinis can transform energy directly through experiences and for this reason it is the Dakini who is associated with Tantric teachings and working with the energies of the body, speech, and mind. Meditation on a Dakini such as Vajra-yogini or the Five Buddha Family Wisdom Dakinis is one way of establishing awareness of Dakini energy in all its forms.
>
> –Keith Dowman

> The unique compassion of the Dakinis is their focus on the embodiment of sanity through the integration of all emotions, not just peaceful or looking-good emotions…Unearthing the primordial feminine brings relief to the tensions of a positive outer image and an inner life in turmoil. We can be angry or fearful, and, at the same time, know that the transformation of those emotions is creativity and grace. When we have exposed the hidden poisons in our psyche, the Dakinis provide a path of soulful living and transformation. With rampant worldwide spiritual hunger, Dakinis offer the synthesis of our emotional, creative, and spiritual realities.
>
> –Mari Selby

The Five Wisdoms are the fulcrum between wisdom da-kinis and worldly dakinis. The particular neurosis of each of the five energies is associated with a corresponding wisdom. By invoking one of them, we can transmute the neurosis of that particular energy into its wisdom aspect. For instance, a da-kini's anger is transmuted into clarity; a dakini's passion is transmuted into compassion. It's almost scientific!

There are many kinds of dakinis. They live in our everyday world with both enlightened and worldly aspects. Some are consciously aware of their feminine potentialities. For a tantric practitioner, to live as a dakini means to be aware of the true meaning of a dakini: one who can transmute confused energy into wisdom. Most women living in our samsaric world are not aware of this capacity.

Nevertheless, whether aware of their power or not, women have the capacity to inspire, seduce, and provoke us. They can be angry, manipulative, yielding, accepting, shy, beautiful, playful, mischievous, and surprising. She can love you and hate you. Trungpa Rinpoche once remarked that our life would be a continual boredom without them.

The power of the dakini cannot be denied. For several dec-ades I have practiced Vajrayogini, both in the ritualized prac-tice and the inner yoga called tummo. My psychophysical being has been transformed.

One of the most powerful and memorable dreams I have had was of a dakini. I was standing in a room facing a large window. A young girl stood next to me. I said, "You know it is really OK that your mother left because it was really a terrible situation." At that, I felt a heightened energy in her. Suddenly "she" was outside the window, but transformed. She hovered in the air, seemingly on fire with a blazing white light. I could not distinguish her form, but her face was very clear and her blue eyes stared at me. I was startled but respond with, "You're so beautiful; you're so brilliant." Yet I felt some fear. I stood there and we looked at each other; there was a pause. Suddenly, I was swept off of my feet and drawn feet first into her, completely consumed.

I woke up abruptly. I felt some fear but mostly I felt awed by her power to destroy. I wondered if my words were a way of denying her destructive power, being naive. Should I have been more scared? I wondered who the child was, but came to feel that she was my daughter. Why did she say that my mother left? Was it my mother (who died of cancer at the age of 57) or was I the mother? My daughter and I have gone through years of deep searching into the dynamic play in our mother lineage. It has been both excruciatingly painful as well as brilliantly illuminating. My daughter has always been a dakini, a teacher, for me.

Gender In Our Times

As wonderful as our potential is for nondual union, unfortunately our societal patterns seem perpetually locked into a feminine and masculine duality. We live in a patriarchal world focused on application, practicality, efficiency, and accomplishment. This is all well and good, but it creates a world of tight bureaucratic rules and regulations, aggressive politics, and focus on the bottom line. There is a demand for dominance over the world. Masculine energy, whether in a man or woman, is always trying to make something happen. The dominance of science and the necessity for expertise in our overly complicated world creates segmentation. It feels solid and unchanging. We can't relax, can't stop, and so are unable to start fresh. We want space but are too nervous to enjoy it. Within this tangle, the feminine is undervalued, distorted, and cheapened. In some sense the fate of nature and women have gone together.

In a provocative Bryn Mawr Commencement Address in 1986, Ursula Le Guin talked about language, specifically the father tongue of power and the mother tongue of communication. I find it powerfully descriptive of the tangible qualities of the masculine and feminine. I highly recommend you check out this speech to really bask in the richness of the text. I will include only a small excerpt here:

>...many believe the expository, particularly the scientific discourse, is the highest form of language, the true language, of which all other uses of words are primitive vestiges. It is the language of thought that seeks objectivity... When either the political or the scientific discourse announces itself as the voice of reason, it is playing God...[in fact] it is distancing-making...between the subject or self and the object or other...it enables it to dominate every other culture, so that everywhere now everybody speaks the same language in laboratories and government buildings and head-quarters and offices of business, and those who don't know it or won't speak it are silent, or silenced or unheard...[you] learn the language of power-to be empowered...if you want to succeed, you have to be fluent in the language in which "success" is a meaningful word... The father tongue is spoken from above. It goes one way. No answer is expected, or heard. [It is] immensely noble and indispensably useful. When it claims a privileged relationship to reality, it becomes dangerous and potentially destructive.

>...[as a child] You were learning your mother tongue. It is the other, inferior. It is primitive: inaccurate, unclear, coarse, limited, trivial, banal. It's repetitive, the same over and over, like the work called women's work; earthbound, housebound. It's vulgar, the vulgar tongue, common, common speech, colloquial, low, ordinary, plebeian...The mother tongue, spoken or written, expects an answer. It is

conversation, a word the root of which means "turning to-gether." The mother tongue is language not as mere com-munication but as relation, relationship. It connects. It goes two ways, many ways, an exchange, a network. Its power is not in dividing but in binding, not in distancing but in unit-ing…it flies from the mouth on the breath that is our life and is gone, like the outbreath, utterly gone and yet return-ing, repeated, the breath the same again always, everywhere, and we all know it by heart…It is the language stories are told in. It is the language spoken by all children and most women, and so I call it the mother tongue, for we learn it from our mothers, and speak it to our kids.

● ● ●

The universe is made of stories, not atoms.

–Muriel Rukeyser

Looking through history, the time of hunter gatherers was patrilineal because their social ties and structure were organized around the masculinized work of hunting. Later, many horticul-tural societies were matrilineal, based on kinship with the mother or the female line, because the social ties and structure were organized around the feminized work of crop cultivation. In matriarchies, women hold the primary power positions in roles of political leadership, moral authority, social privilege, and control of property. Later still, agrarian societies with land and animal ownership societies became more patriarchal.

Matriarchal societies and primitive cultures have honored the feminine. Feminine wisdom is a very earthy and embodied wisdom. Women are more in touch with nature and the world of the senses. They don't dominate nature but mingle with it. They are very attuned to their bodies. Their monthly cycles go with the natural rhythms of the moon. They give birth and pro-duce milk to feed their babies. There is an intermingling of the creative, spiritual, and healing journeys. In many cultures these are one and the same. There is a sense of inclusiveness and interconnectedness. The feminine leads with the heart.

There have been, and still are, pockets of full-blown feminine energy. The geisha in Japan, for example, live in their own enclaves. Men visit these houses but never speak of it to their wives. In the Ottoman Empire, harem women were locked away from the rest of society and guarded by eunuchs. The harems constituted the sultans' private treasury of feminine energy. Though these traditions are dying out, similar elements exist in many cultures. On another note, we can also consider that in the West, women have more freedom than they did 1,000 years ago. And look at the differences in how women manifested in the 1950s versus in 2024!

There is constant change in the dance of gender. Energies are at times oppositional and at times complementary. There is attraction and repulsion. It's always dynamic. When the neurotic aspects are heightened, the imbalance is exaggerated and solidified. In a primary relationship, a woman becomes more emotional and a man more obstinate or harsh. By acknowledging the gifts of both genders, perhaps we can learn to nurture a healthy balance between masculine and feminine energies in our lives and work environments.

Not long ago, someone in a training presented themselves as they. Out of curiosity, I asked them why they had chosen to do this. Their answer was very straightforward: it was a spiritual choice, not wanting to leave out any part of themselves. Yes! Gender is such a big topic these days, creating a lot of pain and confusion. It has induced some people to go to the extreme measure of making a sex change. But outer appearance and genitalia are not the main point. We can heal ourself by realizing that both feminine and masculine energies exist innately within us. It's about energy, a more subtle but also more profound relationship to ourself.

A Possible Trajectory

If the problem on our spiritual path is too much masculine energy, the solution would seem to be to emphasize feminine energy. What happens with religions is that as they become more institutionalized, they become more masculine. To have a more genuine spirituality, we need to become primordial feminists, over-emphasizing emptiness. Emptiness is, after all, the most profound teaching of Buddhism and ultimately neither feminine nor masculine, but nondual.

All who have tread on a spiritual path are in essence longing to reunite with the primordial mother, to lose ourself in her embrace, to release ourself from the painful egoic separation from reality. When we don't feel her warm embrace, we continue to look for her outside. We keep looking for that sense of connection, that love. We become fixated, always longing, searching, and striving for more. Yet we haven't been able to find her in any of the constant things we do to entertain ourself. And we certainly have not found her in the material world.

We long to feel full, but it is actually emptiness we seek. Let's wake up: what we so desperately seek is already right here. We could simply direct our gaze inward to find it. We long for this truest sense of our self, yet always feel the subliminal tension of our solid sense of self, so it constantly eludes us. At the deepest level we are looking for the release from looking itself. At some point, the truth dawns on us and we stop looking. Some sort of renunciation is the demand of any genuine spiritual path. Only then will we experience the formless emptiness that is our primordial mother. At that point we discover who we truly are, ourself as no-self.

Emptiness is a cosmic release from self. We actually feel fullness at moments of experiencing emptiness and rest in the release of not wanting or looking. We feel full because we have tasted emptiness, a glimpse of no-thing. It is almost too good, too simple, to be true.

CHAPTER 22

Passion: Opening
to Ultimate Love

The world of real passion is a different atmosphere, a limitless world. When you have a glimpse of this, when some un-programmed moment of ventilation allows you to feel something outside the ego, that could inspire you to try to step out altogether. You realize that it's possible to go beyond your habitual patterns—the maze of ego...The only way out is to directly see another parallel dimension, outside the egoistic setup. That could appear as a momentary perception...In one moment, you can step out of the maze completely.

–Chögyam Trungpa Rinpoche

In essence, the hallmark of Tantra is passion. A distinctive feature of the Kagyü sect of Tibetan Buddhism, which is my own lineage, puts an emphasis on passion with a tradition of teachings on emotion, passion, and devotion. Kagyüs are said to be very emotional people, very devotional people. Trungpa Rinpoche commented that Kagyü lineage-holders tend to be padma people. They have tremendous love and devotion that they manifest in themselves and spark in their students.

In Tantric Buddhism, having a teacher is very important. They have the ability to dissolve us completely into the world of passion. We want to merge with our teacher's mind. It brings a magical quality to the lineage. As Trungpa Rinpoche's student, I had private meetings with him. In retrospect, I realize that all I really wanted to say was that I just wanted to be with him.

Let's begin with the birth of passion. As we have seen, the feminine principle is the primeval background, the basic ground of our existence, what is unborn, unconditioned, and beyond our control. Passion arises as a life force from that primordial ground. Its fundamental impulse is to create. In our passionate exuberance we create ourself. So, passion is the root of our being, our life-blood. Passion, or desire, gives us life and keeps us living. Most are created from the passion of our parents. We are reading this book because of our passion for dharma, to understand what is real. We desire to eat, to sleep, to make love, to work, and all the rest. Desire is what keeps us going. When we have passionate engagement, we experience the liberated qualities of the Five Wisdoms Energies, which is to say that we have a passion to be, know, enrich, feel, and act.

The sticky part is that we are so driven by trying to get what we want that we are tormented if we don't get it. We are always running after the object of desire. For sure, we do feel momentary fulfillment in the connection. We eat and feel full; we make love and feel blissful; we get the job and feel we have arrived. But then there is the desire for the next meal, the next embrace, the next promotion. Human life is driven by unfulfilled desire and those desires never end. In essence, passion and all that it brings up about being lonely, separate, and without, keeps us always on the move. This is what binds us.

Since desire and passion are so basic to our human life, it is important that we work with them properly, employing them as fuel for wakefulness and compassion. So, the emphasis on passion is due to our habitual or conventional fear of it. It's an energy that can provoke, seduce, and inspire. It is the one emotion that ego cannot really capture, contain, or confine. This is why it is so powerful. It is so important to understand passion as we have so much difficulty relating with it.

There is a basic shyness, embarrassment, even panic or bewilderment, with our relationship to passion. A friend of mine was researching aggression and checked out many books from the library. He told me he was always very self-conscious when checking out books on passion and sexuality.

While on the one hand, we are self-conscious in relating to passion, on the other hand, it is always on our mind. Our desire to be loved is even stronger than our fear of death. The irony is that we ignore our passion but crave it constantly. So, we suffer. As well, passion is dangerous. It is vehement, overpowering, explosive. Frustrated passion is deadly and leads to anger, violence, rape, murder, and wars as well as depression and suicide.

There is a hit-and-miss quality in relating to passion. Sometimes we relate to our passion in a skillful way, but most often we do not. Passion is the desire to own what we desire, anything, anywhere, anytime, anyhow. It is present in all of our relationships, family, raising children, and work interactions. It creates enormous complexity. In our dualistic human realm, our primary mantra is "I want." It is the padma neurosis of clinging to what is pleasurable. But we are never satisfied because we have tried to control our passion and, therefore, we cannot experience passion freely.

Fire is the essence of passion. We are hot with passion, burning with intensified emotions. We are consumed by them. But we cannot find any satisfaction so we are tormented, constantly looking for something to satisfy our desire. The irony is that we go against the fundamental energy of passion. In trying to possess the object of our desire, we destroy it. It is like trying to catch a butterfly. We grab it and, in so doing, kill it. When we destroy it, we no longer want it. Then we go on to the next butterfly.

The pure or liberated dimension of passionate relationship relies on the energy of no-mind…in the experience of pure passion, mind transcends logic. It requires courage to access that dimension of life. Generally, logical answers provide security. Logical conclusions bring us some comfort… It requires the bravery that is willing not to involve itself with that comfort…The only way to turn off that process of logical thinking is just to step out of it…[It] may feel very bleak and cold because it seems so unfamiliar. So when we experience it, we usually try to reestablish our familiar territory further and further…you should just step into that cold and bleak area—because it is not participating in the logical process of ego. That's all you can do. In a way, what you do is to just not do anything.

–Chögyam Trungpa Rinpoche

Tantra is noted for its inclusiveness of sexuality in a spiritual context. Tantric practices use this most powerful source of energy and intensifies it. It has the ability to open us completely. The liberation of passion and the experience of bliss is a powerful expedient in the practice of Tantra. Think of it. Making love, at its best, is a time when we pay attention to something fully. We are called upon to abandon ourself and experience a fuller state of being. We experience intimacy that is rare in our life. In this form, the openness and intensity is fulfilling. However, because of its power it can lead to extreme states of mind, so it is dangerous.

Passion is both intelligent and destructive. At best, it can intoxicate us into great bliss. At worst, it can make us obsessively addicted to it. Therefore, Tantra is often considered as outlawed, illegal, beyond the conventions of morality. We can only talk about passion in an awakened way when we are introduced to tantric teachings. However, it is imperative to first have some stability of mind. Then we are able to relate to it in a wholesome way.

In many ways pure passion is just passion in the ordinary sense, but at the same time, it is what is called vajra passion. It is vajra, which means indestructible in nature. It is called vajra passion because it is wild passion, in that it has no egoistic networks or wire mesh around it. It is free passion, wild passion, unleashed passion. It is passion that hasn't been directed by any sort of switchboard…It contains qualities of sparkling light—a wisdom quality—as well. It has tremendous consuming energy, which does not pass through any filters or networks. That kind of passion, whether it is connected with sex or anything else desirable that arises in life, is genuinely wild passion…[Ego] complicates our efforts to liberate this pure passion. The more we try to step out of ego's game, the more logical answers ego supplies, attempting to block our efforts.

–Chögyam Trungpa Rinpoche

Let's backtrack a bit here. When we first hear the dharma, it is the message of passionlessness. To work with our self-centered desire we learn self-restraint, renunciation, and simplicity. Our meditation cools the heat of passion and we experience openness of mind. We don't feed the fire. We cut off the gasoline supply. We cut the karmic momentum of ego-centered passion. We cultivate the simplicity of being alone. And we to learn to love ourself, the basic ground from which all else is possible. We could say that the most important relationship is the one with ourself. We take loneliness, aloneness, as our consort. There is a sense of sad joy, unrequited love. We don't fear losing our lover because we are always with our lover.

When we learn to love ourself it is taking the first step. It opens us up. Then the question is what do we do with all these people? The progression is actually a very natural one. To love is to open our heart. To open our heart means to let everyone in. Therefore, to love ourself means we inherit everybody.

When we are in a relationship to one person, we are in relationship with everyone. When we understand the interconnectedness of the mandala principle, love extends to all sentient beings. We then develop compassion for all beings. It is an interesting twist to loneliness.

> When our habitual self-centered desire turns toward care for others, a kind of spiritual transformation is possible... The fuel for this practice is desire, which has been transformed into the awakened heart, a spontaneous openness and warmth which liberates habitual self-centeredness... transformed desire is a kind of contagious fever of compassion.
>
> –Judith Simmer-Brown

From a tantric perspective, extinguishing the fire does not solve the problem. It dismisses the intelligence of passion as a path to liberate ourself and it cuts us off from our compassion for others. So, we have to work with the fire. The intensity of passion can only be liberated by passion itself. We need very skillful methods to liberate this fundamental quality of human existence. It is what constricts us and it is what liberates us. The problem isn't that we are on fire. It is that we don't burn freely and completely. The interesting twist here is that we are not passionate enough! Tantric practices work with passion to increase our passion. The fulfillment of passion is coming to great bliss, a merging of fire and space, blissful emptiness. Ultimately, it is a passion to unite with space, connecting back to the primeval background. It takes a certain fearlessness as it can be threatening. Bliss has a quality of deep satisfaction which we can experience in anything we encounter.

We have to be passionate people in order to practice Tantra. Being lukewarm is a problem. It is stuck in duality. It misses the point. Fundamentally it is not that we want "other," it is that we want complete union. The twist here is that we can only have real union when we are not clouded by projections and fantasies or blinded by enmeshment, not being able to separate self from other. Instead, we could have a sense of individuation and separateness, which allows more space. Separation makes complete union possible because longing is intensified and we long to surrender.

Since our nature is passion, it is not something new we have to take on. It is more of relaxing and letting go. Passion is connected to sacred outlook. There is a sense that we hold life as something sacred and precious. There is a sense of blessings which are often described as heat wave, like a summer day. So, we have a physical sensation of sacredness which comes from a sense of physical well-being. We are confident and cheerful. We appreciate our desires and are more compassionate.

In summary, the path is first freeing ourself from fixated passion, then discovering self-love and compassion, and finally conducting ourself with passionate engagement.

Let's look at the difference between passion and love. While passion has an intense enthusiasm or desire, love is a tender feeling. Passion is more primal and impacts every aspect of our life. Love is the deep feeling we have for others.

Love

All you need is love. It sounds almost corny. After 50 years of being a practitioner, plumbing the depths of esoteric Tantric Buddhism, is this what I've come to? That love is all you need? Yes! Not a dependently needy love, but an unconditional love.

We all want to love and be loved. But we often desperately seek love from others or love blindly without reserve. What we most need is to love ourself. I call this romancing the self. How can we be our best friend? We could even dissolve our loneliness and make friends with our solitude. We are not lonely; we are just alone. When we love ourself, we can love others. Moreover, when we love ourself, we become lovable.

> Love is to be kind to yourself, to be compassionate to yourself, to generate images of joy…In the Buddhist teaching, it's clear that to love oneself is the foundation of the love of other people. Love is truly a practice…When people love each other, the distinction, the limits, the frontier between them begins to dissolve, and they become one with the person they love…To love one person is a great opportunity for you to love many more. That nourishes you, that nourishes the other person, and finally your love will have no limit.

> –Thich Nhat Hanh

We have to go deeper and define what we want. At one point, my personal experience was quite profound. I started by saying I wanted to be in a relationship. What was deeper? A sense of joining with another, having physical intimacy. What was deeper than that? The pleasure and enjoyment of padma energy, which can manifest in many ways. So, I took up tango. And then? Blissful emptiness that I experienced at times on the meditation cushion and in life became more permanent. I moved from a constant sense of loneliness to a delight in being alone. I even questioned getting back into a relationship because I would lose my blissful aloneness.

My daughter Karuna and I were talking about loneliness and desire. She said that in her busy life surrounded by people, she finds that she gets most lonely for herself. I find this to be true as well. I shared the Robert Browning line in an earlier chapter. ("Every woman of true royalty owns a secret land more real to her than this pale outer world.") This line has resonated with me since I was a teenager. As a Buddhist practitioner, the sense of having a secret land still rings true but has taken on a new meaning.

Experiencing loneliness, feeling separate, is a primary aspect of the human condition: our first experience of existence is being in a warm, nurturing womb. Our second is of being born, being separated from that. Coming into this world is a rather dramatic story of being totally at one with another and then disconnected. Feeling the warmth and nurturing of another human being is our motivation to be in a love relationship. We desire another and long for someone with whom to join, to unite. It is human nature but it is indeed a sad story that primary love relationships so often sabotage feeling joined.

It's really all about the heart. Being in the heart, we are not thinking, just feeling. Thinking constricts us. Being in our heart, opens us. There is much to learn from the heart. We have a natural interest in others so the discipline of benefiting others brings delight to them and happiness to ourself. To develop universal love, we must accept both the light and the dark, the good and the bad.

The teachings of the Four Limitless Ones offer guidelines as to how we can expand our understanding of loving others. We can practice these for ourself, someone we love, someone we feel neutral toward, and someone who challenges us. A feeling of warmth or a flash of insight could arise. We could let go of the words and rest in the feeling.

1. Maitri, Loving Kindness: May all beings enjoy happiness and the root of happiness.

2. Compassion: May all beings be free from suffering and the root of suffering.

3. Joy: May all beings not be separated from the great happiness, devoid of suffering.

4. Equanimity: May all beings dwell in the great equanimity, free from passion, aggression, and ignorance.

When I feel my daughter's pain my default so often is to try to fix it. I just want to relieve her pain, and mine, as quickly as possible. It doesn't work. She is a smart cookie and actually knows what to do. She doesn't want advice. What she wants from me is empathy: to be embraced and held by my love, my compassion. I'm learning. For one thing, advice is often felt as criticism by the recipient. I also know this as a professional. I practice providing a container of unconditional love and kindness so that whatever arises is workable.

The Drama of Romance

There is nothing as delicious as falling in love. We get high on it. It's our new religion. We have just met a person who is compellingly attractive to us. It can be extremely gripping and keep people in fixated relationships for years. As Fred Kofman, author of *Conscious Business* commented, "I fell in love, and I did not calculate whether it was a good or a bad decision." However, romantic love is fraught with obstacles and falling out of love is devastating. Our intimate relationships, which could be a source of real nourishment in our lives, are often more painful than supportive.

We are wired for love. There is a spark and then the flame. We are pulled toward another to satisfy our longing to join. Our hormones make sure that this is so. Ultimately, what we do when we love is break down the barrier between ourself and another. We dare to let down our protective shield and feel vulnerable, exposed. It is also possible that we could freeze at the prospect as we are so wired to look for threats. What happens if the bubble bursts? What happens if we are rejected when what we long for is acceptance?

Let's look at the drama in an ego-centered love. We fall in love and experience the most open we have ever been. There is a feeling of excitement and mystery. We are in love with love and feed on its intensity. At a very visceral level, we feel we can't live without the other. We take our love to be solid and eternal. So, when the relationship doesn't hold-up to our expectation, we get manipulative, needy, and grasping. It becomes a push/pull, love/hate relationship. We are attracted to our love experience and also burned by it. We may become cynical, angry, and hardened.

Being in love, overcome with passion for someone, blinds us to who they are. When the bubble bursts and we wake up, we see them more clearly. We discover they are not who we thought they were as well as discovering volumes about ourself. This was certainly my experience on the break-up of my long-term marriage. Our fantasies and projections make them who we want them to be so we see them as just an extension of ourself. Then we are resentful when they don't live up to our expectations. So, a basic issue is whether we see another as an extension of ourself or as another person. Have we fallen in love with our projection? In this push and pull, there are always four people involved: ourself, the other, our projection of them, and their projection of us. How confusing is that?

Our world culture has created an especially difficult environment in which to work with our romantic expectations as we are taught that the solution to life's problems is romantic love. We have a fascination with beautiful and powerful people, padma and karma energies. For those with a heterosexual orientation, popular role models for women are movie stars and models; for men, politicians and business men. Beauty and power are fine values to have, but are easily corrupted by our obsessive fascination with them. When they are the dominant values, they leave out wonderful aspects of who we are. For those who are gender identified in other ways, it is no wonder people get confused, depressed, and suicidal. No wonder we cannot find relationships that resonate with us at a deeper level.

The Dharma of Romantic Love

The myth of romantic relationships is that it is someone else who is supposed to make us happy. We think that the object of our desire is something we have to grasp. But we can never really possess the object of our desire. In truth, we can't love someone until we don't *need* to love them. The more we depend, the less we love. In any case, why would we want to depend on another person for our own happiness? Additionally, if we always got everything we wanted, there would be no passion. What fun would that be? When we embody our energy fully, we are fulfilled, so more independent. Self-love makes us better partners.

We can cut through fixation on another by understanding energy. If we feel a particular energy is missing in ourself, we tend to seek it in another. When we can cultivate that energy in ourself, we become what we long for. Then we can dissolve our fixation on "other" and feel joined with them. In fact, we see we are already joined. There is a powerful shift from being in love to being love.

From a dharmic perspective, the teachings on unrequited love are profound and powerful. We could love unconditionally without expecting our love to be returned. When our love is not rewarded, we can still stay with a tender heart. Do you want to live on the edge? Try romantic love without attachment! I am a true believer, but also find it tricky to do. The mind is so slippery. We have to ask ourself, "Do I love him with all of my heart but don't depend on him for my own happiness?"

What does that do to romantic love? We dance with others. The decorum of tango, when taken to heart, is a model of this. We are asked to dance, we dance in a warm and intimate way, sharing our energy, and when the dance ends, we thank each other for the dance. Then we go on to the next partner, the next dance. It's fullness and emptiness right there on the dance floor!

A most profound and paradoxical aspect of a loving relationship is that unconditional love of another can liberate us to more fully realize our individuality. How can this be? When we surrender to another, we open our heart and, at best, are self-less. It's not one plus one equals two, but one plus one equals one. Two people who can unconditionally love without being dependent on each other is powerfully fulfilling. The most basic understanding of our existence is that we are already joined.

We often seek out an intimate relationship because we are lonely. The loneliness feels like an empty hole inside. The fire went out. There is no vitality. It also feels like there is not enough substance, earth; no nurturance. When we let go of who is feeling, the "I," then we are ready to love. Being alone and practicing meditation allows us to connect with the deepest part of ourself. Desiring to join with another in this deep place, to have a soul mate, can be deeply enriching. But watch out! Grasping can kill it!

Most importantly, the deepest self transcends the self. It is the no-self. No-self rests in being completely fulfilled. There is no place to go, no one to seek. Loneliness is transmuted into an open-hearted state of love that requires no need to seek further. When we love, it is with an open heart, without attachment. Having no attachment allows us to be big-hearted toward everyone. Though there is no self, there is self-existing non-appropriated energy. We can go for the ride.

When Trungpa Rinpoche died, I actually felt closer to him. Instead of longing to be with my teacher in that chair, in that room, I felt him everywhere. There was no radiator, just the omnipresent radiation of his warmth and brilliance. My love for him was not interrupted by the absence of his physical presence.

Some day after we have mastered the winds, the waves, the tides, and gravity, we shall harness the energies of love. And then for the second time in the history of the world, man will have discovered fire.

–Teilhard de Chardin

CHAPTER 23

A Sacred Way
of Seeing

The sun has a sense of all-pervasive brilliance, which does not discriminate in the slightest. It is the goodness that exists in a situation, in oneself, and in one's world, which is expressed without doubt, hesitation, or regret. The sun principle also includes the notion of blessings descending upon us and creating sacred world. It also represents clarity, without doubt.

–Chögyam Trungpa Rinpoche

Some kind of celebration is necessary rather than being a good student.

–Chögyam Trungpa Rinpoche

Having a sacred outlook is the fruition of our journey. An intuitive knowing, captured in nowness, experiences the world as sacred. We have a sense of awe, a sense of reverence. When we open our mind to space, the world pours in. We could feel powerfully present and synchronized, experiencing heightened energy, vitality, and delight. The world becomes alive with energy and replete with meaning. There is a tremendous appreciation for all things great and small. It invites the arts and all forms of expression and diversity. The view of living in a sacred world is an inspiring vision. We can celebrate.

We have been on the runway. Tantra is the take-off: that magical moment when the wheels lift off the ground and we are in the air. There is a willing suspension of disbelief that we could actually be in the air. Rather than trying to get somewhere, it is about being right here right now: flying! It is truly a different world, a sacred world. The most provocative thing we could say is that ultimately there is nowhere to go, no one going anywhere, and nothing to do. We could let go of our self-importance and earnestness and relax. It can be the atmosphere in which we live.

The result of the journey through the stages of dharmic realization is that we have transformed from ordinary people to awakened people. We have developed a certain understanding of ourself and the world. Our tantric world is a more cheerful place to be than the pure emptiness approach. There is emptiness but also a sense of brilliance. The phenomenal world has become a self-existing dynamic mandala, not for or against us. We have nothing to regret and everything is appreciated just as it is.

At first, we were bound by our neurosis. Now we have an even greater bondage: to not waver from the big mind. We have run out of coping strategies, and we are bound by that particular "run-outness," as Trungpa Rinpoche liked to put it. We have unconditional appreciation and feel tremendous dignity, trust, and fearlessness. We could feel how incredible it is to be alive. We could have moments of *just that*, what is immediately real at the moment. We call this "suchness" or "thatness" or "things as they are."

Sacredness can sound theistic when we first hear it, but it is not. Rather, it is a sense of awe at the splendor, intensity, and potential of our world. As I have said, Quakers express this beautifully as the light within and the light in the world. The light within is an inner teacher. The path has no creed but is defined by a search for the light. I grew up as a Quaker. In meetings for worship, we sat in silence. Anyone could rise and share their inspiration. It creates empathy, intimacy, and aliveness in the community.

> Transplanting the moon of wakefulness into your heart and the sun of wisdom into your head can be natural and obvious. It is not so much trying to look for the bright side of life and using that side of things as a stepping stone, but it is discovering unconditional cheerfulness, which has no other side. It is just one side, one taste. From that, the natural sense of goodness begins to dawn in your heart. Therefore, whatever we experience, whatever we see, whatever we hear, whatever we think—all those activities begin to have some sense of holiness or sacredness in them. The world is full of hospitality at that point. Sharp corners begin to dissolve and the darkness begins to be uplifted in our lives. That kind of goodness is unconditionally good, and at that point, we become a decent human being and a warrior.
>
> –Chögyam Trungpa Rinpoche

The sacredness of the world is always available to us. Our problem in realizing sacredness, is feeling that we are separated from it. It seems foreign, in great contrast to our mundane everyday life, so we don't want, or don't know how, to go there. We just move along in our day-to-day world and take things for granted. We are conditioned to doing what needs to be done and just become functional, going through life like a robot. Our thinking is aligned with self-preservation and life's comforts. And to make really sure there is no gap, we endlessly entertain ourself and indulge in distractions.

The sad news is that when we do not cultivate a sacred outlook, everything we do becomes flat. When we lose our awe and respect, the sense of our world shrinks. We could feel small and awkward. It's an implosion of the heart and mind. When we experience the goodness of being alive, we respect who and what we are. With a sense of greater confidence, we allow ourself to just stop and look and feel. We could have a sacred outlook in simple gestures and actions. We could see that there is an indivisibility between the secular and sacred worlds in bringing together the notion of immense emptiness of space and manifestation within it.

Sacred possibilities always exist in our lives, right here now. This is not about some transcendent realm or religious outlook. The goodness and the gentleness of the world are always there for us to appreciate. Nothing needs to be rejected but can be embraced. So, we find that the secular becomes sacred, very real, completely genuine.

> The heart of the vajrayāna teachings is the realization that the phenomenal world and one's mind form an indestructible unity, which includes the defilements of ego as well as the purity of practice...every element of existence is seen as sacred; nothing is rejected...we begin with the proclamation of vajra nature, the indestructible and primordially pure nature of all beings. Because all beings possess vajra nature, enlightenment is no longer viewed as a conclusion, but as the starting point of practice. Practice is not seen as a means to an end, but as the expression of awakened mind in everyday life.
>
> —Vajra Regent Ösel Tendzin

Appreciating sacredness begins very simply by taking an interest in all the details of our life. Pure sense perceptions are the gateway to experiencing the sacred world. We engage with a world that is radiating its essence. We are drawn to listen to a beautiful piece of music, smell a flower, sit and watch the clouds go by. However, we can only catch their radiance, their vitality, when we are open to them. We need the sacred space of silence to feel the world's vibrancy. Our ordinary perception is so ordinary that it is super-ordinary. We also note that nothing stays the same; everything is inherently in flux, impermanent, ephemeral, and illusory. There could be a sense of what Trungpa Rinpoche called "transcendental indulgence." We experience feeling completely adequate in the moment. The past is fiction and the future is a dream. It can be heartbreakingly beautiful and we could stay there forever.

> When playfulness and pleasure begin to take place...We have a sense of complete joy and complete freedom... indulgence is the sense of utmost celebration. There is light-heartedness because the things that happen in our life do not mean very much...and at the same time, they mean a great deal...a lot more fun and a lot more inquisitiveness takes place in our life.
>
> –Chögyam Trungpa Rinpoche

Taking the idea of sacred world a step further, new theories in neuroscience suggest the idea of a universal consciousness. This is an understanding that consciousness is intrinsic, a fundamental and ubiquitous feature of reality. This means that everything material, however small, has an element of individual consciousness. Of course, this idea is not exactly new. It is fundamental to many indigenous spiritual traditions like paganism and shamanism. What excites scientists is that, with more research and testing, they will be able to measure the degree of sentience in a given person or object. They could *prove* that everything is sentient.

Let's look at the remarkable experience of Dr. Jill Bolte Taylor, a neuroscientist working at the Harvard brain research center. She had a literally mind-blowing experience when a blood vessel in her brain popped. Within minutes her left lobe, the source of ego, analysis, judgment, and context, began to fail her. She said, "My perception of physical boundaries was no longer limited to where my skin met air...The energy of my spirit seemed to flow like a great whale gliding through a sea of silent euphoria." Once recovered, she said she became a new person, one who "can step into the consciousness of my right hemisphere" on command and be "one with all that is."

She now has a deep personal understanding of something she long studied: that the two lobes of the brain have very different personalities. She comments that the experience of deep contentment "is a part of the capacity of the human mind." She goes on to say, "There is no doubt that it is a beautiful state and that we can get there...I believe that the more time we spend choosing to run the deep inner peace circuitry of our right hemispheres, the more peace we will project into the world, and the more peaceful our planet will be." For me this story gives us confirmation that we are wisdom beings living in a sacred world.

Interestingly, the end of the journey toward realization is the beginning of how we participate in the world. We turn around and come back. This will be brought out in Part VI when we talk about our life's purpose.

PART V

Mandala: Our Ever-Shifting Kaleidoscope

CHAPTER 24

The Five Wisdoms Mandala

...The visualization becomes just a mixture of colors. The dazzling rays of the five wisdoms are bright red, deep green, clear blue, pure yellow and bright white. They are not static but oscillating all the time, and they fill the whole of heaven and earth...and you lose the clear-cut concept of "here" and "there" and become dizzy...

—Chögyam Trungpa Rinpoche,
the Sadhana of Mahāmudrā

By now we should have a sense of the energetic dimension of both our outer and inner worlds. Moreover, we should understand the inseparability of these two worlds. We see how we color the external world, and how all external phenomena colors us. We begin to see that everything we experience is the energetic play of the mandala, a matrix of interconnected energies. It is primordially perfect, spontaneously present, timeless, spaceless, and without beginning or end. It brings together immense emptiness and manifestation within it. We know this intuitively, free from concept. Our small mind acts as reminder to open to this vast mind, the big mind. It becomes impossible to stray from the big mind.

This total energetic field is the playground of the Five Wisdoms. It has five types of intelligence—sometimes constricted, sometimes flowing—which merge and layer in infinite combinations. It points to the myriads of connections and immense diversity of our world. As well, the mandala is exquisitely sensitive so that one energy always influences the whole. We begin to see each situation has an inevitable and predictable pattern. Because there is a predictable dynamic between energies, we can see their inevitable outcome. This is not magic. It is just being aware.

> Life is an ever-shifting kaleidoscope. A slight change and all patterns alter.
>
> –Sharon Salzberg

The Toxic Energy of the Samsaric Mandala

Traditionally, each energy is in a particular direction which is not geographical but metaphysical. The following examples are when a person has a dominance of an energy.

East/Vajra: The dominant intensified emotion is anger. People are intellectual, have an analytical mind, and depend on logic. They are severe toward themselves and rarely enjoy themselves. They have a sense of austerity, and sacrifice their health and comfort. They can be pushy, cutting, and destructive.

South/Ratna: The dominant intensified emotion is pride. People are arrogant and self-assertive without much sense of dignity or confidence. They want to be acknowledged and sometimes have a perverted way of demonstrating their generosity. They can become overwhelming, demonic, and heavy-handed. Any sense of comfort or entertainment becomes more than is needed, uninviting and claustrophobic.

West/Padma: The dominant intensified emotion is passion, grasping. People are tremendously seductive. Others feel constantly sucked into their territory. There is no room for equal exchange. Someone could want to be sucked in because they feel insignificant and want to be loved.

North/Karma: The dominant intensified emotion is jealously fed by paranoia and competitiveness. People are very heavy-handed because they are always trying to get ahead and be in control. They undermine or crush any object of their jealousy. They think of themself as top dog and see others as insignificant so they are not threatened by them.

The Awakened Energy of the Wisdom Mandala

East/Vajra: Mirror-like wisdom, reflecting everything in an unbiased way.

South/Ratna: The wisdom of equanimity, a fulfilled sense of richness.

West/Padma: Discriminating wisdom, a profound intimacy with the world.

North/Karma: All-accomplishing action for the benefit of all beings.

Five Wisdoms Cycles

The most common cycle arising from primal space: buddha, vajra, ratna, padma, and karma.

Times of the day: vajra or karma in the morning, ratna in the mid-day, and padma in the evening.

The seasons: winter is vajra, spring is padma, summer is karma, fall is ratna.

Understanding the Five Wisdoms
Through Sense Perceptions

Sense perceptions give us the potential to experience the five energies because they open us to five distinct fields of awareness. Each sense has a different sense-ability. Each one puts us in a different psychophysical relationship to our world. We might seem to become different people. What is your experience when hearing your favorite song? Smelling a rose? Tasting chocolate? Chairing a business meeting? Being touched?

Becoming sensate enables us to become multi-dimensional and so discover this multi-dimensional reality. We become more receptive to different experiences, widen our palate of permissible energies, and have more fullness of being. We see things as they are and experience their essence, their energy. They make experiential sense to us. This sense could be a very ordinary down-to-earth experience. We also find we have our preferences and aversions. An affinity to one sense gives us an understanding of who we are and how we experience the world. Experiencing is believing: we can have a non-conceptual trust in our senses.

When we focus intently on *seeing*, as in writing a book on a computer, we arouse a sharp mental acuity. Taking a photograph, we like relating to how things are lined up: their form, shape, and texture. We are meticulous about how things are arranged in space. Visual perception creates a subject-object relationship.

When we fully focus on *smelling and tasting*—as when cooking and eating—we enter a ratna world. For many, it is satisfying and nurturing to savor good food. Ratna is also associated with the very visceral experience of *touch*. We feel our body from the inside, as in kinesthetics, the sensations of the body at rest or in movement. We awaken our body through the awareness of it and open to the deep inner-dance of sensation. Touch is the only perception that is below the neck.

When we pick up on the vibrations of a person or situation, we tune in to padma, a *feeling* energy. We sense the emotion or feeling state and not just the words being said. Music, particularly love songs or romantic pieces, permeate our body and strongly affect us. It stirs our emotions and can change our mood instantaneously. We might want to express the feeling by dancing. Speech in poetry, politics, or theatrical performances can have the same effect. Sound exists in time, so when we hear, we are in the moment. The capacity for attunement makes the padma energy the most receptive to the energetic dimension of reality.

When we swing an ax, kick a ball, or put our foot on the gas pedal — *touch something in a functional way* — we are in karma energy. This touch is functional rather than sensational, as in ratna's touch. We engage muscles to make a movement happen. We become active. We physically connect to an object or make a movement.

There is no particular sense perception associated with buddha. We are in space, just being. It is open to all of the senses and so acts like a switchboard, a receptor, for the other energies.

Becoming sensate has to do with:

Vajra's looking and then seeing

Padma's listening and then hearing

Ratna's smelling and tasting and then savoring

Ratna's touching and then feeling

Karma's touching and then making something happen

Most often, we use several sense perceptions in any given moment. Chefs know that a meal must taste good, be pleasing to the eye, and communicate that it is pleasurable. So, there is an implicit interconnection of the five senses. Each sensory perception opens us to the others. We could see, smell, hear, and touch with our eyes. When we hear something, we could see it, smell it, touch it.

Let's look at how we might experience an object through all of the senses. Let's take a peach. We move from the outside and get deeper into the object, finally merging with it. Initially, we acknowledge the space (buddha) in which the object exists. Then we see its form, shape, and design (vajra). Next, we sense the radiation, communication, particular vibrations of the object (padma). When we begin to merge with the object, we could actually smell or taste it (ratna). Now that we have taken an immense interest in our peach, we could pick it up and, in a sense, become one with it by eating it (karma).

Sense Perceptions, Projections, and the Five Wisdoms

To review, in Chapter 7 we looked at the Five Psychophysical Aspects in the development of ego leading to projections and Intensified Realities. A moment of perception quickly gets linked to a subtle process of picking and choosing, having opinions, taking a stance, and creating a dualistic world.

How do we get out of this knee-jerk reaction to our sensory perception? How could we have a cleaner relationship to our world? Be more ecological? We have to be clear on the difference between projection and perception. A projection is ego's expression, a way of identifying with what we have projected to confirm our existence. "This is my rose." Pure perceptions see directly without commentary. We don't even name things. We experience roseness.

When we slow down, we are able to see through our self-referencing dualistic fixation. Rather than identifying with our projections, we could merge and play with the illusory nature of our world. With this attitude, our senses are purified and our projections are not a problem. They are what they are, illusory forms, apparent and yet not inherently there. They can be exciting and dynamic: a simple display of colors, emotions, dramas, and interactions. We could relax our control and simply delight in the world. The development of ego through the chaining together of the psychophysical aspects, projections, and Intensified Realities are dissolved. We discover that when we are open, the aspects are experienced as five qualities of intrinsic sanity, the Five Wisdoms. We could embody and act out of these qualities:

The spaciousness of buddha energy

The mirror-like wisdom of vajra energy

The equanimity of ratna energy

The discriminating awareness of padma energy

The skillful means of karma energy

An Extraordinary Panoramic Vision

Experiencing our world as an energetic display of people, places, and situations brings us one step closer to the ultimate truth: what underlines the display is the insubstantiality of it all. All is apparently manifesting in its magnificent, colorful, fleeting, and ephemeral display, but nothing is inherently enduring or permanent. This is both scary and liberating. It's scary in that we have nothing to hold onto: we so love looking good, being right, and knowing what to do. Yet it's liberating in that we can relax that perpetual struggle.

We realize the ultimate truth of emptiness—not in a nihilistic way—that emptiness is full of dynamic energy, a pervasive and extraordinarily awake ground. It is directionless, timeless, and spaceless; lively, vivid, and luminous; illusory, ephemeral, and fleeting. We find that it is vastly more enjoyable than our constricted self can possibly imagine. We have tuned into the magical possibilities of life, a self-existing greater atmosphere. There is no separation between us and our world. We are part of life's flow. The ultimate experience is the vibrancy of all we experience.

CHAPTER 25

The Five Wisdoms
Journey

T he Five Wisdoms Energies provide us with an opportunity to make a big leap beyond our tunnel vision that
is "all about me." We circumvent our biased perspective
and join the dance of self-existing energy. Energy is just there,
doing its thing; it does not need our confirmation or ownership.
Our understanding goes from the inner-personal, to the interpersonal, to the world view, to a cosmic perspective. It's a journey that goes from all-about-me, to all-about-us, to all-about-
humanity, to transpersonal. We go from being driven by our
subconscious habitual patterns, to being self-aware, to having
a "we" consciousness, to unbiased wisdom.

That there is a rock bed of energy in which our wisdom and
our confusion co-exist gives us an unparalleled opportunity to
transform all of our challenges into opportunities. As we gain
more awareness of how we interact with our world—our patterns of behavior, emotional responses, and relationships—we
can have a sense of friendly curiosity toward our struggles and
appreciate our brilliance. Our willingness to see ourself clearly,
without judgment and criticism, is the first step. We train ourself to align with our best and find wisdom present in whatever
we do. We regard our stuck places as work points. Moreover,
by knowing ourself deeply, we understand others and are
more skilled in engaging with them.

Energy is just there, doing its thing, and we go for the ride. Going for the ride, rather than steering the ride, means we have found a way out of our constricted ego sphere of constantly manipulating the world to our own advantage. By not taking ourself so seriously, we find our difficulties are not personal but a manifestation of energy. "Oh, isn't this interesting: this person's energy and mine are clashing (or attracting) each other. What (not who) is that about? What is going on here?" We can drop the story line, relax, and relate with what is happening without trying to control or influence it.

Each stage of this journey brings us into a bigger perspective of the Five Wisdoms. Many find that relating to the wisdoms from the perspective of a typology has brought tremendous understanding into their lives. Others see the potential for a meaningful life only when the sense of self falls away to become one with the play of energies.

There is a natural progression to acquainting ourself with the energetic qualities: learning, contemplating, and embodying. First, we learn about them. Second, we contemplate them as they reflect in life experiences. The more experiences we have where situations are illuminated by them, the more they become a language through which we experience our world. Third and finally, they become our guide to living a fulfilling life and reflect in everything we think, feel, say, and do. This work is subtle and deep, predictable and surprising. Our journey of self-discovery can be both exciting and uncomfortable, but it always makes us feel more alive!

Maitri Space Awareness and the Great Switcheroo

Trungpa Rinpoche skillfully named this body of teachings Maitri Space Awareness. We see that maitri is the key to transmute our constrictions and gain more spaciousness of mind.

We then open to the dynamic energy of space. We can't manufacture or create it. It is discovered on the spot.

Just when we feel we might be tamed and processed by Hīnayāna and Mahayāna, we jump into the tantric view that space is full of energy. Emptiness has left us in no man's land. With Tantra, we are re-introduced to the nitty gritty of the relative world. A key to our understanding is that confusion and space are inseparable: the claustrophobia of confusion and the brilliance of sanity coexist. This is not something we can conceptualize or manufacture, it's an experience.

Here is the big switcheroo. Up to this point, our approach has likely been "I am a solid identity (ego); what's out there is to be manipulated to my desires." Here, the idea of space gets flipped around completely and our approach becomes, "Space is solid, real, tangible, colorful, vivid and I am open, fluid, roll with the punches, sail with the wind, surf the waves." We realize we can't dictate what happens, not because we give up trying, but because it is more effortless to go with the flow. The practice is to be open to the present moment, enter the confusion, and stay there. What happens happens.

As we have seen, ego has a tendency to project. However, we can develop clear perception, unsullied by our particular story line. Projections can be completely fluid and workable and we can dance with them. Ego is manipulative; going with the flow is spontaneous. Projections are not a bad thing in this sense. Instead of our tendency to have projections that are frozen, stiff, and solid, we could have projections that are exciting, fluid, dynamic, and playful. When we are open and responding to the energy, we are not projecting.

This indestructible space accommodates the five energies. When we are open to the energetic dynamic of space, our experience becomes more vivid and intense because we are unmasked, naked, vulnerable. It is all extremely shifty because we can't box experience into neat little categories. There are always twists and turns because energetic space can't be reduced to something graspable or definable. Eventually, we learn to relax in an intensified world.

Fruition: Balancing Our Energies

Each of our wisdoms has the ability to serve us. However, if locked into hours and hours of one energy—inevitably making that energy neurotic—we deplete that energy and become energetically unbalanced. Moreover, if we don't balance them, they either explode or collapse. We could monitor this by asking some simple questions. Do we feel a balance of energies or are we stuck in one? Are we accomplishing what needs to get done or are we getting sluggish? Do we need to change gears and try another energy? On a daily basis, are we able to accomplish more for longer periods of time if we practice balancing our energies?

The good news is that we are all multi-dimensional. We can learn to balance our energies throughout our day. I call this the daily diet of five.

1. rest in the spaciousness of basic being
2. have insightful clear thinking
3. be resourceful and generous
4. engage and speak from our heart
5. accomplish our tasks efficiently

At different times in different circumstances, one or more of these qualities is needed. Being more balanced brings our full being into whatever we do.

Contemplating Our Personal Mandala: Involvement in Five Areas of Life

1. Intellect, vision
Study, reading, having a life perspective

2. Nurturance, resourcefulness
Health, mind/body disciplines, food, domestic comfort, cultural pursuits

3. Relationships
Friendships, marriage or primary partner, artistic pursuits

4. Livelihood
Involvement with a career, profession, job

5. Spirituality
Formal practice, inspiration for higher understanding

Ask:
- What areas seem wholesome?
- What areas seem lacking and how could they be developed?

Fruition: Wisdom Activity

We know we have developed wisdom activity when we tune into what is happening and respond with the energy needed in the moment. We are no longer operating from ego's agenda. We ride the wave of coincidence with actions that are spontaneous and appropriate. Surrendering to the natural flow of energy is more effective than trying to control it. When we surrender, we know what to do. We can bring wisdom activity, motivated by compassion, into play. Allowing ourself to fit into the big picture—without manipulating or scheming—is a powerful experience. This is traditionally called buddha activity. Our slogan becomes. "When I have fully embodied the Five Wisdoms, I can go anywhere and do anything, as long as it benefits others."

Fruition: The Ultimate Truth

As we learned in Chapter 20—the dimensions of reality—emptiness is a more primal dimension than the energetic play of the Five Wisdoms. The ultimate truth underlies the energetic display of people, places, and situations. It sees the insubstantiality of all, *apparently* manifesting in their magnificent, colorful display but it is *inherently nonexistent*, fleeting and ephemeral.

Emptiness is difficult to describe in words, but we can experience it. It allows us to view the world as a psychological and phenomenal process without the need to centralize the energy on ourself. This then enables us to relate with life straightforwardly and directly. When we tune into this magical possibility, we have a positive experience of nonexistence. As a Zen Roshi friend says, "Roshis just like having a good time."

The Five Wisdoms are not mundane sanity but brilliant sanity. They give us a sense of confidence and soft heart. At the same time, we don't forget the pain and confusion that lurks around the corner. Our lives are felt fully and thoroughly, so we appreciate ourself as authentic. We feel both joy and sadness fully. Things feel real and ring true.

Practicing With the Energies

The process of coming into our wisdom could be quite messy because we first need to expose our solidified neurosis. We might have avoided this our whole life. However, if we bypass our juicy neurosis, we never know who we really are. Generally, we are only part of who we are, part of our potential. If we drop the fixation, the energy is more available to us. We could hide out in a cocoon or we could wake up and express our brilliance.

In any given moment we could say yes or no. No is the inertia of our confusion; yes is the innate confidence of our wisdom. We do this all of the time. We wake up or we go to sleep. When we are open and welcoming, we feel a sense of well-being. We sense ourself as fundamentally good, sane, and intelligent and invite a life full of possibility. When closed and resistant, we become constricted and confused. We identify with our confusion, not our intrinsic goodness. We feel stuck, dense, and claustrophobic. We could either freeze or explode. In time, we can learn to align with wakefulness.

Life is constantly challenging us to open to the situation at hand. Do we embrace the fullness of the moment or shrink from it and withdraw? Do we forget what is good and believe in confusion? When we are aware of energy, we can align with it; when we are not aware of it, things are confusing. When aware of our habitual patterns, we have a choice; if not, we are a slave to them. Transmutation is key. We transmute neurotic energy by knowing it intimately. It is helpful to note that outer circumstances can either enhance our sanity or exacerbate our confusion. Mostly, we cannot change external situations, but we can always work with ourself.

The Five Wisdoms are not something to acquire but a contemplation; not something to learn but something to become; not a tool to get but becoming a tool. They are about an expanded awareness of everything in the field of our experience more than a formal practice. It is empowering. Our best teachers are the ones who embody this.

Practices

Now let's look at ways we can put these understandings into practice, train ourself. Training means repeating, practicing in an ongoing way. It is re-aligning toward another way of being. The journey is the teacher and whatever comes up is the path. Contemplative training is tracking experiences in our body, speech, and mind, and how we move through our world twenty-four hours a day.

We work with deep embodied energetic practices. Philosophizing, intellectualizing, or analyzing blunts the experience and doesn't integrate sensuality and sexuality. Mind/body practices allow energy circulation and reinvigorate and re-tune the energetic body. They work with very deep conditioning and develop a relationship with the dark forces within us. We pay attention to:

1. Physical sensations.
2. Felt sense of emotion.
3. Discursive thoughts.

Children do not have the conceptual armoring that adults have, so their experience is more direct. My daughter, then aged 7, and I went into the specifically designed Five Wisdoms rooms. In moments she picked up on the different energies. Then she said, "I'm going to do a dance for you and show you what moods we got into in each room."

The Five Wisdoms Posture Practice

Trungpa Rinpoche created the practice of using postures and colors. Though it is essentially a tantric practice, rather

than keeping it secret as is traditional with esoteric practices, it can be practiced by anyone. It is based on the understanding that our wisdom is embedded in the very energy we experience as neurotic. The postures—working with our body's subtle energy or inner yoga—are designed to bring to light our physical, energetic, and mental states. They are like a pandora's box. We have no idea what will happen. The color is a code. It is not so much that we see the color but enter a whole world.

For years I wondered how the postures work. Unfortunately, Rinpoche had passed before I could ask this burning question. Other teachers have given general answers. There was a very humorous moment when I asked a chi gong teacher about them. He said that the Tibetan body was not his body!

But here is the gist. The basic principle is that our energy moves in specific directions in our subtle channels and accumulates at our energy centers (chakras). However, in the course of life, our neurotic tendencies and physical illnesses block this movement. The postures are designed to heighten the flow of energy in specific channels to "flush out" the blocked energy, often locked in our body for years. Each posture is designed to evoke, intensify, and transmute a specific neurotic pattern by releasing blockages. They work with intensification to penetrate and illuminate our dark corners and make the experience of our energies more vivid.

As we come into a felt sense of each energy, we discover the tangible qualities of all five in our make-up. When the channels are functioning smoothly, our mind and body are relaxed and we have an unconditional acceptance of ourself. When not, we get confused. Once we get a taste of each energy, we can re-experience and align with its wisdom in a flash. I call this a homeopathic dose.

In some sense, posture practice is the best teacher of the energies as they give us direct experience of who we are. We could have intensified experiences of claustrophobia, confusion, irritation, or our favorite emotional upheaval. We could also have a very spacious, very low-key experience. We could go to sleep, or have an adverse reaction, or love the energy. It could feel totally familiar or completely foreign. There is no experience we are meant to have. We all bring our mix of colors to the posture.

The practice is extremely simple but may also be challenging. Thoughts can run wild and emotions can get very full-blown and, as you can imagine, quite messy. We might never have thought we had that much red energy or blue energy! We become connoisseurs of our confusion. Insights could arise spontaneously. If we can handle the intensity, that's fine, but sometimes it gets too much. If we are spiraling into a dark place, sitting practice could lighten it. It is also part of what makes maitri happen, a tool to regulate the intensity. By embracing the intensified energy and surrounding it with an attitude of unconditional friendliness, we become more open, expressive, and sensitive to all of the different textures and qualities around us. We also become more aware of how we color the space.

Sitting practice is always done in conjunction with posture practice. I like to think of it as if we are as a glass of muddy water and sitting practice helps to settle the sediment. If we were to put color into the muddy water before the sediment has settled, it would just create more mud. If we put color into a clear glass of water, they become brilliant. It creates the space to accommodate some of the intensity of the experience.

The Five Wisdoms arise out of our neurosis as sane manifestations of who we are. Our neurotic pimples are turned into ornaments with which we adorn ourself. Constriction resolves into simple presence, confusion into clarity, neediness into richness, emotional intensity into love, and hesitation into action. We open. There is no struggle when we open to the moment. As Trungpa Rinpoche says, "You can't get stuck in space." This is the transformative power of posture practice.

The practice balances the feminine and masculine energies innately within us. Padma and ratna are associated with passion and are feminine qualities; vajra and karma are associated with aggression and are masculine qualities; buddha is neutral but cosmically it is more feminine. With practice, we come into a balance and naturally manifest both energies. This has the potential to heal our inner fragmentation, confusion, and turmoil of these seemingly oppositional energies. Societally we have been conditioned to be one or other, but this has limited us. We can discover the personal integration of the five and come into the full spectrum — an embodied unification — of who we are.

The Effects of Posture Practice

The practice is done by taking a posture in specifically designed rooms or with colored glasses we call Wise Eyes. The postures are only done under guidance as they can be quite provocative.

- The buddha posture suggests drawing inward, creating a closed, secure place. It works with laziness and a tendency to ignore. It works with the central channel and life force and opens our heart. As energy starts to flow through our channels, we become aware of larger space and relax into a sense of basic being.

- The vajra posture frustrates the desire to scan our surroundings and take an overview. It thwarts our preoccupation with details, our desire to know what is going on. We may become irritated or angry. It's primary energy is in the chest and forehead. As our channels become unblocked, we discover a confidence in what we already know, an inherent knowing.

- The ratna posture gives a feeling of expansion. We want to embrace the whole world. We feel there is much more to be appreciated, but the richness is beyond our reach. Most affected areas are the solar plexus, stomach, and skin. All the channels are straight so it can be healing. The posture reinforces a sense of poverty and insubstantiality until we relax and begin to feel the richness inside of us.

- The padma posture frustrates the longing to possess. We long for the object of our desire but can't grasp it. We are stuck in mediocrity and boredom. The body parts most effected are the three communication centers: throat, heart, and genitals. We discover our innate passion and that all we desire is within us.

- The karma posture's immobility frustrates our desire for action, to always make something happen. In this restricted state, all we can do is look at the impulse. Our limbs are most effected. Eventually we give up the struggle and experience a powerful potential within us.

Forty years later I still remain in awe. These postures—one of Trungpa Rinpoche's gifts to the world—have the potency to transmute all we struggle with into our natural intelligence. They validate this whole body of teachings. I am continually amazed at how people often do a posture briefly, with no idea of what to expect, and then give a textbook description of the energy. At the same time, people have a wide range of experiences. However we display our energy, we are always celebrating our strengths and working with our stuck places!

Aimless Wandering

Aimless wandering is done after posture practice as a way to experience our world after being dipped in a color. We simply wander around our house or outside, in silence, with absolutely no agenda. We have the sense of opening to what is around us, mingle ourself with the sights and sounds and smells of your environment. We can pause at times and sense the play of energy in the world.

Creative Expression and Sharing

Exploring the energies creatively helps to bring out non-conceptual experiences. We can color, move, write poetry. No talent necessary! Sharing experiences allows us to see the full spectrum of possibility with each energy. We freely learn from others. The insights that emerge from our shared experiences are powerfully illuminating.

Community

It is helpful to be with like-minded people in environments that, support our practice. The Five Wisdoms are generally practiced in the context of a community which allows for both the intensification of energy and the accommodation of that energy—as the danger surfaces, the maitri permeates. As I wrote in *The Five Wisdoms Energies*, a group provides "a nonjudgmental, supportive container with an attitude of fundamental acceptance of whatever arises. It is a safe, nurturing place where we support one another in being genuine. In such a community, we can explore without censure, so our neuroses are neither repressed nor indulged but are openly recognized. It allows the best and the worst to come out."

PART VI

Your Life Purpose

CHAPTER 26

Envisioning
Your Purpose

Tell me, what is it you plan to do with your one wild and
precious life?

–Mary Oliver

There are seasons in your life in the same way as there are
seasons in nature. There are times to cultivate and create,
when you nurture your world and give birth to new ideas
and ventures. There are times of flourishing and abundance, when life feels in full bloom, energized and expanding. And there are times of fruition, when things come to
an end. They have reached their climax and must be har-
vested before they begin to fade. And finally, of course,
there are times that are cold and cutting and empty, times
when the spring of new beginnings seems like a distant
dream. Those rhythms in life are natural events. They
weave into one another as day follows night, bringing, not
messages of hope and fear, but messages of how things
are. If you realize that each phase of your life is a natural
occurrence, then you need not be swayed, pushed up and
down by the changes in circumstance and mood that life
brings. You find that you have an opportunity to be fully
in the world at all times and to show yourself as a brave
and proud individual in any situation.

–Chögyam Trungpa Rinpoche

More and more I resonate with the words of systems scientist Peter Senge who said, "People are our best resource." This really hit home for me when I was presenting at a conference on sustainability. At first, I was confused as to why I was there. I wasn't talking about the earth and the water and climate change and all the rest. I realized that my primary calling was to cultivate sustainable people. I totally resonate with how Trungpa Rinpoche says it, "People are our business." I feel fortunate that my calling is so clear for me. After four decades of honing my work as a trainer and coach in personal and professional development, I have come up with three primary slogans which form the basis of my work.

Three Slogans

"Be who you are," is a slogan that has long been bandied about. My version is, "Be *the best* of who you are," which ups the ante considerably. It points to a path of working with ourself. It is not striving to change ourself but actually has more to do with relaxing, unconditionally accepting, and fully embracing who we are. When we relax, we come into our essence, our personal authenticity.

Our world abounds with miscommunication and tension in our dealings with others. It paralyzes both our work and personal relationships. Coming to any resolution seems insurmountable. In a situation of tension with another, I have made it a priority to work on the relationship. Making the relationship a priority, more than getting the job done, produces ease in communication because it creates trust and openness. So, the second slogan is, "Put people first."

My third slogan is, "Do what is needed." We are needed in this world to respond with benevolence rather than react with our fixated ideas. Habitually, we *react* to situations. We come from our small mind, defending the "I," our ego. It is a survival mentality. When we *respond* to situations, we see things as they are and offer what is needed. We take a big mind attitude. We can react with a small mind or respond with a big mind. One makes us a victim, the other a warrior. We can put our fully empowered self to work.

Taking these slogans with us on our journey of self-discovery may help us discover where we struggle as well as our unique style of intelligence and potential. We could join the best of who we are with work that brings us alive.

> Healing our society goes hand and hand with healing our personal, elemental connection with the phenomenal world.
>
> —Chögyam Trungpa Rinpoche

Clarifying Our Intention

Clarifying our intention in working with others is crucial. We must ask several important questions. What are our aspirations? How can we best serve? What is needed? What aspects of ourself stand in the way of realizing our vision? The bigger our vision, the more we need to face our dark side. Envisioning how we want to be in the world keeps us honest about how we lead our life. We must also have a sense of really loving that vision, a vision of ourself at our best. We have to embrace all that we are: our values, strengths, capacities, and abilities.

Fulfilling the vision could be arduous and it could take a long time, so we need to commit to whatever it takes. It all boils down to this: do we have enough passion? When coaching people, one of my first questions is, "What is your passion?" It gives me a sense of both who the person is and what they might do in life. When we have passion for what we do, we have sustainable performance.

Everyone begins the journey on the path [of working with oneself] by experiencing dissatisfaction. Something is missing somewhere, and we are frantically looking for it. But even though we run faster and faster, we do not discover anything at all. There is the constant sense that we are missing the point. So we start to ask questions.

–Chögyam Trungpa Rinpoche

For a period of time—a week, a month, a year—keep a journal to write your answers to the following questions. As you do so, you will see that there will be a growing understanding of who you are in the world. The more you do it, the more you will access your inner wisdom.

1. What are your deepest values?
2. What do you do in your life to align yourself with your deepest values?
3. Would you like to do more? If so, what?

Three Aspects of a Genuine Path

1. Discipline is developing trust in one's self
2. Meditation is practicing one's trust
3. Intellectual understanding and direct intuitive insight give clarity

By thoroughly marinating ourself in the dharma, whatever we do is in service to others. It feels wholesome and creates a sense of doubtlessness and delight. We develop tremendous power and strength to help others. We learn to dance together.

Too often our intentions could be confused by our own needs. We need to be aware of our own predilections and unspoken agendas. We could lay our trip on another, or try to change them. Work with others will reveal our habitual ways of interacting. There are three primary obstacles based on the primary intensified emotions: passion, aggression, and ignorance.

- Trying to rescue someone is based on passion—
  We want to take over the situation, become a savior

- Trying to cure someone is based on aggression—
  We become authoritarian, in charge, want to fix it

- Professionalism is based on ignorance—
  We have a detached concern, operate by rote

These all arise out of fear and insecurity so we need to clarify and purify our intention.

Our highest intention is to create an awake space to align with wisdom. So, we could model rather than tell, feel rather than think. We could model that all energetic states are workable. Then others can have a direct experience of confidence within confusion.

When we connect to our natural brilliance, our basic goodness, we shine. We empower ourself, our life, with basic principles and core practices. When we are receptive to our world in the immediacy of the moment, we experience the light in the world. This is nourishing, opens our heart, and is empowering. It is from where we can lead. There is a synchronicity in finding our seat, our spot, our place in the world. When we do, we access great power. We are not the center of the universe but we have our place in it.

A major factor affecting whether we have smooth sailing or capsize in any situation is our ability to manage our emotions. We can get defensive, or we can take full responsibility toward a win-win solution. In this stressful world, we need to train to be players and warriors, rather than being trapped in victimhood.

The Five Wisdoms Training in personal and professional development I created focuses on understanding personalities, emotions, and relationships. Successes are most powerful when matched with the sense of purpose that comes from knowing ourself. It is key to a life worth living.

CHAPTER 27

Engaging Effectively

Our plan is to make sure that individuals, whoever we
meet, have a good life. At the same time, you should
keep in contact with people, in whatever way you can.
That's very important, not because we're into converting
others, but because we are into communicating... There
are hundreds of thousands of people who need your
help, which makes you feel sad, so sad. Compassion automatically invites you to relate with people, because
you no longer regard people as a drain on your energy.

–Chögyam Trungpa Rinpoche

This chapter is on how to bring out our best in engaging
with others. There is a primary shift here in that following a genuine path is now done for others. Employing
tools for skillful communication is extremely helpful, but most
importantly, we become the tool. The more we rely on our own
insight and intuition, the more creative and appropriate our responses will be.

Our formal practices are to engender compassion in all of
our interactions:

- Meditation — we work with ourself to be a tool to work
  with others

- Tonglen — we break down the barrier between self and other
- Four Wisdoms Actions (see Chapter 29) are skillful means

We have a deepening sense of being a compassionate person and discover that our actions are more spontaneous, effortless, and heartfelt. We are not as much concerned with ourself as available for others. We readily meet people where they are, always being sensitive to the unconscious impact we might have on another.

We are not trying to figure someone out, but connect on a different level. They are not Jane but Janeness, a mix of energies that is Jane. Knowing someone's energetic make up gives us a skillful edge in all of our interactions. We begin to see their predictability and what we can and cannot expect from them. We also find that people simply do not have certain capacities to move into a more wholesome version of themselves.

Highlights of the contemplative approach in working with others:

- Set your aspiration to benefit beings.
- Make ongoing work with yourself the ground for working with others.
- Cultivate the warmth of an open heart to fully appreciate another.
- Willingly enter someone's world as the first step in helping them.
- Practice energetic exchange and unbiased perception.
- Align yourself with the basic goodness and sanity in everyone.
- Take action based on clarity and benevolence.

Defining Your Role

In whatever role we play with others, there are many ways in which we can be helpful. Every relationship is an opportunity to manifest wisdom and compassion. Different relationships and circumstances require different approaches. How deep we go depends on our capacity, the depth of someone's stuckness, the container we can provide, and the degree of mutual openness and trust. For each situation, we need to clarify what we are doing and set appropriate boundaries. We may have to protect ourself from what is unconscious in someone without judging them. If we blame them, we become the victim which disempowers us.

By far, our most challenging relationships are with our intimate partners and family members. They press our buttons and we press theirs. So, we are often the last person who will be heard in trying to be helpful. I find it quite distressing that there is no requirement in our educational system—until there is a crisis—for education on relationships, parenting, and family. Such an education would have a lasting and profound influence on a person's development affecting the way they think, feel, and act. No wonder there is rampant trauma! No wonder there is a plethora of personal growth trainings!

Possible Ways to Engage With Others

- As a friend, we can continuously take a big mind approach and help in dealing with the vicissitudes of life. True friends can run the rapids together and come out the better for it.

- As a life or work coach, we can relate to situational issues and recognize if someone's particular style is meeting them.

- As a psychotherapist—in particular body-oriented psychotherapy—we work with life-long chronic neurosis or psychosis often triggered by past trauma.

- As a meditation instructor, we focus on bringing whatever is coming up to the practice.

I have engaged with others in all of these ways. I have found that working with meditation practitioners has been more fruitful as they have a practice and path. They take more responsibility for themselves. Others are more reliant on another.

Some guidelines, somewhat edited, to follow in workplace communication from Boris Groysberg and Michael Slind:

1. To learn more, listen better. Leaders who earn a reputation among their people for communicating well don't just *say* that they listen to employees...they create regular, intimately structured occasions when leaders resolve to shut up, and when employees at every organizational level are able to speak up. [This could include mirroring back what you heard and engaging in authentic inquiry.]

2. To have a big impact, meet in a small group. Leaders who want to hear about what's really happening in their company, and to hear from more than just a few "usual suspects," make an effort to meet with people in an up-close-and-personal setting.

3. To build trust, show trust. Before they ask employees to trust them, they take steps to demonstrate that they trust employees—by, for example, entrusting them with potentially sensitive information.

4. To be a better communicator, be who you are. One way to get close to employees is to show a willingness to get personal. Leaders who take organizational conversation seriously appreciate the value of authenticity, and they understand that being honest with people sometimes means being vulnerable. They don't hide behind a veil of corporate authority.

We can be grateful to everyone. We could appreciate that they are presenting us with tremendous obstacles, even threats or challenges. By triggering us, they heighten our efforts to deal with our neurosis. We could feel grateful to people who push us onto the path of dharma.

Taking Our Seat

Finding our seat joins us with the spaciousness of heaven, the groundedness of earth, and human dignity. We can take our seat and create a proper environment. Then we can extend to others.

> In my experience, the most important element of engaging in good conversation is to embrace our own visceral experience. Interestingly enough, in order to deeply connect with another human being, first we can come home to our own body...Once arriving in our own body, we can extend our awareness out into the space around us. You can actually begin to feel the other person, and notice how they might be feeling...Landing in the present moment by embodying our experience allows us to communicate with genuine expression. When our expression arises in this genuine way, there is not only a deeper level of kindness in our interaction, but there is fluidity and availability—we can be whoever we need to be to meet this particular conversation.
>
> –Sarah Lipton

We use meditation practice so we can be stable, consistent. It cuts through our fixed views and agenda and gives us access to innate qualities in ourself: strength, clarity, and insight. In meditation, sometimes we are present and sometimes we are not. When we stay with our experience, we gently hold our mind. When we don't stay with our experience, we harden. The same thing happens when we are with another. We can continually come back to what is alive in the present moment, a gentle wakefulness. We feel less anxiety and less pressure so we don't have to try so hard. We could have a big sigh of relief.

Five Qualities to Develop in Relating to Others

Buddha Presence
- Embodied, spacious, awake
- Listening deeply

Vajra Mental Clarity
- Insight into someone and their circumstance
- Having tremendous curiosity

Ratna Equanimity
- A deep sense of satisfaction and fulfillment
- Being resourceful as to what is needed

Padma Energetic Resonance, Attunement
- An open heart full of warmth and empathy
- Being attuned to another

Karma Action
- Knowing what to do
- Making an intervention from a sense of spaciousness, clarity, warmth, and equanimity

Basic Instruction in Relating to Someone: Authentic, Aware, Engaged, Effective

- **Authenticity:** Stay in the present and radiate out
- **Awareness:** See their mix of sanity and confusion
- **Engaging:** Align with their sanity and mirror their confusion, a work point
- **Effectiveness:** Offer an intervention, knowing what to do

Beginning, Middle, and End

In any communication have a sense of:
- **Beginning:** setting the agenda
- **Middle:** discussing the topics
- **End:** a clear summary, focusing on action items, which seals the meeting

• • •

Engaging effectively takes years of practice with like-minded people to hone our understanding.

CHAPTER 28

Creating Your World

The wisdom of dealing with situations as they are, and that is what wisdom is, contains tremendous precision that could not come from anywhere else but the physical situations of sight, smell, feelings, touchable objects, and sounds. The earthy situation of actual things as they are is the source of wisdom.

–Chögyam Trungpa Rinpoche

What does our world look like? We live in a time of great confluence between all cultures and religions of the world. We take great delight in mastering our external world, having the best technology, the most efficiency, and more possibilities. We live in the information age with the internet as a vast resource. Anything we want to know is a few clicks away. How seductive is that? We are connected to events in a global community by a world-wide network of media. We can communicate with almost anyone in the world in a matter of moments. With our technological advances, any daily task is made more efficient and more things are more possible. With the exponential growth of material goods, with a well-paying job, we can live like royalty. We know more (mental clarity), own more (richness), have more enjoyable diversions (passion), and can accomplish more (activity). We live in the land of opportunity. We are the elite of the world. Great! Wonderful!

That we have increased opportunities is grand, but life has become increasingly complex and stressful. Wanting to take advantage of every opportunity, we move through life with great speed. We pile meeting on meeting, task on task, madly trying to accomplish things. Our infatuation with technology takes us down the rabbit hole again and again. Pleasure has been computerized which encourages a shallowness. We forget the simple pleasures of listening to music, reading a book, or strolling in a park, most of which are free. We have forgotten how to be simply human. Despite our riches, we are confused, anxious, and psychologically hungry. We lack contentment, so we seek constant excitement. We have wings to fly, even rockets into outer space, with nowhere to go. So, we go around in circles. Going around in circles is, in fact, the Buddhist definition of a life without wisdom: samsara.

We could take all this for granted. But we also could ask a few questions. "What's wrong with this picture? What have been the costs to this climb to greater seeming satisfaction?"

There is stress in the land of opportunity! We do not have the capacity to cope with the amount of stimulation offered by this bountiful global village. There is simply too much data for our minds to manage. Each gadget or technical tool meant to "simplify" our life comes with detailed instructions, from the back of the package to a two-inch thick operating manual. External demands are out of proportion to what we can handle. We can't remember things. Preoccupied by what came before and what happens next, we are not in the present moment. We revisit decisions because we can't remember we made them before. We are confused as to how to prioritize the day, not knowing what to accept and reject. The dis-ease of stress is a daily occurrence.

The news overloads us with data that we feel powerless to change: wars, corruption, global warming, species dying off, natural disasters, poverty, disease, and the list goes on. Just reading this list may bring a sense of oppression. Whether it is work or managing our home and domestic affairs, we get over-whelmed. Multitasking is the name of the game and it is ex-hausting. Being forced to track a million things in our day, no wonder Attention Deficit Disorder (ADD) and chronic fatigue are our new diseases. No wonder we become self-protective: "It's all about me."

No wonder life guidance has become so necessary. We, hopefully, all have a therapist, a life coach, a spiritual teacher, or a friend we count on to be there for us. Many of us have had profound realizations and our consciousness has expanded ex-ponentially in this new age. Yet there is a much larger percent-age of people who simply can't manage the tasks of life.

Indeed, the tasks of the world, both great and small, are ac-complished through a forward-moving energy. However, the force of that energy is like a cyclone and, once caught up in it, we are buffeted about, losing our direction. Technology has many benefits. I use it all of the time. However, there is the vain assumption that it will provide us with more leisure time. In fact, the speed of life has increased to the point of a technolog-ical tsunami, killing us in a vain attempt to find inner peace. But has it occurred to us that we might be winning at the wrong game?

An article titled "Americans Work More, Seem to Accom-plish Less" shows that these truths are commonly known:

> Most U.S. workers say they feel rushed on the job, but they are getting less accomplished than a decade ago, according to newly released research. The biggest culprit is the tech-nology that was supposed to make work quicker and eas-ier, experts say… "Technology has sped everything up and, by speeding everything up, it's slowed everything down, paradoxically," said John Challenger, at Challenger, Gray & Christmas Inc. "We never concentrate on one task anymore. You take a little chip out of it, and then you're on to the next thing…It's harder to feel like you're accom-plishing something."

In a job interview at a major corporation, the Human Relations person to whom I was talking said that if people were not working sixty to eighty hours a week, their job was on the line. I asked how people could possibly cope with such a demand. She confessed that she did not know but assumed many people were taking drugs of some sort, or were choosing to leave. In the interview, after I had laid out the benefits of working with the Five Wisdoms, she said bluntly, "They would only be interested in the green energy here." Getting the job done is their only value. I asked myself, "Is this the way we want to spend our waking hours?"

An article on meditation in BusinessWeek online in August 2004 stated that there is a $200 billion loss annually in "absenteeism, subpar performance, tardiness, and worker's compensation claims related to stress. In fact, stress-related ailments account for upwards of 60% of all doctor visit, according to the Mind/Body Medical Institute" [at Harvard University].

What Is This Doing to Us?

We have lost ourself. We have become victims of this monster of progress that we have created. Most days we work in high gear and then all we can do is flop in front of the TV. To cope and get relief from the pressure we turn to sex, alcohol, and drugs. In many ways our life has been disappointing. Filled with the idealism of our teenage years, we have seen our expectations come to naught. Our desires and ambitions have not come to fruition. We struggle with the pressures of the outer world and our emotional upheavals.

Most importantly, we have de-humanized and depersonalized our existence. Contact with another human being has been minimized. The Covid pandemic certainly did not help! Now we mostly get information and make exchanges by punching buttons on our phone or computer as we navigate a website. I have jokingly considered forming an over 50s club. Anyone over 50 is automatically a member. The operating rule is that no matter what transaction you want to make, you get to talk to a real person.

Fundamentally, every one of us feels insecure. We may have material resources, a good education, and close friends, but none of those seem to make much of a difference to our state of mind. We become perpetual seekers in the marketplace where more and more therapies and spiritual traditions—some authentic and some superficial—abound in ever-increasing numbers. Confused by conflicting influences, we become overwhelmed. At times we retreat into a cocoon of self-indulgence where we drug ourself, literally or figuratively, on whatever gives us pleasure. There is something fundamentally threatening about being alive. We need lots of reassurance to keep us going.

In the onrush of life, and in our desperate attempt to escape from it, we seldom stop to consider what we are doing. We are indeed fortunate to live in a time and place of tremendous opportunity, yet has the cost been too high? We need to pay attention to how we navigate this seemingly overwhelming world we have created. We need to find the inner resources that will carry us through times of difficulty. We can't turn back the clock to a time when there was a slower pace of life. We need to work with what we have. How do we do this?

> The stories you tell yourself and believe day-in and day-out are literally creating your future. Change your stories, change your brain, change the game and create your own destiny.
>
> —Fleet Maull

From a Five Wisdoms perspective, the answer to these questions is crystal clear: the spacious white energy is missing. Most of us do not realize this is a core problem. Yet we might have been one of those to say, "Stop the world. I want to get off." We might have decided to retreat into an inner sanctum and meditate all day. But there are other ways. At the center of the cyclone is stillness. As a metaphor for our life, we can remember to come out of the whirlwind to that stillness again and again. It is in silence and stillness that we plummet to the vast resource of our wisdom and strength. It is wise eyes that see the wisdom world. We can experience the pervasiveness of spacious energy that permeates all occurrence. Then we can learn to ride a cyclone. What fun!

Envisioning a Good Human Society

When I envision an awake world, I see a place where there is a fundamental trust in goodness, a willingness to do the personal work to bring out our best, and a life where we are not threatened by others or situations. We have personal authenticity that is full of integrity, clarity, and warmth, and is both gentle and fearless. Every challenging situation is an opportunity. We are able to serve because we are not biased. We take 400% responsibility for what we think, feel, say, and do. We have an allegiance to put others first and continually extend friendship, wishing for their happiness and well-being. We create environments and situations to make this possible. We become a warrior of goodness in the world.

There is an art to living our life. First, we need to appreciate and cultivate who we are. We become a reasonable person. We are well-groomed, pay attention to our clothing, and keep our house tidy. We speak properly and manage our emotions. We pay attention to every detail of our life in a natural and dignified way. Our attitude toward our world has a sense of preciousness, respect, and dignity. We create a worthwhile situation, appreciating reality at its fullest level. We feel good when we handle our world properly and fully. We have more genuine humor, sadness, and joy. When all of our activities are an extension of our sanity, we can have an influence on others.

We encounter obstacles to waking up. We are lazy and are more apt to turn away from fulfilling this kind of vision. We identify with the clouds and forget the sun. We have trouble trusting our own goodness and intelligence. We keep up a good facade but shrink from life. Identify with the sun, we wake up and give up the struggle. The sun *is* always shinning! When we have a glimpse of an awakened world, we yearn for it. It is ordinary and magical. It is so ordinary and simple that we could miss it and never appreciate what we have. It could feel so mundane, we take it for granted. We miss seeing magic, the innate wisdom in the ordinary world. It is wondrous and inconceivable because it is beyond anything we can conceive.

Feminine and Masculine
in the Workplace and Society

Feminine and masculine qualities in ourself, the workplace, and our society are always at play. To reiterate, the masculine energy is focused, direct, clear, logical, action oriented, goal oriented, reason based, problem oriented, and practical. Feminine energy is nurturing, receptive, emotional, process oriented, collaborative, relational, spontaneous, and spacious. From the perspective of the Five Wisdoms, vajra and karma are associated with masculine qualities and padma and ratna are imbued with feminine qualities. There is always friction between rigid masculine hierarchy and the feminine interest in being interpersonal and collaborative.

Our world culture is imbalanced, dominated by masculine energy, partly because of fear of survival. It brings home the bacon and gets the job done. But it is very competitive and paranoid. In my opinion, the women's liberation was a failure. Women seemed to want to take on masculine qualities rather than liberating themselves to feel the power of their feminine. That men also need liberation from their role has largely been ignored. Most importantly, it did not honor the potential for feminine qualities to make a significant contribution to our world. Only in small off-shoots of mainstream society do we find any real effort to stay attuned to the feminine.

> The most important problem for our world to solve is the inequality of men and women...When women come into their full power, a balance will occur which has not been seen for so long that no one remembers it...Until women assume their rightful place on earth there will never be an end to wars, cruelty and oppression.
>
> –Dr. Frederick P. Lenz

Business is the most powerful force in the modern world. Churches used to be at the center of a city. Now it is high-rise office buildings. We spend most of our time at work so the workplace is pivotal in this conversation. It could be a vehicle for transformation where we could manifest deeper ideals and purpose. Let's do it! Let's bring in more padma and ratna energies which truly address the problems of the 21st century: anxiety, stress, and aggression. The challenge is in infiltrating the mainstream, as much as it is needed. It's the truth: the soft stuff is the hard stuff. It is too threatening, especially for men, like going naked to your next board meeting. That some large corporations now offer meditation, buddha energy, is a big step.

Let's see how this plays out in therapeutic approaches. The more goal-oriented, reason-based, problem-solving masculine approach is powerful at fixing certain problems like trauma and addiction. The feminine approach is based on being in the present moment with the process. It creates a compassionate space where there is no agenda because what unfolds is based on the innate wisdom of the client. It is about discovering wholeness rather than fixing a broken person. From the perspective of equine-assisted psychotherapy, my daughter has this to say:

> The best way for the therapist to assist in the process is for her to be willing to let go into the unknown, be present, and trust whatever arises. The therapist must truly accept that all experiences and emotions hold meaningful information on the journey to healing. From this trust, the therapist can assist by drawing the client's awareness to the little shifts or insights that do occur. In this space of collaboration, spontaneous transformations take place.
>
> –Karuna Rockwell

And yes, please let's not forget:

> Since everything is an apparition, perfect
>   and being what it is,
> Having nothing to do with good or bad,
>   acceptance or rejection,
> You may well burst out in laughter.
>
> –Longchenpa

CHAPTER 29

Five Wisdoms in Your Life

The spontaneity of the true nature is based on having a notion of being and a notion of nowness. There is no need for panic. Everything is clear and precise, and you act depending on what the situation demands. Sometimes one has to be tough and sometimes one has to be gentle. That is dictated by the situation. There is no goal orientation at all, other than what is required at that very moment.

–Chögyam Trungpa Rinpoche

E xperiencing the world as a living web of interconnectedness, sensitive to the natural rhythms and structures of events and of society serves as the basis for action that is both compassionate and effective. This view of profound connection marks the common wisdom shared by humanity. Could we come to see society as a dynamic mandala? See that all that happens is just energy — constricted or flowing, predictable or surprising? Could we learn to lean into the powerful energy of the constriction and see the wisdom within it? This is the profundity and ultimate skillful means of the Five Wisdoms mandala.

Five Wisdoms in Our Life in Quadrants

Here is an overview of how we can manifest.

Core Practices

- Mindful awareness
- Five Wisdoms postures
- Tonglen
- Experiential learning modalities

Personal

- Personal authenticity
- Embodying Five Wisdoms qualities
- Emotional intelligence
- Sensory awareness
- BSMQA* of BVRPK**
- Personal energetic constellation

*Body, speech, mind, quality, action

**Buddha spaciousness, vajra clarity, ratna richness, padma passion, karma activity

Interpersonal

- Authentic relationships
- Energetic exchange
- Unbiased perception
- Skillful communication
- BSMQA of BVRPK in relationship
- Relational energetic constellation

Professional/Worldly

- Manifestation
- Engaging effectively
- Five ways of engaging
- Four Wisdoms actions
- Service to others
- BSMQA of BVRPK in situations
- Situational energetic constellation

Society and Culture

- Enlivened environments
- Creative expression
- Arts
- Nature
- BSMQA of BVRPK in places
- Societal energetic constellation

A Learning Organization

A learning organization is like a thriving ecosystem, transforming in effective ways because its members are continually adapting and learning together. It cultivates a quality of individual and shared learning that enables everyone to hone in on their goals with extraordinary focus, resiliency, energy, and creativity. It is able to continually transform itself to better address its ever-changing challenges and opportunities. It could look like a dance troupe moving in unison to a tacit beat.

The interplay of three relational spheres creates organizational health and vitality: the formal/structural/objective, the social/relational/intersubjective, and the trans-personal. This is a rephrasing of what we became acquainted with in Chapter 20,

The Dimensions of Reality. All three spheres interact continuously and transform in response to each other.

The formal context is compromised when a single perspective dominates, which results in bureaucracy. The social context is compromised when cliques take over, like the politics of old-boy networks. The transsubjective realm is sabotaged by various sorts of fundamentalism. In this ecology of overlapping, interpenetrating spheres, leadership is both deeply personal and inherently collaborative. Being an authentic leader is greatly enhanced by a transpersonal understanding.

Systems Therapy is another way of looking at how a family or community learn together. The goal is to gain insight into each member's role as it relates to the healthy functioning of the whole. problematic behavior patterns helps group members attain good relationships. People learn how to transform their patterns to more adaptive, productive behaviors. It does not focus on causes or symptoms, but gives living systems nudges that help them to develop new patterns together. Many conflicting situations and issues can be effectively treated in organizations, communities, or families.

Four Wisdom Actions or Four Powers

The Four Wisdom Actions, traditionally called the four karmas or buddha activity, has to do with egoless activity. They are four different ways of being active: pacifying, enriching, magnetizing, and destroying/subduing. It is egoless and therefore it responds to whatever is needed. It goes with the flow. If somebody is coming at us with aggression, we pacify; if somebody needs to be drawn out, we magnetize; if something needs to be stopped in its tracks, we destroy it. There is a sense of being able to completely manifest without any reference back to a self.

As mentioned previously when looking at Maitri Space Awareness, it is about awareness of space and having a friendly relationship with it, dancing with it. We see that space is the medium in which everything happens and we are open, so we can go with the flow. When we are hooked into the energy, there is no duality. We don't impose ourself on a situation and try to change it, instead we merge with the situation and act in accord with what is needed. Being in the space and responding to the space, we are not projecting. Ego is manipulative; responding to what is needed is more spontaneous. Our actions happen in a larger context as we see the totality of what's going on, how everything is pervasive and interconnected. This is the magic dance of no self. People call it a "high" or "being in the groove."

The Five Wisdoms and the Four Powers

1. Buddha (white) and vajra (blue) combine in the calmness and evenness of just being, with a pacifying, unyielding, immovable quality.

2. Ratna (yellow) is enriching and resourceful.

3. Padma (red) is magnetizing, embracing and inspiring.

4. Karma (green) is actualizing or fulfilling, destroying anything that is too fixated.

What these accomplish:

1. Pacifying energy allays our fears and suffering.

2. Enriching energy increases our long life and health.

3. Magnetizing energy draws together the necessary circumstances for our support.

4. Destroying energy is wrathful intervention to quickly cut through obstacles.

Each of these activities has a profound ultimate function as well:

1. Ultimate pacification is the pacification of the mind's poisons.

2. Ultimate enrichment is the full accumulation of merit and wisdom.

3. Ultimate magnetizing is awakening the true nature.

4. Ultimate destroying is annihilating all the ways we create solidity.

Examples of Five Wisdoms in Action

Experience Integral, founded by Anouk Brack, hosted a seminar on Embodying Integral Sustainability. As a final exercise, three groups were given thirty minutes to create a product or service that related to sustainability. Each team member held the perspective of one of the wisdom energies. Team members reported on both what they had created and their process. Here are excerpts from their reports, slightly edited:

From Marilyn Hamilton, founder of Integral City Meshworks: "We moved into our sustainability work with an invitation to notice how the Five Wisdoms contributed to organizational design as defined by the Integral City master principles: take care of yourself, others, and the environment. We brainstormed possible organizations, missions, and goals aligned with each of these principles. The Five Wisdoms provided a deeply spacious, integrative, rich, activating, and resourceful framework. It was most satisfying to recognize the Five Wisdoms as an evolutionary intelligence."

From Foreno van der Hulst, Circling workshops leader: "Having all the wisdoms present allowed us to design a robust project in a short amount of time in a very fluid way. Having vajra and karma energies divided meant one person could really focus on the vision while the other was making sure that we stayed productive and on time. The padma person made sure the team stayed connected internally. The ratna person made sure that we would invest time and energy in teaching each other about our particular fields of expertise as well as look at the local resources of the region and people. The buddha person can be overlooked so was regularly asked for their thoughts, feelings, and ideas. We gained new perspectives as a result."

From Miriam van Groen, founder of Catalyze Circling: "We all got a glimpse into our energy and what it wants to do under time pressure. I chose the buddha energy. This is an energy I am not really familiar with in my daily life, and I decided to try it out for this exercise. Many of us struggled to let go of our ego and ideas in order for the energy of the color we represented to shine. I got annoyed with myself and others in the group for not representing their colors correctly (vajra), tried to hold space for the group but got stuck in just not participating (buddha), wanted to make sure everyone was included in the process (ratna), and wanted us to have something to present on time, that was better than what the other groups came up with (karma). The process was not as smooth as might have been possible but in the end we made a good pitch. We presented an app that would help reduce your ecological footprint by combining GPS information for travel and product information for purchases. Then it would make suggestions for sustainable products or services that would fit your lifestyle."

Five Wisdoms Training

Graduates have brought the Five Wisdoms into nine countries.

Sydney Leijenhorst is the Director of KenKon Integral Life and Training Center, Wageningen, The Netherlands. KenKon engages in Five Vital Wisdoms Weeks twice a year. They have become integrative journeys for colleagues and students in all disciplines: karate, qigong, meditation, Zen, judo, aikido, and dance. The energies become a shared source of inspiration, a language where they connect at a new and meaningful depth. It enlivens the way they are present in their bodies and world.

Maureen White is the Co-Founder/Executive Program Director of Red Mountain Sedona, Transitional Living Program for Young Adults, Sedona, AZ. Maureen created the core-values for their business and a curriculum in order to develop greater familiarity with their own patterns. White trains both staff and clients on the Five Wisdoms.

Jean Gunner is the Director of Operations in pediatric primary care, Buffalo, NY. Jean created STAAR (Sustainability, Transparency, Accountability, Adaptability, Reliability) based on the Five Wisdoms to work with Human Resources in building capacities and partnership, and in strategic development. She and Craig Zink founded the Five Wisdoms Center, an affiliate of the Five Wisdoms Institute, in Hamburg, New York. Working with them are graduates Peggy Galantowicz and Brigitte Kihn.

Nem Bajra is the CEO and President at Calsoft Systems and teacher at the Zen Center of Los Angeles. He offers Mindfulness in Entrepreneurship courses that include working with the Five Wisdoms for his employees and business associates in both the US and Japan.

Kelly Petrie is the founder of the Maitri Center for Mindful Living, Oregon, Wisconsin. Kelly is a contemplative educator. Her specialty is using the Five Wisdoms in working with autistic clients in schools and privately.

Klara Molnar is the co-director of 5 Elements Food, Miskolc, Hungary. Klara uses the Five Wisdoms as the primary vision for their company. Their mission is to create daily practices for people to connect to themselves and others, their bodies, nutrition, the environment, and nature. Their goal is to create a compassionate community where people help each other, listen to each other, and ultimately find their passion to do what they love.

Francesco Melita is an independent coach, trainer and storyteller, Wageningen, Netherlands. The Five Wisdoms influences all he does. He creates an atmosphere that offers space for freedom to express passion, humor, and creativity. He coaches teachers and marketing students in professional presentations, has led a creativity training for employees of the four biggest civil-engineering bureaus in the Netherlands, and led a workshop for the Dutch Association of Psychologists.

Those engaged as life coaches or therapists: Carucha Schwencke, Den Haag, Netherlands; Tessa Racine, Mas Marvant, France; Monika Steinberg-Békeffy, Budapest Hungary; Arthur Souza, Recife, Brazil; Seweryn Julien, Poland.

Those applying the Five Wisdoms in healing arenas: Zung Nguyen, Paris, France, incorporates the Five Wisdoms as an osteopath. Kate Summers, Santa Monica, CA, created a model for hospice workers. Mike Brown, Program Director at Red Mountain Sedona, created a protocol to regulate intensified energy in staff and clients, Sedona, AZ. Andrea Casetti, Tenerife, Spain, works with a spiritual connection through the elemental energies. Those offering courses to their Zen communities and beyond are Joanna Jakubowicz and Sabina Steckiewicz, Warsaw, Poland.

To have an understanding of how the wisdoms can be applied in health, education, leadership, and the arts, please visit the Professional Applications page on the Five Wisdoms Institute website.

Five Wisdoms Slogans

- There is no such thing as black and white; everything is very colorful.

- There is no such thing as independence; we are all interdependent.

- Nothing is static: everything is always in flux, in constant change, and unstable.

- Chaos is good news.

- Wake up, wake up! It's all right here.

- What's wrong with this picture? Nothing. Change your attitude and relax as it is.

I will leave you with the overriding slogan for all Five Wisdoms activities:

- When we have fully realized the wisdom energies, we could be anywhere and become anything but always connected to whatever is needed.

Good luck!

Irini Rockwell:
Illuminating the Path
of the Five Wisdoms

Irini Rockwell's journey is a testament to the transformative power of ancient wisdom in modern life. She has been deeply interested in the essence of who we are and how we can bring out our best to serve the world. With over four decades of experience in Buddhism, meditation, and the expressive arts, she has become a beacon of light for those seeking personal growth and spiritual awakening. Her unique ability to bridge the gap between esoteric teachings and practical application has touched the lives of countless individuals across the globe.

With an innate curiosity about the human experience, Irini's path began in the world of dance. A graduate of the prestigious Juilliard School in New York and the Arts Educational School in London, she initially expressed her passion for understanding human nature through movement and artistic expression. Her early career saw her directing her dance company, Footloose, in the San Francisco Bay Area, where she explored the intricate connections between body, mind, and spirit.

It was during her time as the director of dance and dance therapy at Naropa University in Boulder, Colorado, that Irini's life took a profound turn. Here, she encountered the teachings of Chögyam Trungpa Rinpoche, a seminal figure in bringing Tibetan Buddhism to the West. This meeting sparked a lifelong dedication to Buddhist studies and practice, particularly the profound wisdom of the Five Wisdoms, which would later become the cornerstone of her work.

Driven by an insatiable thirst for knowledge and a deep commitment to personal growth, Irini immersed herself in a diverse range of studies. She completed a master's degree in Contemplative Psychotherapy/Buddhist Psychology and the Authentic Leadership certificate at Naropa University. She studied trauma at The National Institute for the Clinical Application of Behavioral Medicine. Khenpo Tsültrim Gyamtso Rinpoche was a significant teacher in her spiritual journey. Mind-body disciplines are a passion and she has explored many. As a perpetual student of life, a commitment to ongoing learning infuses her work with freshness and authenticity. This rich tapestry of learning lays the foundation for her unique approach to personal and spiritual development.

In 2002, Irini founded the Five Wisdoms Institute and in 2006 she launched the Five Wisdoms Training. Both are a culmination of her life's work and passion. Through this platform, she has shared the transformative power of the Five Wisdoms – an ancient system that illuminates our innate intelligence and provides a roadmap for personal growth. Her approach is both deeply rooted in traditional Buddhist teachings and refreshingly modern, making timeless wisdom accessible and relevant to contemporary life.

As a teacher, Irini is known for her warmth, authenticity, and ability to connect with people from all walks of life. Her workshops and trainings are more than just educational experiences; they are invitations to embark on a journey of self-discovery and transformation. Participants often speak of Irini's unique gift for creating a safe, nurturing space where profound insights and personal breakthroughs can occur.

Irini's impact extends far beyond the walls of her institute. She has taught internationally at Buddhist centers, spiritual retreats, and personal growth venues, touching lives across continents. Her work has found resonance in diverse settings, from corporate boardrooms to meditation halls. She has created customized trainings for organizations such as the National Institute for School Development in the Netherlands, Karuna Training in Germany, and the EastWind Institute in Canada, demonstrating the universal applicability of the Five Wisdoms.

As an author, Irini has shared her insights through two acclaimed books: *The Five Wisdom Energies: A Buddhist Way of Understanding Personalities, Emotions, and Relationships* and *Natural Brilliance: A Buddhist System for Uncovering Your Strengths and Letting Them Shine.* These works have been translated into multiple languages, spreading the transformative power of the Five Wisdoms to readers around the world.

Irini's latest book, *Unfolding the Mystery of Your Life on the Five Wisdoms Path*, represents the culmination of her decades of study, practice, and teaching. In this profound yet accessible work, she delves deeper into the spiritual dimensions of the Five Wisdoms, offering readers a roadmap to navigate life's complexities with grace and wisdom.

At the heart of Irini's teaching is a profound belief in the innate brilliance of every individual. She sees her role not as imparting knowledge, but as a guide helping others uncover their own inner wisdom. Her approach is holistic, integrating the intellectual, emotional, and somatic aspects of experience to facilitate deep, lasting transformation.

In her personal life, Irini embodies the principles she teaches. Those close to her speak of her genuine warmth, her ability to be fully present, and her capacity to find joy in the simple moments of life. She approaches each day as an opportunity for growth and discovery, bringing mindfulness and compassion to her interactions with others.

As Irini Rockwell continues to shine her light, she invites us all to join her on the Five Wisdoms path – a journey of self-discovery, healing, and awakening to our true potential. Through her work, she reminds us that within each of us lies a wellspring of wisdom, waiting to be uncovered and shared with the world.

APPENDIX B.

Extended
Table of Contents